T0331977

The Systems Work of Social Change

"Doers and donors alike will find in this book indispensable tools for ambitious, forward-thinking systemic work."

—**Ambassador Don Gips ret., Chief Executive Officer, Skoll Foundation**

"'Systems Thinking' is all the rage, but too often, it is just that — thinking, without much practical consequence for those of us intent on changing the world. Systems Work will be of great utility to social change activists and practitioners everywhere."

—**Duncan Green, Senior Strategic Adviser, Oxfam GB and author of** *How Change Happens* **and** *From Poverty to Power*

"Through insightful, practical frameworks and clear, compelling examples Bonnici and Rayner get to the heart of the "work" of systems change. In doing so, they have created an indispensable guide for social change aspirants everywhere."

—**John Kania, Founder and Executive Director, Collective Change Lab**

"Too few discussions of systemic social change are grounded in deep understanding of human relationships. Highly recommended."

—**Harvey Koh, Managing Director, FSG and Board Member, Social Innovation Exchange**

"I especially appreciated the discussions about reconfiguring power towards those who have lived experienced of issues and are rooted in the communities where they seek change. Highly recommend this book for practitioners and funders alike."

—**Olivia Leland, Founder and CEO of Co-Impact**

"An honest taking stock of what system work entails. A must read for researchers and practitioners interested in system change."

—**Johanna Mair, Professor of Organization, Strategy and Leadership, Hertie School of Governance, Academic Editor of the** *Stanford Social Innovation Review*

"By listening to and observing the deep work of organizations that place mothers, families, young people, teachers and informal workers at the forefront of decision making, Rayner and Bonnici demonstrate

The Systems Work of Social Change

How to Harness Connection, Context, and Power to Cultivate Deep and Enduring Change

Cynthia Rayner and François Bonnici

Great Clarendon Street, Oxford, OX2 6DP,
United Kingdom

Oxford University Press is a department of the University of Oxford.
It furthers the University's objective of excellence in research, scholarship,
and education by publishing worldwide. Oxford is a registered trade mark of
Oxford University Press in the UK and in certain other countries

Published in the United States of America by Oxford University Press
198 Madison Avenue, New York, NY 10016, United States of America

British Library Cataloguing in Publication Data
Data available

Library of Congress Control Number: 2021909382

ISBN 978-0-19-885745-7

Printed and bound in the UK by
CPI Group (UK) Ltd, Croydon CR0 4YY

Links to third party websites are provided by Oxford in good faith and
for information only. Oxford disclaims any responsibility for the materials
contained in any third party website referenced in this work.

The manufacturer's authorised representative in the EU for product safety
is Oxford University Press España S.A. of el Parque Empresarial San
Fernando de Henares, Avenida de Castilla,
2 – 28830 Madrid (www.oup.es/en).

Foreword

Mirai Chatterjee, Chairperson, Self-Employed Women's Association (SEWA) Cooperative Federation

The COVID-19 pandemic has touched the very lives and livelihoods of all of us on our planet, leading to reflection and reimagination of our approaches to life and living. Cynthia Rayner and François Bonnici's book, *The Systems Work of Social Change*, is a timely and welcome addition to the debates and discussions taking place in our homes, societies, nations and—importantly—the millions of organizations across the globe who are committed to a world that works for all.

Given their position both as practitioners and academics with a deep belief in the need for social change, they are uniquely positioned to share their own experiences and those of the many social change organizations with whom they have worked. By analysing their own experiences with candour, and reflecting on the experiences of others, what emerges is a lucidly written and cogently argued book putting forward the case for a systemic approach to social change. They argue that a fundamental restructuring of social and environmental systems is necessary to undo the deep inequalities and multi-level injustices of our social and global environmental crises.

This insightful book emphasizes the need for systems work: creating systems that are responsive to changing realities and more inclusive and representative of all. They have attempted to answer several important questions that face us today, and most importantly, how organizations can create systemic change. Their focus is on civil society organizations —non-governmental organizations, social enterprises, self-help groups, and people's organizations. The authors have drawn from eight such organizations on almost every continent, organizations that have worked deeply, diligently, sincerely and with commitment to improve the living and working conditions of millions in every corner of the globe.

These organizations are examples of what Mahatma Gandhi called 'constructive action'. He believed that all such action showed us the path towards an alternative vision of society based on truth, non-violence and social justice. Their work is values-based, starting as local, community-based efforts, and addressing a felt need of vulnerable people and communities. Many have grown into large organizations with global reach, attempting to fix broken services and systems. Yet they have remained true to their calling with a focus on decentralised and democratic functioning. While many began with one or more visionary leaders, they are committed to supporting grassroots leaders to take their shared vision forward.

The authors start by drawing on lessons from two hundred years of history, pointing out that there have been moments when opportunities have presented themselves—following wars, during social upheavals like the civil rights movement and amidst struggles, such as in their own country of South Africa—to effect systemic social change. But they caution that the complexity, scale and depth of social problems must be considered carefully as we plan and strategize for change. They outline two approaches to social change: the technical approach as in the Green Revolution and the transformational one which seeks to start afresh and re-build structures, arguing that each alone are insufficient and, instead, *both* are required. Most importantly, it is the *process* of change that is important as change is an ongoing journey. Change is messy and non-linear. We do not always see outcomes at once—and even if we do, we often miss the nuances and the underlying shifts. There are no easy solutions or short-cuts.

In the last two decades, our field has been intensely focused on "scaling up." Yet this preoccupation with scale and speed can have adverse consequences. Many of us face this in our daily work. As a long-time practitioner/worker in the Self-Employed Women's Association, SEWA, I am often asked: "Why are you reaching only 1.8 million in a country of 1.3 billion?" We have resisted the exhortation to rush processes and go in with a "cookie-cutter" approach. Organizing people for social change is a slow and steady process of ups and downs, of forward movements and some backward steps as well. At all times, people, especially the poorest and most vulnerable—

whom the authors call primary actors—must lead and determine the pace of change.

In addition, Cynthia and François stress the importance of context—one size does not fit all. Diversity and plurality of approaches are to be welcomed and these offer important lessons in different contexts. As many countries move towards negation or downplaying of diversity, we would do well to remind ourselves of the richness of pluralistic approaches which comes out clearly in this volume.

Finally, the authors stress that power is yet another critical aspect to be considered in social change work. Who controls what and to what extent, are among the questions to be grappled with in the process of organising for change. Organizations face powerful social, economic and political interests as they push for changes that focus on democratization, inclusion and power-sharing. I have been fortunate to witness at SEWA the power of collectives and how they can change power balances in the home, in villages or urban neighborhoods, and in my own country, India.

Part II of this book focuses on the practices of organizations engaged in systems change work and shows how power can be challenged, with the collective strength and bargaining power of local people, especially the poorest and most vulnerable. It would be interesting to examine further the types of organizations which best work to effect lasting systems change and how regulations and laws can enhance or hinder the process.

Binding all of this work together is the principle of starting the journey of systems change where people *are,* putting people in the centre of all their efforts. No top-down approaches here. In my own experience, with a strong base of people's organizations demanding change, one slowly sees that policies and plans are changed from the top as well, and with far-reaching impact on the lives of people. The organizations profiled herein show the power of platforms or alliances, building solidarity networks for change.

Finally, the authors share their views on measurement, and how conventional, linear methods are being challenged and replaced by holistic and multi-dimensional ways of measuring outcomes. These include qualitative as well as quantitative yardsticks. In my experience, it is often these real life stories that change hearts and minds, not least those of funders, policy-makers and others who shape public opinion. They have also proposed new ways of thinking about resourcing, and how funders can be partners and co-creators in the systems change process, creating spaces where all actors can exchange ideas in the spirit of mutual learning and humility.

The authors end with a call to action in these challenging times—where a tiny virus has wreaked havoc on every continent. We are faced with a chance to re-think, re-set and re-build. While each of the profiled organizations are innovative and exemplary in their own way, it's worth thinking about how these efforts might be knitted together in future for a movement for a very different world—a world centred on justice, equity, inclusion, democratic functioning, and respect for Nature and all who share the earth with us. My experience points to the need for strengthening organizations *and* building movements based on a shared vision and values. Only these efforts together will create the lasting social change which is respectful of both people and our planet.

Cynthia Rayner and François Bonnici have launched us on a journey of reflection and exploration and one which is rich with empirical data, unique organizational insights, and lived experiences. It is a journey of hope, inspiring stories and action which will surely encourage us to act collectively for the common good of all of humanity.

Preface

We live in a world where a small group of billionaires has more wealth than half the planet's population, where global warming and a global pandemic are widening the gap between the richest and poorest countries, and where pervasive racism restricts opportunities in health, wealth, and education. The need to reimagine the systems that support these inequalities is urgent. Yet, how do organizations create systemic social change? How do funders and policymakers support these organizations in their work? These questions defy simple answers, particularly when grappling with the defining challenges of our time—issues like inequality, climate change, and racial justice. After a five-year journey to learn from a group of committed social change practitioners, we believe the answers are right in front of us. However, they are not the answers that got us to where we are today—the approaches currently promoted, celebrated, and widely funded in pursuit of social change.

Organizations of all shapes and sizes—and the myriad practitioners working in them—seek to make a positive difference in the world. Charitable and faith-based organizations, as well as relief workers and emergency volunteers, provide aid to the poor and underserved. Development practitioners encourage economic growth at the same time that environmentalists drive awareness of ecological limits. Activists use protest and civil disobedience, both nonviolent and violent, to shift power in favor of those who have been marginalized, while human rights advocates use the courts to tackle unjust rules. More recently, social entrepreneurs, impact investors, and even big businesses endeavor to bring new models and capital to social change. And, increasingly, social media gives voice to the "digital grassroots," allowing anyone with a media account to create momentum for change. The work of social change is burgeoning like never before.

It might be easy to think that these approaches alone can be used to combat the challenges that lie ahead. However, signs of trouble have emerged: the pace of change over the last few decades, and the way it has unfolded with power concentrating in the hands of a few, and exacerbated by a global pandemic, have left many groups under-represented and the natural resources of our planet dangerously depleted. Significant political upheavals, rising authoritarianism, and co-optation of seemingly benign technologies have challenged the bedrocks of national and global institutions. Indeed, the unintended consequences of progress—driven by the very strategies that have gotten us to this point—are now creating unrest, division, and unprecedented environmental destruction. These events have revealed too plainly the inadequacy of our current approaches, but they have also created the conditions for a reflection on how to move forward.

This book represents our exploration of "systems change," a term that has emerged in recent years to reflect a systemic approach to social change. Here, we journey with several organizations that are shifting what social change can and should look like. From them, we have come to understand that the day-to-day work in the long arc of social change is messy and non-linear: effects can rarely be traced to single root causes and outputs are rarely proportional to inputs. Rather than just promote successful outcomes, these organizations are focusing on the *process* of change, creating new systems that are more *responsive* to a rapidly changing world, and more *representative* of a diverse and growing global populace. The values and approaches with which these organizations are operating are not new, but have generally been happening beneath the surface. We believe that the current context requires us to bring this work to the fore. We have come to call these principles and practices *systems work*.

How *We* Got Here

We embarked on this project as social change practitioners who have had our minds changed. Each of us spent the beginning of our careers with a strong faith in the type of social change that got us to where we are today. As a medical doctor, François was trained to think that the answers to society's greatest challenges had already been worked out by unprecedented scientific advancement. However, as a junior medical officer in Namibia, he discovered that the biomedical approach alone was inadequate. Working at the height of the HIV/AIDS pandemic, amongst casualties of war returning from the Democratic Republic of Congo, he was struck by how poverty, the history of colonialism, and the legacy of apartheid undermined many attempts to fundamentally improve people's lives.

Cynthia's work in social change began when, fresh out of business school, she launched into a nonprofit fundraising role for a South African non-governmental organization (NGO) in New York City. As a former management consultant with a corporate career, Cynthia thought her background, based on the principles of efficiency and efficacy, primed her to make positive change. Yet when she arrived in South Africa and became immersed in the organizations she had been funding, these principles seemed to raise more problems than solutions.

As our careers progressed, an unsettling realization came to us slowly—too slowly for our own liking. The truth was that we, and the institutions in which we were positioned, were messing up a lot of the time. We were failing the communities with whom we worked and forming part of the very problems we were trying to solve. We saw issues with our approaches: strategies developed with superficial input from "beneficiaries," project plans written by officials or consultants with little appreciation for ground-level dynamics, funding that ran out just as we were making headway. Communities at times seemed to resent "interventions," while the discussions we had with funders and policymakers felt increasingly disconnected from reality. The deeper we got into our work, the more questions bubbled to the surface. Truth be told, we got scared. Was this how it was supposed to go? Why didn't it feel like anything was getting better, despite the significant investment and effort on the part of so many organizations and individuals?

These questions crystallized when our paths overlapped in 2011 at the Bertha Centre for Social Innovation at the University of Cape Town Graduate School of Business, a research center and academic community committed to effecting social change in the context of South Africa that was established in partnership with the Bertha Foundation. Nearly two decades after its political rebirth from the unjust system of apartheid, the country was coming to terms with extreme inequality, the twin pandemics of HIV and tuberculosis, widespread unemployment, and the early effects of climate change. At the same time, the Bertha Centre was connected to the emerging conversation around systems change at many global conferences and convenings. From this vantage point, we could see more clearly the disconnect between the conversations about systems change and the lived reality. It was this disconnect that guided the Bertha Centre's work to bring the people least likely to be represented in a business school—community workers, activists, and social justice champions—into the systems change conversation.

Over the next five years, we hosted dialogues with policymakers and protestors, presented short courses alongside radicals and activists, engaged with movement-makers, community organizers, and emerging-economy entrepreneurs. We were provoked by colleagues and peers, and followed up on every exchange that would allow us to understand systems change across this diverse pool of practitioners. In the process, we connected with funders, scholars, and advisors from around the world who were engaging with systems change in deeper ways than we originally anticipated.

First and foremost, we learned from these forward-thinking organizations and individuals that systems change is not an outcome but rather a process. In them, we have seen ways of working—specific *practices*—that are different than the ones highlighted in our textbooks and funding applications. Diverse though they are in roles and structures, they share certain unifying values, the *principles* behind their change work. These principles and practices are, on one hand, simple and accessible, yet, on the other, difficult to detect and quantify. Simply put, they are not easy to pin down, prove, and fund. For these reasons, we think they have been over-looked by well-intentioned practitioners, funders, and researchers like ourselves. We have come to believe that if we can bring these practices to light, and give them credence among funders and policymakers, we will have far more success in our collective efforts to achieve just and enduring social and environmental change.

Reading This Book

We have constructed this book in four sections :

In the Introduction, we explore the origins of the term "systems change" and highlight the principles and practices of systems work that we will expand upon in the remainder of the book.

In Part I, we give highlights from two hundred years of social change-making and break down systemic problems in terms of three features—complexity, scale, and depth—with the aim of understanding why the social and environmental challenges we face today seem intractable, in spite of two centuries of ostensible progress. We then outline the *principles of systems work* that drive a particular type of systems change aimed at creating systems that are more responsive and representative of the people who live in them.

In Part II, we describe *practices of systems work*, a collection of approaches we have gathered from our research with thoughtful practitioners. Here, we will share the many stories and conversations that allowed us to fundamentally shift our own thinking. Some of these practices may seem obvious at first (as they did to us), but we think you will share our revelation that they really are the deep work of social change.

Finally, in Part III, we discuss what it takes to support systems work—from those who work externally, providing funding and resources, to those who work internally, as professional managers and advisors. Since systems work is far more about the process of change than outcomes, means are just as important as ends. This requires a new way of looking at how we measure and resource the work of social change.

Throughout, we have attempted to amplify the voices and stories of those people who have taught us from their experiences and challenged us with their efforts. We have encapsulated the key themes in a series of learning notes at the end of each case-based chapter, and further detail each organization's practices and tactics in the Appendix, to emphasize the practical take-aways for busy practitioners.

Above all, this book venerates those social change practitioners who continuously reflect on the work they are doing and aim to put their insights on paper for others to learn.

Acknowledgments

This book has been a five-year endeavor, and we have been humbled by the many individuals and institutions who have shared this journey with us.

This book, at its core, is a tribute to social change practitioners whose systems work provides the inspiration and empirical basis for our analysis. The case studies in this book involved many interviews, conversations, and observations in person and over phone and email. We are grateful for the gift and privilege of sharing their stories through the lens of systems work. We want to extend a sincere thank you to Jos de Blok from Buurtzorg; Jeroo Billimoria, Bram van Eijk, Lubna Shaban, Jared Penner, Bianca Isaincu, Rob Becker, and Koen Vermeltfoort from Child & Youth Finance International (CYFI); Mauricio Lim Miller and Jesús Garena from Community Independence Initiative (CII) and Family Independence Initiative (FII); Vicky Colbert, Clarita Arboleda, Heriberto Castro, and Luz Dary Rojas from Fundación Escuela Nueva (FEN); Frank Beadle de Palomo, Mitch Besser, and David Torres from mothers2mothers (m2m); Arbind Singh, Rakesh Tripathi and Ratnish Verma from Nidan; Marlon Parker and Rene Parker from RLabs; and Sheela Patel, Nancy MacPherson and Ariana Karamallis from Slum Dwellers International (SDI). All these organizations have been active in the networks of Ashoka, Skoll Foundation and Schwab Foundation and thus we are grateful to each of those organizations for highlighting their work allowing us to build our knowledge collectively. We also learned extensively from those representing the supporting case studies in the book, including Kisimbi Thomas from AMP Health; Alice Evans from Lankelly Chase; Andrew Darnton and Andrew Harrison from Revaluation, and Anand Arkalgud from Socion.

Unfortunately, any book has its limitations as to how many stories and organizations can be profiled. A long list of practitioners and organizations were generous with their time and thinking, even if we were unable to profile their work as we sincerely would have liked— to them, we are beholden. We would like to thank Ruth Bechtel, Aida Coehlo, Jessica Crawford, Anisa Draboo, Ashifi Gogo, Danielle Goldschneider, Pinaki Halder, Katia Hamida, Tim Hanstad, Gregorio Janeiro, Chris Jochnick, Jordan Kassalow, Margarida Matsinhe, Anand Mehta, Luvuyo Rani, Evan Simpson, Elizabeth Smith, Hien Tran, and Allen Wilcox for the conversations which advanced our thinking in so many ways.

This book could not have been written without Tony Tabatznik and Laura Horwitz from the Bertha Foundation, who graciously provided the ongoing support, provocation, and encouragement to make all this work possible through their partnership with the University of Cape Town Graduate School of Business and the Bertha Centre for Social Innovation. We also wish to thank Hilde and Klaus Schwab, Katherine Milligan, Mirjam Schoening, Goy Phumtim, Pavitra Raja, Carolien de Bruin, Maria Inés Martin, Gabriela Henchoz, Shiv Verkaran and the Schwab Foundation for Social Entrepreneurship who commissioned the research that formed the backbone of the manuscript, and in particular Precious Moloi-Motsepe and the Motsepe Foundation, who provided the funding for the research. Geraldine Reymenants and Katrien Vanderplaudutse and the Government of Flanders, with their support for research and development of case studies and teaching materials on this topic at the Bertha Centre, also made this work possible. These individuals and organizations have been more than funders—they have been true thought partners in every sense of the term.

We are also indebted to the talents and energy of several people who worked closely with us to turn our ideas into words: Sarah Boyd, originally a research assistant who quickly segued into co-writer, editor, and true collaborator; Jane Notten, who skillfully put much of our thinking into readable prose; and Michael Schellenberg, who patiently gave us editorial support when we needed a professional and experienced hand. Gayle Northrop read several drafts of this work and improved it considerably with her clear thinking, encouraging guidance, and substantial expertise. Camilla Thorogood and Deon Cloete enthusiastically joined us early in the journey to help with case research and reviewing the substantial literature, and Janet Kinghorn who joined us later to bring our work to life in art and design Finally, a substantial thank you to Adam Swallow and Jenny King at Oxford University Press, who believed in this work and kept the project going longer than anyone originally anticipated, as well as Susan Framptom for the final copy editing and Saravanan Anandan for his diligence and step by step support to the finish line.

We are privileged to work alongside an incredible group of thoughtful individuals at the Bertha Centre for Social Innovation and the University of Cape Town , who are blending academic theory and practical action on a daily basis. In particular, we are grateful for our colleagues Warren Nilsson, Ncedisa Nkonyeni, Ella Scheepers, Tana Paddock, Ralph Hamann, Kosheek Sewchurran, Walter Baets, Mills Soko, as well as Claire Barnardo, Thato Bereng, Katusha de Villiers, Susan de Witt, Tine Fisker Henriksen, Olwen Manuel, Luvuyo Maseko, Barry Panulo, Aunnie Patton Power, Sulona Reddy, Solange Rosa, Fergus Turner, Simnikiwe Xanga, and Ndileka Zantsi, who inspired and challenged us with their own systems work in the academic and institutional sphere of the university. Equally important, the research would not have been possible without the administrative prowess, warmth, and humor of Nicolette Laubscher, Saadick Davids, and Stacey Thorne. Finally, the Pavalax community, provided a welcome water break from the focus of writing during François' sabbatical period at the university.

Over the last five years, we had the opportunity and pleasure to engage with many people and organizations we greatly respect and admire who have influenced our thinking, guided our assessments and tested our conclusions. We have benefited from these exchanges immensely. In particular, we would like to thank Julie Battilana, Amira Bliss, Mille Bojer, David Bornstein, Winne Byanyima, Stephan Chambers, Ernest Darkoh, Nomvula Dlamini, Cheryl Dorsey, Bill Drayton, Peter Drobac, Alnoor Ebrahim, Carol-Ann Foulis, Marshall Ganz, Don Gips, Duncan Green, David Harrison, Senzo Hlophe, Janet Jobson, Kippy Joseph, Philippa Kabali-Kagwa, Tom Kagerer, John Kania, Olivia Leland, Vanessa Lowndes, Johanna

Mair, Roger Martin, Mario Meyer, Michelle-Lee Moore, Odin Muehlenbein, James Mwangi, Alex Nicholls, Phumlani Nkontwana, Iris Nxumalo, Per Olssen, Shrashtant Patara, Raj Patel, Doug Reeler, Cheryl Rose, Loretta Rose, Florian Rutsch, Asif Saleh, Courtney Schoon, Christian Seelos, Peter Senge, Judy Sikuza, Peter Tufano, Roberto Unger, Marc Ventresca, Diana Wells, and Frances Westley. We were also lucky to spend time with cohorts of dynamic and thought-provoking students, fellows, and practitioners in our teaching and learning engagements, through the Systems Change & Social Impact course at the University of Cape Town, the Rockefeller Global Social Innovation Fellowship with the Waterloo Institute for Social Innovation and Resilience, Stockholm Resilience Centre, and the University of Victoria, and the Fellowship for Organisational Innovation led by the D.G. Murray Trust. We especially wish to extend our gratitude to the late Pamela Hartigan, whose leadership at the Schwab Foundation for Social Entrepreneurship and Skoll Centre at the University of Oxford's Saïd Business School was a motivating force for so many in the field of social change.

Lastly, we wish to express our deepest appreciation for our families. We are exceptionally thankful for François' wife, Heidre Bezuidenhout, the medical geneticist who spurred us on with patience, encouragement, and caffeine, and for Cynthia's husband, Chris Rayner, a ceaseless champion who never hesitated to talk through a particularly challenging day of writing over the dinner table. Their love, intelligence, and friendship have been our foundation. We are also grateful for our parents, Areti and François (snr) Bonnici and Angie and Roland Schweer, whose hearts for service and social justice nurtured our own; our siblings, Gigi Bonnici (a role model with a lifelong commitment to justice in migration) and Erica Whalen and Julie Wilhite, for their enduring cheerleading and camaraderie; and finally, our young children, Luc, Leonardo, Harry, and Eva, who continually remind us that relationships are the defining feature of human systems, and whose generosity of spirit and playful approach keep us hopeful and enthusiastic for the systems workers of the future.

Contents

Introduction: Working in Systems   xxv

PART I. PRINCIPLES OF SYSTEMS WORK

1. **An Industry of Social Change**   3
2. **Complexity, Scale, and Depth**   18
3. **Connection, Context, and Power**   33

PART II. PRACTICES OF SYSTEMS WORK

4. **Cultivating Collectives**   51
5. **Equipping Problem-solvers**   68
6. **Promoting Platforms**   86
7. **Disrupting Policies *and* Patterns**   103

PART III. REIMAGINING THE FUTURE

8. **Measuring for Learning**   123
9. **Funding for Partnership**   141
10. **The Principles and Practices in Action**   162

*Appendix: Case Studies: Organizational Practices
and Tactics of Systems Work*   179

Endnotes   197
Index   239

We have arrived at a point in our human evolution where we *know* a lot, but we *understand* very little. Our chosen navigation has been piloted by reason, leading to the port of knowledge. As such it has been an overwhelmingly successful. We have never, in all of our existence, accumulated more knowledge than during the last 100 years. We are celebrating the apotheosis of reason, but in the midst of celebration we suddenly have the feeling that something is missing...Perhaps the moment to pause and reflect has arrived.

—Chilean economist Manfred A. Max-Neef, *What Next?*

Introduction

Working in Systems

It takes a significant leap of confidence to believe we can make the world a better place. For most of human history, people have left this task to divine intervention. In the last two hundred years, however—a span including a succession of scientific and technological revolutions, two World Wars, and significant political and social upheaval—an audacious, distributed project to secure a world "free from want"[1] has been well underway. Paul Hawken, author of *Blessed Unrest*, has described this as the "largest social movement in history."[2]

We refer to this movement as social change: the intentional restructuring of social and environmental arrangements to improve society. The project of social change is both exciting and daunting, and it already has some notable achievements. Extreme poverty, while persistent in some geographies, has been reduced to just 10 percent of the global population.[3] Health and longevity have experienced extensive gains: a person born in 1800 could, on average, expect to live to just twenty-nine years old. That average, globally, has more than doubled to seventy-one.[4] Hunger and malnutrition, while still deplorably high, were once problems faced by the majority and are now experienced by the few:[5] developing countries have reduced the prevalence of malnourishment by two-thirds, to just 13 percent of their populations, since 1970.[6] These figures paint an overwhelmingly positive picture, suggesting that improvement of livelihoods has become, in short order, a taken-for-granted objective of our political, social, and even commercial arrangements.

One would think that these successes would boost our shared confidence considerably. And yet, they have not. In survey after survey, respondents around the world indicate that they believe the world is getting worse off.[7] Our own informal polls among students in the classrooms where we teach bear these statistics out. Even in our conversations with those who are courageous enough to devote their life's work to improve the world—the nonprofit leaders, activists, environmentalists, community organizers, social innovators and entrepreneurs whom we refer to collectively as *social change practitioners*—we sense a growing unease.

Systems Work Terms 1: *Social change practitioners*

social change practitioners	*nonprofit leaders, activists, environmentalists, community organizers, social innovators and entrepreneurs who work to influence social change*

Swedish physician and statistician Hans Rosling achieved a level of fame through a TED talk that explored this very conundrum, reaching the conclusion that our ignorance of statistics and "cognitive dissonance" were to blame for our global pessimism.[8] However, we believe that there is something more fundamental at work. Social challenges are not like ordinary problems, the ones we are trained to solve at school or even in our workplaces. Social challenges are inextricably linked to the historical contexts and the natural environments in which they manifest, meaning that we cannot address these challenges in isolation. They share key characteristics that create confounding results when we try to solve them, tempering any level of progress that we may feel while working on them. We believe that these characteristics—notably, the complexity, scale, and depth of social problems—explain the lack of confidence, even overwhelming cynicism, that pervade our attempts to "change the world" for the better.

The complexity of social change implies many different variables interacting with one another in dynamic and unpredictable ways. It means that even while we seemingly make progress, our audacious efforts often feel as if they are in vain. Many social problems are what design theorists Horst Rittel and Melvin Webber dubbed "wicked problems."[9] Wicked problems are uniquely unsolvable; they are always symptomatic of other problems. Just when we think we have found a solution, they wriggle out of our grasp and present us with new, unknowable consequences. These unintended consequences of social change confoundingly emerge as new problems, such as rising obesity rates in contrast to malnourishment, and climate change as a result of industrialization and economic development.

Meanwhile, the scale of social problems means that we necessarily learn more about problems as we attempt to solve them. As we traverse new geographies, we become aware of similarities and differences across contexts and, as we look closer, we discover that root causes are merely symptoms. This feature of wickedness is the lack of a stopping point: once we understand a problem, we are able to do better, and our satisfaction at having arrived at some level of success is vanquished by the prospect of yet another mountain to climb. Hence, our aspirations for social change have become ever more expansive. What economist Jeffrey Sachs dubbed our "common fate on a crowded planet" is now part and parcel of both global and national policies.[10] In September 2015, 193 countries agreed to a global agenda, the Sustainable Development Goals (SDGs), which seeks not only to end poverty and hunger, but also to secure a laudable list of human and environmental rights for both people and planet. This set of goals followed the already ambitious Millennium Development Goals (MDGs), a set of eight goals which aimed to halve extreme poverty and halt the spread of HIV/AIDS, against which many countries made significant progress. While this boldness is commendable, addressing the scale of social and ecological change is also daunting. Each context which we attempt to change or improve involves a different set of variables and a widely divergent set of outcomes.

Finally, and most importantly, social problems have depth, meaning they derive from the values, norms, and beliefs that we bring into our daily lives. This is the most elusive and controversial of the three characteristics of social problems. Over the past five years, we have watched as funders, policymakers, and change practitioners have recognized the issues of complexity and scale, looking for ways to account for unintended consequences and non-linear growth trajectories. Depth, however, remains a blind spot. Yet, as many practitioners can attest, the further we go with our change efforts, the more it becomes clear that our work can actually entrench the very order of things that need to change. We can reinforce rooted problems such as racism, gender inequality, and multi-generational poverty, even as we fight against them. It is perhaps because of our failures in this regard that we have been reluctant to interrogate them further. Those who attempt social change do not receive "immunity" for good works. In fact, we are liable for the consequences we create.[11] And as mega-challenges like climate change and racial justice exceed political and generational timescales, our culpability is not just to those who live now, but to those who are not yet born.

It is because of their complexity, scale, and depth that social problems are systemic in nature. Due to these features, systemic problems require a more comprehensive way of thinking about social change—a concept that is increasingly being referred to as "systems change". These are not problems to be solved, but rather dismantled and reimagined, with adequate redress and reorganization to set us on a different path to our collective future.

Exploring Systems Change

Our exploration of systems change began at the University of Cape Town's Bertha Centre for Social Innovation: an unlikely partnership between one of the oldest, most conservative universities in Africa and possibly one of the youngest, most radical family foundations in the world. The Bertha Centre was founded on the premise that innovation can solve social challenges by improving critical social services, such as health, education, and youth development. In our own capacities within the Centre—François as director and Cynthia as a senior researcher, both working alongside Bertha's unique team of social change mavericks and misfits—we began to recognize that such a straightforward theory of change seemed naive at best. At the time, in 2011, most of the academic literature on social innovation was coming from North America and Western Europe and didn't seem to encapsulate the on-the-ground realities of the African context, much less the broader Global South.[12]

While partnering with some of the more thoughtful institutions focused on social change, including the Stellenbosch Centre for Complex Systems in Transition, the Stockholm Resilience Centre, and the University of Waterloo Institute for Social Innovation and Resilience (WISER), we were also focused on the immediate challenges posed to us by the entrenched legacy of apartheid and growing inequality in South Africa. We had one foot in the world of institutional change-making, and the other firmly planted in the "grassroots" work of social change.

Against this backdrop, we were invited by the Schwab Foundation for Social Entrepreneurship to generate a new set of learnings from organizations tackling the same kind of complex, large-scale, and deep systemic problems we encountered at the Bertha Centre. The Schwab Foundation, housed within the World Economic Forum,[13] hosts the world's biggest community of late-stage social change practitioners and although it calls these individuals "social entrepreneurs," it uses a very broad definition of the term. The organizations recognized by the Schwab Foundation come in all shapes and sizes, from traditional nonprofits, to commercial social enterprises, to advocacy and activist organizations.

On paper, these are some of the largest, most successful organizations in the world, serving millions of people through direct services, innovative products, and community development initiatives. Yet, despite their apparent successes, many of the founders and leaders of these organizations—several of whom we will introduce as case studies in these chapters—continue to feel that their responses are inadequate. By 2015, several of these leaders had become interested in the emergence of the concept of systems change, but they were not sure how it translated into action.

It was from this practical need that the Schwab Foundation asked us to conduct research on systems change for their community of social entrepreneurs. We were excited about the opportunity, thinking that the project might help us create a definition of systems change that encompassed the real practices we were seeing in the examples around us. During our workshops, short courses, and planning sessions with social change practitioners at the Bertha Centre, we had seen glimmers of the work that one might call systems change, and we already had a sense of the values and activities this work required. However, if pressed to explain what exactly these practitioners were doing differently, we could not readily articulate it. So we set out to examine more closely a group of organizations that embodied the different approaches to systems change as we understood it.

Through the networks we had built with the Bertha Foundation and the Schwab Foundation, we spent the next five years exploring and studying dozens of social change organizations in greater depth than we ever had previously. We sought out local luminaries, revisited standouts from our past work, searched databases, and discovered new groups from the recommendations of colleagues, friends, and beyond. This work took us on an exceptional journey across five continents to conduct conversations with hundreds of individuals. Along the way, we spoke with social change practitioners in boardrooms and hotel conference rooms, as well as under highway overpasses, on bumpy car rides, in classrooms, and even, on one occasion, on a funicular which took us 10,000 feet above sea level. Like any good journey, our final destination ended up being quite far from where we set out to go.

Two Approaches

When we started our research in 2015, the term systems change was growing in use with definitions that had subtle but important differences. These definitions included "addressing the root causes of social problems,"[14] "shifting the conditions that are holding the problem in place,"[15] "changing the way a majority of relevant players solve a big social challenge,"[16] and, most ambitiously, "a fundamental change in policies, processes, relationships, and power structures, as well as deeply held values and norms."[17] Some influential funders, such as the Rockefeller Foundation in the United States and Lankelly Chase in the United Kingdom, were incorporating this language into their strategies, while a few prominent nonprofit consulting firms and intermediaries had begun to publish reports on the topic.[18]

The term itself has an intriguing history. Community psychologists and social work scholars have referred to systems change since the 1990s,[19] however this body of articles has little to no overlap with the practitioner and funder literature that most social change practitioners draw upon. Rather, the funders and consultants who became interested in the term began by drawing from systems and complexity theories, starting in the 1950s with Jay Forrester's systems dynamics group at the Massachusetts Institute of Technology and moving toward the complexity-informed approaches to systems that have grown since the 1960s.[20] However, to really understand the concept of systems change, we have to reach back further to find an even more interesting legacy for systems change.[21]

Systems theory originated in the 1940s, when Austrian biologist Ludwig von Bertalanffy published a series of articles on what he termed "general systems theory."[22] This interdisciplinary theory, which was premised on the idea that parts should be studied in relation to the whole, was quickly adopted by a number of scientists and thinkers, and spread to numerous fields, including sociology, psychology, and economics. As systems thinking was popularized, the expectation that we would be able to "engineer" perfect systems, including social systems, prevailed. In the pursuit of finely tuned systems, many of the scientific disciplines throughout the second half of the twentieth century developed intricate and sophisticated methods of modeling and mapping systems, aided by rapidly developing computer technology.

We were equally seduced by a concept of systems change that enabled the engineering of perfectly functioning social systems at different points in our work. This view seemed to promise that if we could only see the whole picture with all its fine detail, we could change it. We were surprised, therefore, to learn that Bertalanffy's original German text remained widely misunderstood.[23] Bertalanffy's concept of a general system theory ("theory" having a much broader meaning in German) was in fact a cautionary tale to scientists—a reminder that their scientific discoveries were merely pieces of broader systems, each nested within a broader whole for which we have no existing "grand theory" to explain.

While much of what is written about systems change has been described as "abstract in tone, polemical, and more concerned with diagnosing what is wrong than with offering concrete solutions,"[24] there is yet a more subtle danger within the systems change conversation. Discussion around systems change can create the belief that social systems can be "engineered" or "perfected," that our social change ambitions are akin to scientists manipulating variables in a highly controlled lab experiment. This belief is insidious because it implies that complex, large-scale, and deep problems can be solved by "one-size-fits-all" solutions, or "big bets" promoted by powerful actors. More importantly, it shifts the debate of social change away from a central issue: *we are part of the systems that we are changing*. In fact, the work of social change can both alter and perpetuate the deeper structures that entrench our systemic issues.

This realization highlights that there are two divergent approaches to systems change. The first of these is a fundamentally technical approach. For those who believe that social change is a response to a malfunction in society, mechanical glitches that can be fixed, the approach to systems change is largely a technical matter. This *technical approach* assumes that problems can ultimately be solved as long as the right solution is developed and taken up by those who require it. The second approach is focused on the power dynamics inherent in a system. If you believe that systems change requires overturn of the existing order, an uprooting of the deepest norms and beliefs that drive our behaviors, you will approach change with a disruption mindset. This *transformative approach* assumes that existing dynamics must radically evolve or be torn down and rebuilt before change can occur.[25]

Systems Work Terms 2: *Technical vs transformational*

technical	*social change approaches that assume problems can ultimately be solved as long as the right solution is developed and taken up by those who require it*
transformational	*social change approaches that assume existing social structures must be torn down and rebuilt from scratch*

Both approaches have salience, as well as empirical evidence to back them. Yet the definitions of systems change used in both practitioner and scholarly circles seem to vacillate between these two approaches. At times, the two approaches seem compatible, while at other times they feel conflictual.

Due to our unlikely position at the fault line of a school of management and a radical foundation, we often found ourselves translating one side's position to the other's. We were so thoroughly intrigued by this dichotomy that we spent a significant amount of the research for this book uncovering the historical roots that underpin these two approaches (we will delve into this more fully in Chapter 1). We ultimately came to the conclusion that *both* approaches are essential and, in fact, serve as important counterweights to achieving systems change. As systems scientist Yaneer Bar-Yam explains, "the complexity of our approaches needs to match the complexity of the systems we are trying to change."[26]

Discovering the Deeper Work

As we engaged with individuals, organizations, and universities at home and around the world, we were on the lookout for the two approaches. We visited organizations developing innovative products and delivering impressive services, reaching millions of clients or customers. We witnessed the "tipping point" pattern where organizations typically partner with governments, other NGOs, or the private sector to scale their solutions significantly and ultimately create a "new way of doing things" in the world. This was the type of technical systems change that we had read about in books and articles, and it corresponded with many of the conversations we had with practitioners and funders.

Alternatively, we were also on the lookout for transformational systems change, such as influencing policy at the local, national, or international level or forcing political change through community organizing and large-scale protest action. We spent time with groups with long histories of advocacy and activism, generating significant political wins at the local, national, and international levels. Still others were excellent at mobilizing and building collaborative networks, one of them spanning a hundred plus countries and tens of thousands of partners, and another linking up governments and the private sector to spread their models to countless beneficiaries.

What we didn't anticipate was something far deeper—a set of values and beliefs toward the *process* of change that was as important as the change itself. While the accomplishments and achievements were instrumental to achieving change, they were ultimately not the qualities that intrigued us most. We began to realize that the two approaches—technical and transformational—are *necessary but not sufficient* to create systems that are enduring and just. With these organizations, we eventually journeyed to a deeper set of principles which we came to call *systems work.*[27]

Systems Work Terms 3: *Social change, systems change, systems work*

social change	*the intentional restructuring of social and environmental arrangements to improve society*
systems change	*a comprehensive approach to social change that seeks to address the complex, large-scale, and deep characteristics of social issues*
systems work	*the day-to-day principles and practices that guide the actions of organizations and individuals as they undertake to change systems; emphasizes process over outcomes*

Through systems work, these organizations are engaging in day-to-day actions that acknowledge the depth of systemic problems. They are working to fundamentally alter the way a system functions in relation to change. They are ensuring that the people most immersed in the context of a social problem and who live it every day—the people we call *primary actors* in the system—are able to engage with the challenge in new ways. In this way, organizations are working within systems to make them *function in more responsive and representative ways.*

Systems Work Terms 4: *Primary and supporting actors*

primary actors	*the people most immersed in the context of a social issue, often with lived experience of the issue itself*
supporting actors	*professional managers, funders, policymakers and advisors who work in partnership with primary actors to support social change*

Principles and Practices

In the chapters that follow, we will first highlight the principles of systems work at a high level. We will then draw out several practices that illustrate how the principles of systems work can be carried out in the day-to-day activities of social change.

Understandably, with such a diverse group of organizations, the goals, activities, and cultures varied widely amongst the groups. But amongst their diverse practices, we articulate three principles and four practices that encapsulate the values and day-to-day approaches that underpin their systems work.

The Principles of Systems Work

foster connection	*building new collective identities that keep groups together while learning*
embrace context	*equipping primary actors to respond to day-to-day complexity, dynamically adapting as the context requires*
reconfigure power	putting decision-making and resources in the hands of primary actors, ensuring that social systems fully represent the people who live in them

These principles and practices have a fundamentally different target than the ones we were looking for. Rather than providing services to those in need or advocating for change on behalf of others, they aim to bring together people, communities, and institutions that can reimagine and shape alternatives. Many will identify with these principles and practices because they are, in fact, not new at all. However, the emphasis on this work as a fundamental component of systems change is lacking. What we have come to call systems work has really been there all along: the often overlooked, largely unfunded work of successful social change organizations.

Our research coalesces around the idea that systems cannot be "fixed." Change is constant and even the perfect solution is made immediately imperfect by even subtle shifts in the context. However, through the work of the organizations we studied, it is clear that organizations *can* work to ensure that key actors in systems are connected to one another, acting with creativity and dynamism, and thus able to make decisions in responsive and representative ways.

This is also contested work. In our interviews, we encountered social change practitioners who confronted or even courted controversy, some who literally put their lives on the line in their quest for change. This deeper work is not easy. To embrace uncertainty is not a natural human inclination, while the devolution of decision-making is contrary to our twentieth-century ways of organizing. This will necessarily result in new configurations and ways of being that are contrary to prevailing ideologies. Power-shifting is politicized: it requires the reallocation of resources and the dismantling of privilege, much of which will not happen without a fight. This may sound ambitious, even impossible, but in our increasingly polarized and unequal world, we met numerous individuals and innovative organizations who are willing to take up the baton.

We will visit *RLabs*, a social movement that is making "hope contagious" by recruiting former gang members in post-apartheid South Africa and more than twenty other countries to drive new technology start-ups; *mothers2mothers*, an organization working across ten countries in Africa to promote mothers living with HIV as frontline healthworkers; the original version of the *Family Independence Initiative*, an organization in California set up with the premise that poverty doesn't mean families shouldn't make their own decisions; *Buurtzorg*, a Netherlands-based health services provider that has banned bureaucracy in favor of neighborhood nurses; *Slum Dwellers International*, a transnational network elevating the urban poor to the top of the international political agenda; *Child and Youth Finance International*, a global collective that equips children to become fully empowered economic citizens; *Nidan*, the incubator of twenty-two "people's institutions" organizing informal

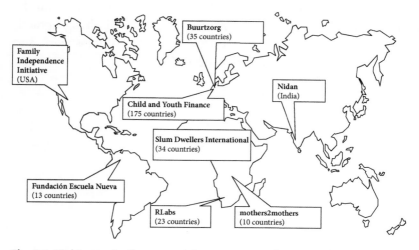

Fig. 0.1 Eight organizations practicing systems work around the world
Source: Authors.

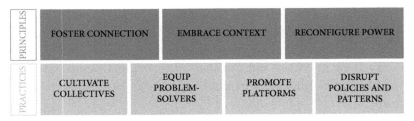

Fig. 0.2 Principles and practices of systems work
Source: Authors.

workers to stand up to exploitation and forming self-governed committees to influence the urban development of India's fastest growing cities; and finally, *Fundación Escuela Nueva*, a nonprofit in Colombia working across Latin America and beyond to improve the quality and relevance of education by putting children at the heart of the learning process.

The principles and practices are inspired by the many organizations we met on our journey, and told through the stories of a few (fig 0.1). This book is not about single success stories, but rather how organizations are working with communities and collectives to channel their power to tackle structural and systemic barriers to change.

Our hope is that these principles and practices (fig 0.2), and the stories that bring them to life, will inspire social change practitioners of all types to uncover their own hidden systems work, and nurture it as the deeper work of social change.

PART I

PRINCIPLES OF SYSTEMS WORK

Although we may not realize it, the prevailing approach to social change is underpinned by an industrial mindset that has been two centuries in the making. Under this mindset, public, private, and nonprofit sectors exchange large sums of money, expertise and resources in pursuit of ambitious goals to stave off poverty, disease, and hunger at a global scale. Yet, despite this massive effort, social problems still seem insurmountable. In Chapter 1, we consider how the *industry of social change* emerged historically, leading to many of the unintended consequences we face today. We then further dissect the *complexity, scale, and depth* of social systems in Chapter 2, in order to gain an understanding of why these features require a different, process-oriented approach. Finally, in Chapter 3, we outline the *principles of systems work*, the values and beliefs organizations uphold to create systems that are responsive to and representative of the people who live in them.

1

An Industry of Social Change

In the summer of 1941, as World War II deepened with Hitler's invasion of the Soviet Union, an envoy of three American scientists began an extensive tour of the Mexican countryside. On paper, their challenge seemed simple. How could Mexico, with a rapidly growing populace, grow enough food to feed its people? The three men chosen for this task were experts in their fields: a maize specialist from Harvard,[1] a farmer and soil specialist from Cornell's agronomy department,[2] and a plant pathologist from the University of Minnesota.[3] These were men who did their jobs thoroughly. Traveling more than five thousand miles by station wagon, trucks, and horse-back,[4] their journey would set the stage for the largest expansion of food production in the history of humankind. It would also mark the start of one of the most controversial social change projects ever funded by private philanthropy.

A powerful group of people awaited their return in Washington, D.C. and New York. Not least of these was Henry A. Wallace, vice president of the United States. Wallace was the eldest son of an Iowa farmer turned politician and had already made his fortune founding the world's first commercial hybrid seed corn company.[5] In addition to entrepreneurial success, Wallace followed in his father's political footsteps, joining President Franklin D. Roosevelt's administration, first as secretary of agriculture and later as vice president in 1940.[6] Fresh off the back of his re-election, President Roosevelt dispatched the Spanish-fluent Wallace to Mexico to attend the inauguration of the country's new president, Manuel Avila Camacho.

Camacho had recently succeeded Lazaro Cardenas, a general turned president who had sent shockwaves through American business interests by nationalizing the country's oil industry and beginning the process of land reform. Camacho, a moderate conservative, was seen as far friendlier to American interests. Wallace knew his task was, in part, to shore up support for Camacho. True to his agricultural roots, he also became interested in Mexico's chronic undersupply of food, which he discerned could easily foment unrest.[7] Soon after his trip, he struck up a conversation with Raymond Fosdick, president of the Rockefeller Foundation (RF), observing[8] that the plight of Mexico's poor could be dramatically improved if the yields of Mexican staple crops could be increased.[9]

Fosdick, a lawyer and an ardent internationalist, was guiding the RF at a precarious time. Established in 1913 to "serve the welfare of mankind throughout the world,"[10] the Foundation was flourishing under his unifying leadership. However, with Europe and China deep in the throes of the war, their most promising international programs had ground to a halt. Wallace's observations appealed to Fosdick and he soon approached the Foundation's head of the natural science division, Warren Weaver, about developing a food security program. Weaver was puzzled by the request.[11] In their strategic planning sessions, no funds had been approved for agricultural work aside from basic research. He anticipated that this would take the RF squarely outside of its comfort zone into a far more operational role than its traditional grant-making activities involved.

Weaver's concern was well founded, since the RF's interest in Mexico encompassed far more than humanitarian objectives. RF staffers had steered clear of being seen as a "tool" of the US government,[12] but a project in Mexico designed to feed a restless populace and keep land reform at bay could not help but have political undertones. FDR's "good neighbor policy" in Latin America, which was headed by none other than Nelson Rockefeller, was strongly committed to increasing influence in the region and preventing communist influence. The Rockefeller family also had substantial business interests in Mexico which had been threatened by Cardenas' populist moves.[13]

Motives aside, the team of agricultural experts that Weaver recruited for the job already had a certain solution in mind. By the 1940s, the field of agricultural science was dominated by industrialized countries, where urbanization and labor mobility had transformed the rural landscape. As a group of scientists who had honed their research in the American South, Weaver's team was heavily focused on higher yields to feed urban centers with fewer inputs, including labor. The Mexican context could not have been more different, with subsistence farming a mainstay of rural livelihoods. Still, the three experts delivered a set of recommendations in line with their experience: set up a team in Mexico City to advise the Mexican government and train local scientists on modern agricultural techniques. The report findings were quickly accepted.

Not everyone was in agreement that a yield-driven approach was the best way forward. The Foundation's International Health Division submitted two studies which raised concerns about the nutritional profile of the proposed agricultural system. RF trustee John Dickey pointed to the political impact of the program, commenting that "these very benefits may introduce fresh economic disparities within the Mexican economy."[14] Critics on the program team repeatedly proposed a more inclusive and multi-disciplinary approach. Investigative journalist Mark Dowie writes, "On several occasions in the years that followed, questions of equity and social fallout were raised again, only to be dismissed or ignored by Rockefeller officials."[15]

By the early 1950s, the skeptics' arguments seemed groundless. RF scientists were developing new varieties of grains that increased yields significantly, particularly for wheat. They trained Mexican agronomists on their findings and the program attracted agricultural science students from throughout Latin America, leading to extensions in other countries and to other food crops.[16] Reports from the field described piles of excess food stacked in the school grounds of Mexican villages. In a victory statement to his RF colleagues, the program's director George Harrar wrote, "The Rockefeller-Mexico program has demonstrated that a mere handful of well-trained scientists can, in an amazingly short time, catalyze the agricultural economy of a nation."[17]

Based on this success, the RF made a calculated decision to expand the agricultural program to India and the Philippines, countries that seemed equally ripe for agricultural economic make-overs. Based on a field study commissioned in 1952,[18] the RF decided to use a strategy similar to Mexico, supporting local scientists to adopt modern Western agricultural methods in these countries. But in scale, these new projects dwarfed the Mexico program in both ambition and funding.

By the 1960s, the investment began to pay off. In 1961, four new maize hybrids were released with characteristics that were favorable in India. By the next year, a national seed bank was created to distribute the seeds to Indian farmers. In 1966, the RF facilitated the "largest single seed transaction in history" when the Indian government purchased 18,000 tons of high-yielding wheat seeds.[19] The World Bank signed onto the project, extending credit to farmers for machinery, chemicals, seeds, and livestock. By 1971, the project was considered complete, earning one of the RF researchers a Nobel Peace Prize and accolades from around the world for his part in what had by now been dubbed the "Green Revolution." But the story was far from over. Just as soon as the Green Revolution declared its mission accomplished, another story of social change began to emerge.[20]

Although the supply of food in Mexico, India, and other Green Revolution countries substantially increased, this did not immediately translate into food for those who were hungry. The RF program was focused solely on yields, a problem that could readily be answered by science and industry. In doing so, it had neglected to account for demand, an issue that required purchasing power by the poor. At the same time, the program required landowners to purchase new seeds, fertilizer, and irrigation to implement the high-yield techniques. Naturally, the World Bank extended credit to larger landowners more readily, and smaller farmers were squeezed out of the market. Thousands of farmers moved off their land, providing cheap labor for more successful landowners and for corporations now manufacturing to meet the increased demand for agricultural inputs. Those who could not find work in the rural areas joined the ranks of the urban poor, increasing the pace of urbanization to already crowded cities.[21] Dowie writes, "The story of this massive undertaking is a valuable case study of an earnest, long-term philanthropic effort to solve a complex, seemingly intractable problem without addressing the fundamental reasons for its existence."[22]

Interconnected and Institutional

The Green Revolution was very much the product of a post-war power structure that laid the foundation for the large-scale social change movement as we know it. Efforts to improve the human condition certainly existed long before the World Wars.[23] However, the lasting impression of two World Wars and the interim Great Depression cannot be overstated. The way we think about social change to this day is dramatically shaped by this psyche. For subsequent generations, it is hard to visualize the aftermath: cities razed to the ground, families torn apart, millions displaced, tens of millions dead.[24] Yet, out of the ash and rubble, rebuilding became a shared project upon which to build a new social compact. In one of those twists of irony that only history can reveal, for those who survived these years, the ability to destroy impressed upon them the imperative to improve. Historian Margaret MacMillan writes, "At the end of the first world war it had been possible to contemplate going back to business as usual. However, 1945 was different, so different that it has been called Year Zero."[25]

The post-war period, in stark contrast to the century prior, marked a turn toward government and other large institutions as instruments of peace and stability.[26] Fueled by unprecedented economic growth, a baby boom, and a sharp reduction in income inequality worldwide,[27] several ambitious projects to construct a new social order emerged. These included the establishment of the United Nations, the International Bank for Reconstruction and Development (which would later merge with the World Bank Group), and the International Monetary Fund. While each of these institutions evolved with different mandates, they represented a dramatic shift in the previous construct of social change: from small-scale, voluntary activities that addressed local or regional issues to large-scale, government-led initiatives that tackled global challenges, spanning nation-states, sectors, and populations. Peace and security were seen in direct proportion to the interconnectedness of global arrangements.

These institutions emerged alongside a growing allegiance to the tenets of scientific disciplines which gained ground as part of the defense-building activities of the World Wars. This mindset was coupled with an unshakeable faith in industry, which had grown in influence through the military conflicts, to support technological development. As conflict drew to a close, military might swiftly broadened into a scientific community with a focus on solving issues related to peace, human progress, and economic growth, rather than just war. However, this entanglement between the technology of warfare and peace would only continue to grow, leading President Dwight D. Eisenhower, a former army general, to warn "against the acquisition of unwarranted influence, whether sought or unsought, by the military-industrial complex" during his 1961 televised farewell address.[28]

The second half of the twentieth century was characterized by the most rapid political upheaval ever experienced by a single generation, starkly divided by economic philosophy. While America and Europe conceptualized their versions of liberal democracy to suit reconstruction, the Soviet Union and China expanded their versions of communism through satellite states both regionally and throughout the world. By mid-century, former European colonies were rapidly winning independence, but subsequent attempts to influence their political allegiances led to continued involvement by former imperial states and new aspiring ones.

In this period, state-led social programs grew in size and importance. In the United States, the Depression-era New Deal and its 1960s counterpart, the Great Society, formed a consistent (albeit fragile) political consensus for the expansion of social welfare programs. The European social model that emerged in the post-war years solidified a set of cultural norms promoting strong employment protection and a social safety net for all citizens. Growth in social spending was consistent, and indeed the source of, increased government spending by the developmental states that emerged in Asia, Latin America, and Africa. This funding, however, was distributed with dual motives. Early programs, the biggest of which was the US$13 billion Marshall Plan (equivalent to US$135 billion in today's dollars),[29] were initiated to instil peace and prosperity in war-ravaged countries that had fundamentally sound democratic processes already in place. As international development attention shifted to the post-colonial context, however, these objectives were largely subsumed by Cold War ambitions. Ideology became a permanent fixture in development, a marriage of idealism and self-interest with far-reaching implications.

By the 1960s, this faith in institutions and science was being challenged by a series of social movements that rocked the period: a growing labor movement; anti-war demonstrations; further pushes for civil, indigenous, LGBTQ, and civil rights; a nascent push for environmentalism; and corresponding lifestyle shifts that threatened to upend conservative values. In the United States, the groundwork laid by civil rights activists built the social networks that inspired much of the leadership for subsequent organizing.[30] Around the world, labor struggles, anti-war activism, and the anti-apartheid movement crystalized into a global resistance to what was increasingly seen as a world of "haves" and "have-nots."

Paradoxically, development and the delivery of state-sponsored social services materialized as an antidote to social radicalism, a mediating influence to associate progress with the staid and comforting measures of health, education, and livelihoods. This approach to social change was *technical* in nature; it was built with the express purpose of creating an interconnected world girded by sound institutions that would never again go to war. At the same time, the world was undergoing profound societal shifts that challenged the values and norms underpinning these very institutions. These changes, led by activists, union leaders, anti-war protestors, and community organizers, envisioned a world free from hierarchy and institutionalization. Therefore, their means and objectives were fundamentally different. While international development technocrats saw economic development as a primary route to peace and prosperity, social justice activists saw a capitalist juggernaut taking advantage of a "continual crisis" mindset context to entrench the growing traditional order. The change they sought was *transformational*, requiring a fundamental rethink as to who was included in the very institutions that were charged with maintaining peace, and who was included in the prosperity they envisioned.

This clash in approaches toward social change came to a violent head in the year of 1968. In a single year, the world seemed to convulse with change: the North Vietnamese launched the Tet Offensive, proving that the United States had entered a long and protracted war; a loosening of the media in Czechoslovakia erupted into the "Prague Spring"; civil rights leader Martin Luther King Jr was assassinated, leading to protests in more than a hundred cities across the United States; 800,000 French teachers and students went on a general strike; the US Apollo 8 orbited the moon. The post-war democratic world, united in its quest for peace, was increasingly divided as to how this should be achieved. Yet, in a strange twist of history, over the coming three decades these competing ideologies would merge together to form an *industry of social change*: the architecture we currently use to imagine, fund, and implement global social change.

Systems Work Terms 5: *Industry of social change*

industry of social change	*the architecture we currently use to imagine, fund, and implement global social change*

Fragmented and Privatized

If 1968 was the apex of the post-war struggle for social change, then 1973 was its nadir. A US stock market crash in February signaled the end of the post-war expansion and proved a sign of more financial troubles ahead. Over the next twenty-one months, the Standard & Poor's Index (S&P 500) declined by more than 50 percent and the Dow Jones Industrial Average sank by 45 percent. It would take a decade for these indices to recover. In October, the Organization of the Petroleum Exporting Countries (OPEC) abruptly raised the price of a barrel of oil by 400 percent.[31] At the same time, the United States, the United Kingdom, and much of Western Europe sank into a recession that was characterized by rising unemployment and rising prices. The era of "stagflation" had begun, with significant consequences for those who were focused on a more just and peaceful planet.

As the post-war economic expansion came to an end, four trends emerged that impacted the way social change was conceptualized. Firstly, crushing economic circumstances and growing dissatisfaction with the "Keynesian consensus" of state-sponsored social spending led to important funding shifts globally. Secondly, as governments reduced their responsibilities for directly delivering social welfare, they began to partner with nonprofit and voluntary organizations to fill the gaps in service provision. Thirdly, in response to fluctuations in funding and stakeholders, these organizations increasingly professionalized, adopting a corporate and managerial culture in pursuit of legitimacy and efficiency. Finally, and most recently, rising inequality and a tidal wave in the transfer of inherited wealth have escalated the influence of private philanthropy, largely toward organizations and initiatives that reflect their backers' economic and political leanings. These four interrelated trends together have had the paradoxical consequence of merging the competing ideologies of big government and radical activism into a professional class of organizations, both nonprofit and for-profit, who see it as their "business" to drive social change.[32]

Shifts in the funding landscape for social service provision and development were a feature of the 1970s onward.[33] In broad strokes, economic stagnation and the rise of conservative forces in the industrialized West led to a contraction of the welfare and developmental states that grew out of post-war largesse. In the United States, policy battles between Democrats and Republicans resulted in a stalemate on the expansion of social welfare provisions. Across the world, the World Bank and IMF's structural adjustment programs encouraged free market policies which placed restrictions on the spending of loans on health, education, or welfare; in many countries, governments spent more servicing their debt than on their own health systems and essential social sectors. While these shifts led to a crisis for state-sponsored social programs, they initiated what nonprofit scholar Lester Salamon has called "an associational revolution" which he describes as "a massive array of self-governing private organizations, not dedicated to distributing profits to shareholders or directors, pursuing public purposes outside the formal apparatus of the state."[34] Contracting of social services to nonprofit service providers, already initiated in the 1960s, expanded as government funds were made available to independent social service organizations.[35] Hollowed-out government agencies, previously responsible for providing direct social services and foreign aid, transformed into overseers of nonprofit and nongovernmental organizations, dispersing funds to these organizations to deliver services independently.

These funding shifts led to a newly conceived partnership between government and nonprofits, even as governments started to reduce these available funds. As free market ideology grew through the 1980s, de-institutionalization and fragmentation of social service provision was held up as a decidedly positive transformation capable of delivering social services even in the absence of government funding.[36] In 1988, US President George H. W. Bush captured this sentiment in his presidential nomination address, likening the nonprofit sector to "a brilliant diversity spread like stars, like a thousand points of light in a broad and peaceful sky."[37] This partnership between civil society and government was, particularly in the United States, billed as a return to "a hypothesized golden age of purely charitable support."[38] However, expecting private philanthropy to foot the now increasing bill of nonprofit activity was decidedly optimistic. While governments reduced their financial support, nonprofits and NGOs increasingly turned toward commercial activities to fund their activities.

During this period and through the 1990s, rising interest in the activities of nonprofits, NGOs, and voluntary associations started to emerge. These organizations, which were previously seen as distinct in their motives and distinguished by their commitment to the two competing approaches described in the preceding section, came to be grouped together in all-encompassing terms.

Terms such as "third sector," "civil society," or "associational revolution" signaled an increasing professionalization for the sector. In the wake of professionalization came the management experts. Social justice expert Ruth Wilson Gilmore writes that the proliferation of nonprofits led to "a flurry of experts to advise on the creation and management of nonprofits and the relationship of public agencies to nonprofits...high profile professors of management, such as Peter F. Drucker, wrote books on the topic, and business schools developed entire curricula devoted to training the nonprofit manager."[39]

Alongside the rise of the "nonprofit manager" came the birth of the "social entrepreneur." At the turn of the millennium, while wealth inequality surged and an unprecedented generational wealth transfer began,[40] the influence of mega-philanthropists, corporate-backed philanthropy, and family foundations sky-rocketed. Although this funding is still small in comparison to state spending and individual donations,[41] these new philanthropists exercise disproportionate power by leveraging their funding through personal and corporate social networks. Mark Zuckerberg and Priscilla Chan guide education policy once reserved for municipalities while Bill Gates commands the global health decisions once reserved for countries. Meanwhile, efforts to pool financial capital traditionally destined for investment vehicles seeking returns, has resulted in entirely new ways of funding social change such as "venture philanthropy," "impact investing," and "outcomes-based financing." Devotees have dubbed these trends "philanthro-capitalism" and "compassionate capitalism," heralding a new economic era for social change.

As we head into the 2020s, our industry of social change now includes an estimated 10 million NGOs globally, contributes on average 4.5 percent to GDP and employs 7.4 percent of the world's workforce, putting it ahead of major industries such as transportation and finance.[42] In recent decades, corporate philanthropy, corporate social responsibility programs, and social impact investing have played an increasing role in the design and funding of social programs. While at first glance this growth appears to be a boon for social progress, it is important to understand what has been lost in this evolution. Nearly 75 percent of the activities conducted by these organizations are related to social service provision, as opposed to advocacy and cultural activities. This growth has been concurrent with the decline of labor unions and other membership-based organizations, historically strong drivers of activist activity that counterbalanced government social service provision in the post-war context. For activist organizations, the trends described above proved nearly fatal. Gradually, as described by social justice scholar Dylan Rodriguez, many followed a path of "assimilation of political resistance projects into quasi-entrepreneurial, corporate-style ventures."[43]

For the individuals, organizations, and movements who drive social change, the conversion to an industrial view of social change is largely complete. Assumptions held by social change practitioners include many if not all of the following: government is incompetent and should rather be led by privately run, "socially entrepreneurial" initiatives; organizations must compete in a "marketplace of ideas" for funding; policies and practices should be based exclusively on scientifically generated, quantitatively proven evidence; advocacy and activism are activities that are largely compatible with philanthropic funding; and civil society is a "service provider" to the public, accountable to taxpayers and "social investors" by the hurdles of measurement and "impact" assessment.

Public sector social change efforts have also adopted much of the industrial view. Discoveries in neuroscience and cognitive science have been picked up by behavioral economists to support individual-focused change initiatives. Policies increasingly use "nudges" and "incentives" to drive individual behavior change from those who are in positions of least power, while the poorest are now "entrepreneurs" and "customers." At the same time, advances in big data and artificial intelligence coupled with social media have provided access to population-level trends that can be used to support policies and programs. "Outcomes-based funding" and "social impact bonds" seek to predict desired social behaviors several decades from now, largely in line with economics that are friendly to financial investors. Meanwhile, companies call themselves "movement-builders," and commercial entrepreneurs are now "activists."

The number of quotation marks in the paragraphs above high-lights the vocabulary that has emerged to support the new industry devoted to social change. Only in hindsight is it possible to see the expansion of this new industry as a mirror to the decline of the post-war consensus and a need to reign in the radical movements that rocked the era. The social change industry has retained its post-war scientific and instrumental orientation, but with new discoveries and technological overhauls on the horizon to expand it. A new generation of professional "change-makers" has accepted this drive toward efficiency and accountability largely uncritically. We know this because, before we did the research for this book, we did the same.

In recent years, a few prominent voices have called out this industrial mindset toward philanthropy in particular, and social change more broadly. Peter Buffett, son of mega-philanthropist Warren Buffet and a philanthropist in his own right, caused an upset in philanthropic circles when he wrote a 2013 *New York Times* op-ed calling out the "charitable industrial complex" and question-ing whether philanthropists were merely "conscience laundering" in their attempts to "give back."[44] Stanford organizational theorists Aaron Horvath and Walter Powell have raised the question as to whether "disruptive philanthropy," as they call it, erodes democracy by altering public conversation and delivering solutions without engaging in the "deliberative processes of civil society."[45] Similarly, social movement scholars Marshall Ganz, Tamara Kay, and Jason Spicer have written that social enterprise "distracts from and under-mines the critical role of an organized citizenry, political action, and democratic government in achieving systemic social change, by offering itself as a private, market-based alternative."[46]

These critiques come at an important juncture for social change. The core premise of this book is that neither the institutionalized, government-driven approach nor the fragmented, private-sector-led approach that emerged out of the post-war environment will get us to the more peaceful and just world that we seek to create. These approaches have resulted in unparalleled prosperity for a lucky few, but they have not generated the widespread equality of opportunity and sense of community and security that results in broad societal flourishing. The industrial approach to social change most surely got us here, but it will not get us to where we want to go. Which is why we need to return to stories like the Green Revolution and understand the accomplishments and mistakes of our predecessors. If we hide behind the overly simplistic conclusions of "it worked" or "it failed," we miss an opportunity for meaningful learning, which, as we will discover, is a fundamental part of systems work.

How We Choose to Change

The story of the Green Revolution did not end in 1971. Rather, the revolution continued, largely in parallel with the global trends that we've described in this chapter. Working in complex political and socio-economic environments, driven by experts with very little exposure to the peasant farmers whom their technologies would impact, and buoyed by geopolitical motives that often trumped humanitarian objectives, the Green Revolution was never the unmitigated success that its backers promoted.

If measured by outcomes—the objectives to raise crop yields and meet the nutritional needs of nations—the RF program achieved its goals by a long margin. Yet, the systemic challenge which prompted the Green Revolution was far more ambitious: to feed the world. By this measure, the numbers don't stack up. Hunger is a wicked problem featuring complexity, scale, and depth, to which the RF program proposed the simple solution of growing more food. Yet, simple solutions for complex problems can reap terrible unintended consequences. The Green Revolution was a harbinger of a bigger agricultural revolution which fundamentally transformed the global food system. And like most revolutions, the transformation that this approach unleashed is far from complete eighty years later.

Today, despite the fact that our planet produces enough food to feed the entire global population, one billion people are malnourished. At the same time, an equal number of people are overweight. As evidenced by the COVID-19 pandemic, our sophisticated food supply chain cannot mobilize to feed the hungry, even in times of dire crisis. Urban migration strains our cities' infrastructure, while rural economies have been hollowed out. Suicide rates of farmers around the world have skyrocketed. Roughly one-third of green-house gas emissions, as well as other environmental issues such as water scarcity and agrochemical pollution, come from this trans-formed food system.[47]

How we "do" social change is not an esoteric question. Those who pursue social change most often do so with good intentions, and we believe this was the case with the RF staff as they pursued the Green Revolution. However, as Rittel and Webber remind us, the "social planner has no right to be wrong."[48] We *must* limit the unintended negative consequences of our attempts at social change and do whatever it takes to learn from our failures. We generally think that the biggest risk of social change is maintenance of the status quo. We believe it's better to "do something" than to do nothing at all. However, the choice to "do" comes with risks in both directions. When we charge ahead with solutions, we can trigger consequences that have long-lasting ramifications. But we can equally squeeze out opportunities to initiate change in more fundamental ways. As activist and writer Raj Patel writes, "The appropriate way...to esti-mate the opportunity-cost of the Green Revolution...was not to do nothing, but to do things in a radically different way."[49]

For those who embark on a journey of systems change, the lesson is clear: we must actively and carefully choose the ways in which we change our systems. However, to *do* things in a radically different way requires us to *understand* in radically different ways.

2
Complexity, Scale, and Depth

It has become almost cliché to speak about the "intractability" of social problems. This apparent intractability stems from the industrial mindset: we have been conditioned to make sense of the world by looking at change in historical episodes with defined markers of success and failure. However, to understand our social issues in a rapidly changing and interconnected world, we need to consider the characteristics of social systems—complexity, scale, and depth—in new ways. This need was highlighted to us in 2015, when we were swept up in a wave of protests on the University of Cape Town (UCT) campus which eventually spread across the country.

Like many uprisings, the opening shot was both shocking and violent. On March 9, a young black university student named Chumani Maxwele picked up a bucket of feces and threw it on a bronze statue of Cecil Rhodes. The statue, which had presided over the campus since it was unveiled in 1934, symbolized both the legacy of colonialism as well as the entrenched racism that persists in the post-apartheid South African university system. Following an open air dialogue and a march to a university administration building, students stormed, occupied, and renamed the building, creating momentum for a wave of protests that rocked university campuses across the country. Exactly one month later,[1] the statue—now covered in graffiti and wrapped in chains—was hoisted off its pedestal by a crane as throngs of students and faculty looked on. While observing the removal, UCT student Rifumo Mdaka said, "I think that the youth of tomorrow will say that the year wasn't 1994, but the year was 2015, when transformation actually began."[2]

Chumani and Rifumo are members of a unique generation in South African history—the last generation born under apartheid, the formal political system which excluded people from social and economic life simply because they were not white. For these young people, currently in their mid-20s and 30s, the release of Nelson Mandela from prison in 1990 and the first democratic elections in 1994 signaled that they could achieve whatever they wanted in life. The promise of South Africa's nascent democracy was a beautiful one, and it captured the imagination of the entire world, particularly in the iconic photograph of Mandela with his wife Winnie making a fisted victory as he walked free. But this beautiful story is a myth, and the photo is as much a symbol as the statues which preceded it.

This myth was manifest in Chumani's own life. The son of a domestic worker and a miner from the Eastern Cape, Chumani had relocated to Cape Town in search of a better life. Chumani spent his days traveling in a minibus taxi from a largely black township on the outskirts of Cape Town to serve affluent shoppers in an upscale suburban neighborhood. He wore a uniform, stood on his feet all day, and served mostly white customers. Traveling through leafy suburbs, past large colonial-style houses, he returned home each night to a neighborhood riddled with violence, where nearly half the population was unemployed. It became abundantly clear: his freedom was a farce. Journalist Eve Fairbanks writes, "The apartheid past, Maxwele realized, was still shaping his life. The realization made him feel more and more angry, because it had not been what he had been taught growing up. His generation had been told they were the 'born frees': an exceptional generation in South African history, the first one raised with almost no direct memory of apartheid's terrors."[3]

Chumani's path seemed to take a turn when he received a scholarship to study at UCT, the top university in the country, perched high above the very same suburbs where he had toiled at the shopping center. Then, in 2010, while taking a study break and jogging on a mountain pass which stretches from the suburbs into Cape Town's city center, he was arrested by special police assigned to then-President Jacob Zuma's blue light motorcade. The police alleged that Chumani stuck his middle finger out at the motorcade, "disrespecting the president,"[4] although Chumani denies he ever did such a thing. The police, toting AK-47s, pulled a black bag over his head and bound his hands with cable ties, shoving him into one of the motorcade vehicles. Chumani was transported to a police station where he was questioned repeatedly about his political allegiances and kept overnight in a cell without food or a place to sleep. Finally, in the late afternoon the next day, he was released. The incident caused an uproar in the press, particularly by political opposition leaders, and the police minister finally issued a reluctant apology to Chumani for his wrongful arrest after a court order to do so.[5] By this time, Chumani had been embroiled in four years of legal battles. He decided to switch his university major from sociology to political science and, less than a year later, he made his stand at the Rhodes statue.

When Chumani lobbed excrement at the statue of Rhodes, he wasn't just angry—he wanted real change, even if it required violence. He yelled out, "Where are our heroes and ancestors?"[6] and told the journalists who assembled, "Decolonization must happen through violence. I think it is highly unlikely South Africa can avoid this."[7] Chumani wasn't simply protesting the apartheid system which had created oppression for his parents and grandparents; he was fighting against those who had tried to change the system and come up short. Living in an under-resourced township on the outskirts of a world-class city, bullied and harassed by the police of his new democracy, Chumani wanted the change that he was promised but never delivered. On paper, South Africa is a multicultural democracy with a constitution that enshrines the most progressive human rights in the world. But on a day-to-day basis, Chumani was living an existence that still bears marked resemblance to the segregated country of his parents and grandparents. His is a generation which was promised a great deal, yet has experienced the disappointment, frustration, and rage that materializes when we believe that change is linear, isolated, and detached from bias and prejudice.

To move away from this straightforward view of social change can feel disorienting. While the "long arc" of social change has become compressed, it can often feel that we are back in the same place that we started, or, worse, that we've unleashed unintended negative consequences, leading to even greater problems. Our trad-itional guideposts for progressive change have been largely tangible: the end of apartheid; winning the vote; the passage of marriage equality; substantial increases in longevity, literacy, and living standards. These are significant markers of change, but they can also give us a false sense of accomplishment. Raj Patel writes, "Social change...isn't a one-step-forward-one-step-back process, a sort of collective Charleston where, after a lot of motion, you end up where you started. It's more like an infinite symphony, with one movement building from the previous one."[8] To accept that social change is an infinite symphony, people and societies adapting to changing real-ities, is a departure in the way we perceive progress itself.

As author and philanthropy advisor John Kania pointed out to us, "systems change is nonlinear, messy, and constantly in flux. Many [social change practitioners] don't want to sign up for that." When we treat social change efforts with defined starts and ends, we nearly always feel frustrated, since our understanding of what needs to change is necessarily a moving target. However, by focus-ing on the *process* of change—asking critical questions such as who deserves? who designs? and who decides?—we can move forward into the future with a greater capacity to adapt.

In the rest of this chapter, we will unpack our understanding of complexity, scale, and depth, discovering *new* ways of addressing these features—a critical first step in embracing a systems work approach to social change. The objective of practitioners must be to live through the learning process and emerge on the other side with a better understanding of what will take them into the next round.

Systems Work Terms 6: *Complexity, scale, and depth*

complexity	*systems that are comprised of many variables interacting with each other, yet functioning as a whole*
scale	*in its most elemental form, how a system responds when its size changes (West)*
depth	*the issues that arise when deeply-held beliefs, values and assumptions no longer serve in a social system*

The Crisis of Complexity

Twenty-first-century organizations—governments, businesses, and social change organizations included—are increasingly grappling with the growing *complexity* of our global society. Yet, what do we really mean by complexity? The term derives from the Latin roots meaning "woven together," which gives us a hint that we are talking about elements that are interconnected, yet function as a whole. Just as cloth is woven from multiple strands of wool, complexity implies that the sum of the whole is greater than the individual parts. As the number of parts and their interconnectedness increases, so does complexity. Systems are complex when they are comprised of many variables interacting with each other. We come across these complex systems on a daily basis. In fact, we live in a nested set of them: our bodies, communities, and the environment. The complex systems in which we live—biological, societal, and ecological—are amazingly and gloriously adaptive. They both self-learn and self-organize. No traffic controller directs the trajectory of antibodies through our blood and lymphatic systems to attack pathogens, nor does a celestial timekeeper guide the crashing of waves to the shore. Despite efforts to predict and control human behavior, we are continuously surprised by the new forms of organizing that emerge. In every action and interaction, people living in societies adapt their behaviors in relation to those around them, resulting in collective behavior that is largely unpredictable. Predicting the behavior of "complex adaptive systems" is a sort of gamble: you can plot and calculate probabilities of known variables, but at the end of the day, your outcome is at best an educated guess.

Indeed, it has become a truism, but our world has grown increasingly complex. It is worth trying to understand why. Since the turn of the last century, our global population has increased by close to 400 percent.[9] As the number of people has increased, so have the potential channels of interacting with one another. Even if the ways we relate and interact with each other had remained static, there would still be an exponential increase in the number of interactions experienced across the human population. However, the number of relationships in which we engage and the interactions per relationship have not stayed static, not even close. Even the most cosmopolitan Londoner living in 1900 would have likely traveled a very minor distance from home each day, received her news reports a maximum of twice daily, and conducted her correspondence via the postal service or a telephone operator working a manual switchboard. Compare that to the commuting habits of modern suburbanites, the 24-7 news cycle of CNN, and the Twitter habits of a former American president. Amongst the now nearly 5 billion internet users, we send more than 60 billion Whatsapp and Facebook messages and 8 billion Snapchat images, and have access to more than 3 billion pieces of new content every single day.[10]

Complexity likewise increases with the architecture of a system. Our organizing strategies, in all their many forms, are now increasingly between end users rather than exchanged through intermediaries. You no longer have to go to the bank branch to conduct business, you connect directly online to your account from anywhere in the world. Employees log into their communications systems from home, an airport lounge, or the cafe down the street, rather than receiving printed memos delivered to a physical inbox from the office of the CEO. Much like the difference between hub-and-spoke versus point-to-point transportation systems, efficiency and complexity act as trade-offs. Imagine if Emirates airlines not only had to contend with a system of 141 destinations, but the destination cities relocated on an hourly basis. Systems which exhibit this sort of architecture may be less efficient, but are far more able to handle the diverse needs of individual users.

When problems arise in complex adaptive systems, you can't treat them like a plumber would a leak, or even a computer scientist would a software bug. The late Brenda Zimmerman, a zoologist turned accountant turned complexity theorist, likened complex problems to the challenge of raising a child.[11] In contrast to baking a cake (simple) or sending a rocket to the moon (complicated), complexity means that recipes and formulas are limited in their application. Since complex adaptive systems are constantly changing and learning, success with one problem gives no assurance of success the next time around—parents of multiple children will undoubtedly agree! The outcome is, yet again, an educated guess.

We often speak about complexity blithely, yet it is actually a deeply philosophical concept. Complexity presents us with the realization that our world is essentially unknowable. Today, the study of complexity is arguably one of the most groundbreaking, interdisciplinary fields in science. Nobel laureate Ilya Prigogine called this "the beginning of a new scientific era" where "we are observing the birth of a science that is no longer limited to idealized and simplified situations but reflects the complexity of the real world."[12] Yet, the "discovery" of complexity from the 1960s came as a sort of scientific existential crisis, mirroring the shift to quantum theories in physics and postmodernism in the social sciences.[13] Suddenly, the aim to fully identify and catalogue the functioning of natural and social systems was not certain. Our views of the world are not only restricted to the data we can access, but to our interpretations of that data. The implications for this are profound, and both scientists and practitioners are still grappling with how to incorporate this into the way we study and perform in the world.

Confronted with "unknowability," we can choose different approaches. We can build models that incorporate complexity to the finest degree possible, narrowing our risk of uncertainty to rare instances and outliers. Many complexity theorists are following this path, working diligently to "decomplexify complexity," and this is certainly an area of exciting scientific discovery, particularly with technological advances incorporating big data and artificial intelligence.

Alternatively, we can acknowledge that complexity means we are fallible in all of our attempts to know and understand, and rather choose a different path altogether. Some scientists have begun to head in this less conventional direction. Paul Cilliers, a South African electrical engineer and philosopher, earned international acclaim in the 1990s by taking this somewhat radical stance. Cilliers was fond of saying that "complexity is a problem word, not a solution word...in other words, we are always in trouble when we act according to our models." Inspired by French philosopher Edgar Morin, he came to believe that complexity is an acknowledgment, a sort of surrender if you will. Even when informed by the most intentional and diverse of groups, with the most robust data, our understanding of reality is inherently reduced, even tainted, by our perception. When working in complex systems, our view will always remain merely a part of the overall picture.

Through our conversations with social change practitioners, we have come to believe that each of these approaches is necessary and valid. Rather than adhere to one approach or the other, we have to learn to *hold both at the same time*. In one hand, we hold the data and models that help explain the complexity we are experiencing. In the other, we surrender to the uncertainty that all complex systems pose. With this dual approach, we are prepared for the opportunity that complexity affords us: the chance to learn.

The Illusion of Scale

In the last century or so, organizations from all sectors and industries—but particularly the public sector—have been learning to deal with the magnitude of social change. After all, big challenges seem to necessitate big solutions. Smallpox claimed the lives of an estimated 300–500 million people in the twentieth century. The fight against a disease that had been with us for 12,000 years was won with a global effort starting in 1950 to inoculate the entire planet. The campaign took just twenty-seven years, bringing vaccines to billions of people worldwide, resulting in a decline from 50 million cases per year to effectively zero.[14] "Big bets" are not simply the preoccupation of technically focused social change practitioners. The first two decades of this century have witnessed the largest protests in human history. Occupy Wall Street, a protest movement against social inequality that began in Lower Manhattan's Zuccotti Park, eventually spread to 951 cities in eighty-two countries.[15] The Women's March of 2017, launched in the United States and then expanding to 673 marches on all seven continents, topped the charts at 7 million people globally.[16] These movements have been surpassed in recent months by the racial justice protests in the United States, in which pollsters estimate that anywhere from 15 to 26 million Americans have participated.[17] Virtual campaigns are able to mobilize in ways never before imagined—the social media movement #MeToo, attributed to activist Tarana Burke and actor Alyssa Milano's use of the hashtag against sexual harassment, virally spread to encompass more than 19 million tweets in a matter of four months, from October 2017 to September 2018.[18]

As the world grows more interconnected, our ambitions for social change grow more expansive. Among social change practitioners, this ripple effect across populations is often referred to as scale—a term which implies that the intervention and its intended effect are the same, only amplified across a broader group. The aim of social change, according to this way of thinking, is to "scale what works," identifying and isolating the element of change that contributes to positive impact and replicating it far and wide. The promise of this approach is appealing to funders and policymakers: it signifies that a solution grounded in evidence can be delivered both reliably and effectively across populations and geographies. It also corresponds with our best business thinking frameworks, which aim to maximize return on investment by creating "economies of scale," essentially getting more bang for our collective buck.

Yet, scale is one of those funny terms that has morphed beyond its original meaning, becoming almost a religion rather than a word. Again, our industrial mindset has a "go to" expectation for scale. Based on industrial economies of scale, first experienced in materials production through assembly lines and factories, and later honed for the services industries through franchising and platform strategies, our expectation is that we can achieve marginally higher impacts by increasing throughput in a system. As one of the executive directors that we worked with put it, "we want social welfare to be like McDonald's." In the last decade or so, many social change practitioners have begun to experiment with other ways of achieving scale, largely by influencing the systems in which they operate through partnerships with other organizations, businesses, or government. Heather Mcleod Grant and Leslie Crutchfield write in their bestseller *Forces for Good*, "If the 1980s and 1990s were all about replicating programs and the last decade was about building effective organizations, we believe the next leap is to see nonprofits as *catalytic agents of change*."[19] However, even this focus on partnership and collaboration overlooks some of the essential features of scale in social systems.

Physicist Geoffrey West, in his book *Scale: The Universal Laws of Growth*, has provided a timely reminder of what we mean by *scale*, writing, "scaling simply refers, in its most elemental form, to how a system responds when its size changes."[20] Yet, he reminds us, we do not really have a good grasp of how scale works in social systems: "Even more challenging and of perhaps greater urgency is the need to understand how to scale organizational structures of increasingly large and complex social organizations such as companies, corporations, cities, and governments, where the underlying principles are typically not well understood because these are continuously evolving complex adaptive systems."[21] Unlike factories and franchises, which have a finite number of variables that can be largely controlled, most social issues arise out of the unique conditions of context and the deeper issues of norms and values, which often exhibit quite confounding responses to changes in size. Systems scientist Yaneer Bar-Yam writes, "As one might expect with a uniform approach to a complex problem, initially there are likely to be misleading successes...At first, the large-scale approach seems to be working and its impact may be felt, but over time it fails in the details, piece by piece. Over time, these pieces add up to form a disastrous failure."[22]

For problems that can be addressed effectively by consistent, large-scale actions, mass intervention is entirely suitable and welcome; these are like the equivalent of a farmer sowing seed by scattering over large areas. Initiatives that emphasize once-off operations—single-dose vaccination campaigns and post-disaster relief efforts, for example—are likely to be solved with large-scale efforts backed by significant capital. However, social change efforts dealing with challenges that exhibit high contextual variability require sustained intervention and more nuanced tactics. In these instances, the social change practitioner is not just responsible for planting the seed, but also for gaining access to land, cultivating the soil, remaining vigilant for pests and disease, and trusting that optimal weather conditions will materialize for that seed to grow.

Ultimately, the conditions are far out of the hands of a single farmer, and will largely rely on the broader ecosystem in which the planting takes place.

Change in complex systems defies singular solutions and rather occurs in unpredictable ways. Scale also has the unintended consequence of "othering" social change. When considering complex systems, and the wicked problems that manifest in them, we have to overcome our exuberance to scale solutions without the contextual variations required. Our colleague at the University of Cape Town, Warren Nilsson, wrote recently, "As the social innovation movement grows larger and more ambitious, it must also become humbler and more intimate."[23] Nilsson's observation reminds us that scale and context are, in fact, not contradictory. However, rather than trying to manage context away, we have to develop ways of continuously adapting to the emerging context.

Depth and Power

While complexity and scale are increasingly part of the global conversation, we believe it is the feature of depth which is still underexplored in the quest for social change. Issues exhibit *depth* when they arise from deeply held beliefs, values, and assumptions—qualities that are extraordinarily difficult to shift. Famed community organizer Saul Alinsky described himself as "the kind of kid who'd never dream of walking on the grass until I'd see a KEEP OFF THE GRASS sign; then I'd stomp all over it." The son of strict orthodox Jewish immigrants growing up in the slums of the South Side of Chicago, Alinsky would go on to write the bestseller *Rules for Radicals*, and become the founder of modern community organizing, inspiring the likes of Barack Obama and Hillary Rodham Clinton, and earning the enmity of the conservative establishment. However, when asked if he had encountered anti-Semitism during his childhood, he replied, "It was so pervasive you didn't really even think about it; you just accepted it as a fact of life."[24]

Working in systems first requires seeing them. Perplexingly, it is most difficult for those who are embedded in systems to make sense of them; by participating in them, we maintain and extend their very existence. The structures that create the architecture of our social systems are built of rules, norms, and cultural beliefs that guide how we interact with one another and our world.[25] When these structures become so deeply held that we barely see them in our daily lives, they are said to be "institutionalized." Many of these structures operate below the cognitive surface and serve important purposes. They provide us with certainty in how we go about our daily activities and give us a degree of comfort about what we can expect when we interact with each other. Imagine if you had to decide each day on which side of the road you would like to drive or whether you should express your pleasure with a smile or a frown. You can suspect the chaos that would ensue or the disagreements that would arise! At its best, this invisible architecture gives us solid expectations and routines so that we can go about the more interesting business of living our lives.

At their worst, however, these pervasive norms and beliefs calcify into values that no longer work for us, or prevent us from assuming new ways of being and behaving that will work better for our societies as they evolve and change. They create cultures of exclusion and derision, and bolster prejudices and injustices. Our institutions fail us when they entrench our beliefs and behaviors to the extent that we cannot only *not change*, we cannot even *imagine change*. It is important to acknowledge that none of these structures act neutrally: power is the greatest feedback loop of all. Author and philosopher Alain de Botton described this feedback loop when he said that "getting to the top has an unfortunate tendency to persuade people that the system is ok after all."[26] We are both the architects and victims of our social constructs.

Power acts as the guiding force to keep our deeply held values and beliefs in place. A classic definition of power comes from the sociologist and scholar of power C. Wright Mills, who wrote in 1956 that the powerful are "those who are able to realize their will, even if others resist it."[27] Mills was writing in a time when the vestiges of power from two World Wars were being parceled out to countries and their elites. Sociologists and political scientists were engaged in a fierce debate about the nature of power: Is it hoarded by a small group of elite decision-makers who remain stable over time? Or is it dynamically distributed in an evolving, pluralistic fashion across interested and invested parties? How to wield and reconfigure power rested on an answer to this important controversy and experiments in governance were being conducted that had implications for millions, if not billions, of people around the world.

In 1962, political scientists Peter Bacharach and Morton Baratz wrote an influential article entitled "Two Faces of Power,"[28] which seemed to turn the debate on its head, saying that neither description of power was accurate and, in fact, both missed the entire point. Rather, power has two dimensions, or "faces," which are used by elites and special interests to control the way that political and social systems are managed. The first face, decision-making power, is the most obvious and public-facing. This is the type of power which confers the ability to make, alter, and assert decisions. Decision-making power is exercised when laws are passed, regulations enforced, and wars declared. While this face of power is certainly important, it doesn't accurately depict the full story of how decisions get made. The second face of power, non-decision-making power, is more under-the-radar but no less important. This power constitutes the ability to "set the agenda" and guide the conversation. Ultimately, this second face of power asserts itself through inclusion *and* omission; the choice of whether to bring an issue forward or place it at the back of the queue provides significant influence. Both elite and democratically driven power structures use this power when they select who gets to attend a conference, who sits next to whom, and what topics make it onto the agenda or get left to the corridor conversations.

Although Bacharach and Baratz changed the dialogue around power, it was yet another scholar who identified the elephant in the room, namely that sometimes people act in a way that is contrary to their own interests. A slim volume of less than a hundred pages, *Power: A Radical View*, written by Steven Lukes in 1974, tackled this paradox head-on, making the case that "we need to attend to those aspects of power that are least accessible to observation...indeed, power is at its most effective when least observable."[29] The third face of power—which he named ideological power—is, in fact, the most subtle and insidious. In this dimension, powerful actors insert their interests into the minds of those less powerful. Ideological power asserts itself in situations where people's preferences are shaped by a world that has already been molded by those who are in power. This face of power is at play when a bright college student chooses a career in banking without ever considering a position as a teacher, or when a young girl raised in poverty sees sleeping with an older man as a ticket to her way out of poverty.

To raise our consciousness and identify the very institutions that make up our day-to-day reality is a crucial step to achieving any sort of meaningful social change. When tackling wicked problems, power is the deep and critical ingredient that cannot be ignored. Explicitly or implicitly, the powerful are those who make the decisions that shape the systems in which we live. Social change approaches that inadequately expose or even attempt to mask the structures that perpetuate oppression or injustice may work for a time, but they will never achieve the social change that we seek. Real, systemic change can only occur when these structures are altered and power dynamics are reconfigured, offering a chance for new actors to step into positions of power and decision-making.

Where Do We Go from Here?

A revised understanding and treatment of the complexity, scale, and depth of social challenges is merely the first step of systems work. As practitioners of social change, we are naturally interested in understanding current reality and using these insights to offer informed mechanisms for change. In those first heady moments of seeing clearly our construction of reality, with all its inherent flaws, it is easy to want to immediately find a solution. As author and organizational behavior scholar Margaret Wheatley describes, "We rush to fix rather than allow the profound discomfort that arises from difficult information."[30] However, our next step is not to scramble for solutions; in fact, as we have seen, these problems defy simple solutions anyway.

In this chapter, we have proposed that our current approaches to understanding social problems are insufficient. Our instincts to "fix" are therefore also flawed. Surrendering to unknowability, organizing for the emerging context, and displacing long-held ideologies are not one-off exercises. There is no end-point to this work. Rather, the most successful examples of social change focus on the process itself, ensuring that systems become *responsive* and *representative*, with learning at the heart of the change process. To do this, they connect people who stay together while learning. They work closely with people to create feedback loops that cycle back information quickly, giving a chance to re-chart the course in real time. And finally, they look deeply at the structures that hold our current systems in place, paving the way for people to have agency in their own lives and communities.

3
Connection, Context, and Power

In 2017, we invited Kisimbi Thomas and Dr Salim Hussein to join the Bertha Centre's annual Executive Education program focused on systems change. We were intrigued to learn more about their experiences building an effective national community health system in Kenya. Kisimbi was one of those participants who is a delight in the classroom. He had relevant stories and anecdotes to share, his contributions in the classroom were revealing and thought-provoking, and he was full of life and fun. He was joined by Salim, who was then head of Kenya's Community Health and Development Unit at the national Ministry of Health (since promoted to lead the country's Department of Primary Health Care). Quiet but wise in his words, Salim brought a gravitas to the group stemming from his years of deep experience. The pair were a perfect complement: while Kisimbi had a birds-eye view of the system and could articulate how community-based change linked to the overall trajectory of population health, Salim had a lens into the practical issues of changing health systems at the community level and the workings of the national government. The week proved to be one of those (not uncommon!) experiences where the learning in the room was truly two-way. Tellingly, we came to realize that their story embodied the three principles that we were beginning to understand as systems work.

At the time, Kisimbi straddled two worlds. While his official role and title was partner of the Aspen Institute's AMP Health, a vast continent-wide multisector partnership between donors, private sector, and governments focusing on improving health systems, he was embedded in the Kenyan Ministry of Health. As a born Kenyan who speaks Swahili fluently, Kisimbi was regarded as an "insider," but as a professional who had been educated in the United States and employed by an American think tank, he was also seen as an "outsider." Along the way, he would find that balancing these two perspectives would be critical to his work.

At the time, the Community Health and Development Unit that Salim was leading was in crisis. The ten staff who made up the team were demoralized. After five years of "boom times," where international funding had flooded the unit at the recommendation of international funders, the plug had been pulled. A recent United States Agency for International Development (USAID) report had difficulty explaining the impact that community health contributed to its investments, and other partners quickly followed by divesting from the Unit almost instantaneously. This was a reminder to the Unit how managing large funders was critical: they tend to signal to the rest where to invest. Under the auspices of AMP Health in Kenya, Kisimbi was tasked with joining Salim to improve performance and outcomes, increase domestic resources for community health, deliver a program to train three thousand community health workers, and build management capacity across forty-seven counties. All in two years.

Over the course of 2016, Kisimbi and Salim doggedly worked to get the Unit back on its feet. They developed an annual planning process, which proved counterproductive as it revealed county executives were not able to make independent decisions for how to respond in their counties. They trained 100 community health workers, delivering an impactful program but falling far short of their workplan which targeted three thousand trainees. They became intimately familiar with the memo-writing process that served as the channel for legislative advocacy in the country, however failed to gain any traction with policymaking. Kisimbi said that "it took nine months just to become effective"[1] and that their initial plan had significant shortcomings. By trying to do too much, the program risked doing nothing at all. One year into the program, the leadership at AMP Health threatened to pull out of the country as the cabinet secretary for health seemed uninterested in the program, rather focusing on the president's re-election campaign and putting off meetings with the program leadership. The cabinet secretary was also dealing with an acrimonious nurses' and doctors' strike, and the Ministry was facing a publicly embarrassing procurement scandal with a little over US$50 million in unaccounted-for, unauthorized, or wasteful spending.

Kisimbi, now deeply embedded in Salim's Unit with a firm commitment to seeing the staff and their mandate succeed, decided to try a new tack. Together, he and Salim identified that county executives—who were the "on-the-ground" implementers of health policy—needed to be brought into the decision-making process and given far more latitude to implement community health strategies for their counties. Kisimbi and Salim refocused their efforts on building the capacity of the ten staff members, realizing that their managerial skills and relationships with county leaders were critical to giving the community health workers the support they needed. With an emerging self-awareness about his "insider-outsider" status, Kisimbi and the team used this ambiguous role to their advantage, allowing him to ask the uncomfortable questions that might not be received as easily if the government Unit's members were to put policymakers on the spot.

Finally, the team worked hard to understand the dynamics within the Ministry, and the relationships that led to the president's ear, and began to undertake the time-consuming task of building these relationships at a personal level. Kisimbi and the team established trust by changing the format of their briefs, highlighting immediately useful aspects such as local employment for youth and women, central to the president's campaign. Kisimbi, Salim, and the team would test out messages on how the Unit could help the president drive National Health Insurance enrolment, get more women to deliver in health facilities, and deploy an "army" of 100,000 workers to reach the households of nearly every Kenyan. Within the year, the Community Health and Development Unit emerged with a decided success: the president committed to a significant excise tax on both sales of mobile phone airtime and bank transactions, resulting in a flood of new funding for community health in the country. He also declared Universal Health Coverage (UHC) as part of his legacy-seeking "Big 4 Agenda"—making clear that community health was going to be critical in helping him achieve it. This signal from the president further resulted in funders and partners returning to the Unit to re-align and co-invest with a key government priority.

The AMP Health initiative had a number of high-profile and well-documented targets that it set out to achieve. Yet, arguably, AMP Health's most important investment was in the relationship between Kisimbi, Salim, and the Ministry team. The *connection* fostered between these two unlikely change-makers and the Community Health and Development Unit was the catalyst for understanding when the program was in jeopardy of losing traction. It also helped them to shift the program's goals when it became clear that a new approach was needed. Salim, with a deep understanding of the community *context*, and Kisimbi, with a critical eye due to his "insider-outsider" position, were able to identify the primary actors in the system who needed attention: the Unit's staff members and the county executives. By focusing their resources on these key individuals—positioning them to respond to the unique needs of each community and county context—the program gained better traction. Finally, by shifting more *power* to the county executives and channeling significant resources to the Unit through the new excise tax, the system was reconfigured in an enduring way.

Systems Work Terms 7: *Connection, context, power*

connection	*new relationships that promote continuous learning*
context	*the particular circumstances or conditions that form the geographic instance of a social issue*
power	*the ability to make decisions, set agendas or create ideologies that influence others' capacity to determine their own actions*

When Kisimbi joined us again on our program in Cape Town in 2018, this time as a special guest faculty and en route to a new role within AMP Health, he sat down with us to reflect on the experience. His observations were both practical and philosophical. He stressed that it was the simple things that made all the difference: the camaraderie built while sitting in the "bull pen" of an open-plan office, a workplan that everyone developed together, and the recognition that accountability goes hand-in-hand with experience. He said that he was conscious of the fact that, for all their informed pre-planning, the project had a life of its own and they had to align the project with practical realities and powerful agendas—almost on a daily basis. Most of all, Kisimbi emphasized how much of his and Salim's work was spent in relationship-building. The ultimate test of their effectiveness in strengthening Kenya's health system was not their expertise, skillful analysis, or political prowess—but rather their willingness to become part of the system itself.

Start with the Process in Mind

Most social change efforts start with an ambitious outcome in mind. AMP Health in Kenya was launched with the aim of improving primary health outcomes by providing training to three thousand community health workers and building management capacity in all counties in a period of two years—all by adding one additional member to the national Community Health and Development Unit team. In 2015, Kenya's public health system was serving a population of nearly fifty million citizens with a budget of just US$169 per person. With almost fifty thousand nurses and ten thousand doctors across ten thousand facilities in forty-seven counties, no single person could grasp the functioning of the entire system.[2] Yet, a new set of relationships between a small group of primary and supporting actors *could* ensure that the entire system began to function in more responsive and representative ways.

As Kisimbi and Salim's story illustrates, systems work is less about ambitious outcomes and more about setting up the process through which further adaptation can happen. First, we see that organizations ensure that primary actors—those fully immersed in a system—feel a strong sense of *connection*, creating new relationships that foster continuous learning. Secondly, they position these actors so that they can act dynamically, solving real time problems in *context*, and sharing this knowledge across the system so that others, including supporting actors, can learn from their activities. Finally, such organizations reconfigure *power* dynamics so that these primary actors are able to take up strong decision-making roles and have the resources to continue their activities. This work may sound simple and intuitive. Indeed, it is already underway in many organizations, projects, and programs. However, too often, this work is hidden beneath the surface rather than highlighted in funding proposals and project plans. It often emerges behind the scenes or as a core activity only after significant efforts have been expended.

In this chapter, we will dive into these three key principles of systems work—which we believe, if revealed as the core work of social change, will lead to deeper and more enduring change.

Principle 1: Foster Connection

Organizations working in systems foster connection, building new collective identities that keep groups together while learning.

As we saw in the previous chapter, the first challenge of social change is that the systems we are seeking to influence are wildly and wondrously complex. Complexity science helps us to better understand the way that social systems behave, giving us tools to better predict the emergent outcomes of social interventions. At the same time, however, we must "surrender" to a level of unknowability. For proponents of industrial social change, this unpredictability is a huge conundrum, an issue to be minimized if not fully eradicated. By contrast, for the organizations we profile in this book we believe the surrender to uncertainty is, in fact, a key aspect of their work. These organizations hold understanding *and* unknowability simultaneously, and are constructed so that learning and responsiveness are central to their organizational design.

As we conducted our research, we found an interesting pattern that led us to this principle. Many of the social change practitioners with whom we spoke explained that their work had started with programs aiming to inspire individual-level behavior change. Over time, however, several of these practitioners became frustrated by the broader systems in which they were working which seemed to limit the changes that individuals could make in their own lives. When Jeroo Billimoria of Child and Youth Finance International (CYFI) reflected on her work at Child Helpline International, an organization which at the time had reached more than eighty million children with their services, she said "It's great that [we] have helped so many people…probably we will reach more and more…but we are not getting to the core of the problem."[3] Similarly, Mauricio Lim Miller who founded the Family Independence Initiative (FII) and now runs its international version, the Community Independence Initiative (CII), wrote, "You can't really change a country as the old saying goes, one person at a time. Success comes when expectations are changed within an entire community."[4]

Discouraged by the tenacity of these social ills, these organizations and others began to work in the opposite direction. They found that building a sense of solidarity among a group of people, changing how they perceive themselves *as a group*, could create far more powerful and enduring effects. In the case of FII (and now CII), families self-organize into peer support groups to champion financial goals to remove themselves from poverty. Through these groups, families are able to respond to their daily challenges and ultimately increase their income and self-sufficiency. In similar fashion, RLabs builds a sense of camaraderie among disaffected youth in communities where joining a gang is seen as the only viable path to adulthood. By introducing technology entrepreneurship as an alternative to gang membership, the organization creates a sense of belonging, inspiring young people to embark on different futures.

Our research also revealed that this type of connection is not limited to the "grassroots," but can be fostered at different levels ranging from neighborhoods to global institutions. For example, CYFI built a global network of finance ministers, central bankers, and NGO leaders, connecting sixty-three thousand organizations across 175 countries. Each of the network members are strongly committed to their national and local institutions, yet through

CYFI activities, they became equally dedicated to a global movement that supports children as "economic citizens." Through this movement, network members begin to see their role not just as promoting economic growth for the short term, but as preparing the next generation for a sustainable economic future.

This principle is supported by much of the scholarly work on social movements. In the 1980s, an Italian scholar named Alberto Melucci was studying social movements emerging in Italy and across Europe, specifically among youth, women, and peace and environmental activists. As a sociologist, Melucci was particularly interested in why these movements seemed so different from the ones he had studied from the past, which were mostly labor-related and focused on class. As he began to delve deeply into the youth movements erupting across Italy in the 1970s and 1980s, he began to see a different set of motivations driving these young activists. They were not organizing around their interests as classes or professions or even a lack of political power, but rather on emerging ideas of who they were as a group. These shared identities were often a construction of their own making and were linked to broader cultural values that transcended traditional class lines. He coined the term "collective identity" for this new way of organizing for social change.

Melucci spent significant time in the field, using his classroom time to discuss what he was finding with his students. Through these conversations, he came to theorize that contemporary social movements are based on a group-constructed sense of "we-ness" that is both intentional and ongoing. He believed that constructing a shared identity is, in fact, the important and primary work of social movements—even more so than the protest and political force traditionally associated with movements. All of the activities that get poured into creating a "we" ultimately build an "action system" which becomes the foundation for broader social change. Melucci's findings came to signal what has been dubbed the "cultural turn" in social movement studies, and is now a widely recognized theory among social movement scholars. As described by social movement scholars Robert Benford and David Hunt, "In a sense, collective identity replaced class consciousness as the factor that accounts for mobilization and individual attachments to new social movements."[5]

A constructed sense of "we-ness" gave us an idea of what we were seeing. Many of the organizations that we studied are building collectives as an "action system" comprising the people who are immersed in a social issue. By forging a collective identity and keeping a group together through a period of change, they are able to gain trust and support from each other and respond to issues by learning from each other's experiences. These collectives are a very human way of dealing with complexity. Complexity requires us to learn how to work together—we may not always agree, but we can stay together while learning. We have always had ways of doing this: families, tribes, communities, even nations. However, many of these traditional ways of accommodating pluralistic collectives have diminished in the contemporary age while more polarizing organizing strategies have emerged in their place. New collectives serve to fill this gap. For example, through the contemporary racial justice and climate movements we are seeing the creation of diffuse, pluralistic movements, across class, race, and age groups, where cross-generational networks of people—including school children, scientists, activists, and policymakers—share a collective identity and learn from each other's campaigns and engagements.

The principle of fostering connection stands in sharp contrast to industrial social change efforts which position experts and heroes who design programs—often with plans synced to funding cycles—to deliver services to those in need of "help." In several of the organizations we studied, experts and outsiders still have a critical role to play, but they step into the systems that they seek to influence, acting as a "host" rather than a "hero."[6] These host organizations foster belonging, provide space for gathering, and keep participants engaged, so that collectives can stay together through the learning process, adapting and experimenting continuously.

Principle 2: Embrace Context

Organizations working in systems embrace context, equipping primary actors to respond to day-to-day complexity, dynamically adapting as the context requires.

The second issue for working in systems is understanding how positive social change can spread to greater numbers of people. This process is often referred to as scale and has arguably become even more urgent in the age of globalization, where problems manifest at a local level but can be seen across regional and global levels. Increasing interdependence and rising complexity have made it difficult to address issues in locally isolated ways. Yet, the ways in which scale is often approached—through replication, partnership, and sharing across networks—too frequently result in diminished quality or unintended consequences.

Our conversations with social change practitioners who have attempted scale by replicating programs or in partnerships with implementers have nearly always revealed frustration. We believe this frustration is because we intuitively assume that with a certain degree of contextualization it should *work*. However, our assumptions are based on industrial views of the world, which do not necessarily hold in complex social systems. Although interdependence and complexity have increased rapidly, we have not yet gained a good grasp of how scale works in social systems. We often make assumptions about the way things will scale from one level to another, from individuals to groups, from local contexts to regional hubs, and beyond. As we explained earlier, these assumptions very often do not hold true.

This principle emerged from another important theme in our research. Many of the organizations that we studied have been encouraged to generalize their models with the expectation that contextual variation can be managed. Often, in the early stages of a pilot program, thoughtful and caring practitioners make modifications at the "grassroots" level to enhance the efficacy of interventions. These often small and inconspicuous modifications to a program—frequently invisible to funders and head offices—are part of the critical elements that create a successful social intervention. However, after proof of concept is obtained, many programs are encouraged to implement "efficiencies," which in fact remove the contextual variation that is delivering local results. Expertise and capacity are anticipated through once-off trainings or delivered through underpaid staff (or even volunteers) while primary investment is channeled into large-scale systems that can replicate the program more widely. Less and less attention is paid to the granular detail that is often poured into the pilot project, with the expectation that a top-down approach will garner more results, faster.

However, many of the organizations that we studied chose to do the opposite, seeking to embrace context rather than mitigate it. Most often, we found that this involved primary actors—those who are most proximate to the problem and primed to drive change through small, often inconspicuous adaptations—improvisations— at the most critical points in a system. Primary actors often have lived experience of the issue or context. Equally, they may be those who have immersed themselves in a context for a significant period of time. Equipped with agency and resources, they are best placed to be responsive to the particular needs and idiosyncrasies of culture and local ecosystems.

Primary actors are, as author Leslie Crutchfield describes in her book, *How Change Happens*, the very people who are "inured to the issue." mothers2mothers, a global health organization operating across sub-Saharan Africa is built on this premise: mothers living with HIV are positioned as frontline health workers in communities and clinics serving pregnant women and new mothers. Although trained to support healthcare providers and patients diagnosed with HIV in the management of their disease, their conversations with women living with HIV are far from scripted; their ability to connect and discern the needs of their clients derives from their intimate experience of being in the patient's place themselves. Equally, the Colombian education nonprofit Fundación Escuela Nueva applies this principle to rural and urban education contexts, positioning students as primary actors in their own education. Learning in Escuela Nueva class-rooms takes place in small groups of students, with teachers act-ing as facilitators. At the same time, student-elected leaders and parents are actively engaged in the running of the schools, thereby enhancing learning opportunities.

Primary actors may also be those people who are fully immersed in a local context, with a type of "insider-outsider" status similar to the way Kisimbi positioned himself in the Kenyan Ministry of

Health. One of the organizations that we studied, Buurtzorg, recruits highly skilled nurses who develop autonomous neighborhood teams that become integrated into the communities in which their patients live. Although these nurses are not necessarily members of the neighborhoods where they work, they become fully immersed in the daily happenings and web of relationships in the community. Based on the intimate knowledge of the conditions in which their patients reside, they can make decisions and adaptations based on what the context requires. Importantly, these improvisations cannot be planned or anticipated. They can only be nurtured so that when they do happen, practitioners can recognize them and make them happen more widely.

To try and manage complex environments so that contextual variation is minimized or managed is not just exhausting, it prevents us from harnessing the power of diversity. In each context, there are abnormalities and responses to these abnormalities. As these aberrations and improvisations add up, they create patterns that are rooted in the context within which they are happening. For social change practitioners, these subtle modifications are the oil that greases the wheels of a program; they are quite often the very actions that make a program effective.

Primary actors have a unique standpoint from which to identify and respond to the needs that they see happening in a social context. When individuals and groups with lived experience of a social issue, or those immersed with "insider-outsider" status, claim agency as a primary actors contextual variability becomes an asset rather than a curse.

Principle 3: Reconfigure Power

Organizations working in systems reconfigure power, putting decision-making and resources in the hands of primary actors, ensuring that social systems fully represent the people who live in them.

Finally, the depth of social problems is largely derived from the "stickiness" of power. Power is the ultimate positive feedback loop: simply put, people in positions of power use their positions of privilege to stay there. In Chapter 2, we introduced the three faces of power. The first two faces of power—decision-making and agenda-setting—are easily acknowledged, but, as we described, it is the third face of power, ideological power, that sits far beneath the surface and drives the deep-seated issues in our social systems. Patterns of behavior, and the motivations and circumstances which drive these patterns, are circumscribed by social norms, values, and beliefs that often go unnoticed and largely uncriticized. Unwittingly or not, the powerful set the parameters within which these norms are followed. In other words, they set the temperature of the water in which everyone must swim.

In our research and dialogues with social change practitioners, we often found that issues of power arose in the aftermath of seemingly straightforward success. For example, we worked closely with several community health organizations on a Bertha Centre-supported systems change initiative toward government adoption of community-based health services in five African countries. Many of the projects were built around exciting technologies that could track patient information and provide timely reminders for hospital visits and medication. However, the uptake of these technologies often had more to do with the promotion of lay workers as decently paid health clinic team members rather than the viability of the technology itself. Several of the organizations with which we worked were in the process of shifting their strategies to elevate community health workers—through policy and practice—into more respected positions in the health system.

Activist strategies designed to confront decision-making and agenda-setting are also challenged by the ideological power issues that sit below the surface. In speaking to Arbind Singh, founder of Nidan, an organization that supports informal workers' rights, we were intrigued to find that while the organization uses traditional protest tactics such as marches and hunger strikes to demand more inclusive policies for informal workers, their more fundamental work has become the implementation of these policies at the local level. Nidan ensures that laws and policies include provision for informal workers to step into positions of decision-making, such as Town Vending Committees with a percentage of seats reserved for informal workers. However, ensuring that these committee members are able to step up into these roles requires a more long-term approach of capacity-building for local leaders contending with entrenched social norms based on the long-standing caste system that pervades Indian culture.

Similarly, Slum Dwellers International (SDI) has spent twenty-four years promoting the role of the urban poor in making decisions about slum clearance and housing development. The organization uses a variety of tactics—protest, negotiation, and international pressure—to challenge evictions and instead promote in situ development so that slum dwellers can remain in their communities while conditions are upgraded. However, much of their work involves contesting the pervasive beliefs that the poor are not legitimate contributors to city life and that they are not capable of generating the data and information needed for the upgrading of their communities. Evictions are often carried out without any prior consultation or warning, clearing the way for powerful developers and businesses to occupy land that has been settled—albeit informally—for decades. SDI's fundamental work is to ensure that informal housing dwellers are recognized and represented in these crucial decisions about the future of cities, and that they are a key source of the crucial data and information that informs decision-making and ongoing management and governance of cities.

Participatory approaches to development are not new. The development community has increasingly embraced the premise of participation since the 1950s. However, the organizations we studied are going beyond a set of practices that "invite in" a set of stakeholders to a process that has already been designed on their behalf. Equally, these organizations are not simply advocating approaches that promote individuals and communities to "claim space" in systems that have already been set up to exclude them. While these approaches have validity, and have had significant attention in other places, we became most interested in the way that these organizations were rather putting in place consistent patterns that allowed new power configurations to replace the status quo.

To engage in systems work is to recognize when existing power configurations no longer serve. As we mentioned in the previous chapter, institutions and long-standing social norms often influence our beliefs and behaviors to the extent that we cannot only *not change*, we cannot even *imagine change*. To alter power dynamics that are entrenched in our current global paradigm will require a collective reimagining of what is valued and to whom that value accrues. It will necessitate tough decisions on issues that are key to our daily lives, such as the food we eat, the energy we use, and the wealth we get to keep. There will be situations which are decidedly not "win-win". For some who have held positions of primacy, it will feel as if the world is changing too fast, that they are losing. It will take strong connections, attention to the idiosyncrasies of context, and new types of leadership to ensure that the benefits awaiting on the other side can sustain us through the transition.

PART II
PRACTICES OF SYSTEMS WORK

How do the principles of systems work show up in the day-to-day activities of organizations? In Part II, we describe four *practices of systems work*, demonstrating how the principles from Part I are put into action. For simplicity, each practice is introduced through the stories of a few organizations from our study. However, we met many organizations engaged in these practices through our years of research. In each of the chapters, we further explore some of the specific tactics that organizations are using to "live out" these practices in their work. We also consider some of the theories and frameworks that explain why these practices and tactics are effective at building responsiveness and representativeness in systems that feature complexity, scale, and depth.

4
Cultivating Collectives

Late one evening in 2006, Brent Williams returned to his parents' house after a three-day binge. He went to the kitchen, rummaged around in the cutlery drawer, grabbed a knife, and headed to his parents' bedroom. High and hallucinating, he wasn't fully aware of what he was doing, but he had decided that he needed to make a name for himself—killing his mother seemed like a good way to get some attention. His mom recalls it vividly. "I don't know if he was aware it was Mother's Day, but this was the day. And I thought, God help me, I need to do something. I think the cat was in his way, he kicked the cat and at that time I got my getaway...I think I was faster than him that day."[1]

Brent and his parents live in Bridgetown, a suburb on the Cape Flats of Cape Town known as "apartheid's dumping ground." Access to education, jobs, and opportunities is limited: too often, kids drop out of school, get involved with gangs, and become drug addicts and dealers. Brent started using drugs at the age of twenty-one, and moved on to selling them at the age of twenty-three. Although he knew deep down he needed to change, he kept falling back into his old habits of drug-using and dealing. He simply couldn't conceive of an alternative to his current way of life.

Then, Brent met Marlon Parker.

Marlon was a Bridgetown boy whose dream was simple—he wanted to wear a shirt and a tie. As he described it, "Very few people in my community had a job where they could wear a shirt and a tie and I felt if I did this, I could go anywhere and people would think: 'There's Marlon going to his office job. He's arrived.'"[2] Marlon studied information technology, mortgaging his mom's two-bedroom house to pay the fees. Eventually, his dreams were realized when he was offered a job as a lecturer at the Cape Institute of Technology.

At the time, Marlon's father-in-law, a pastor, was running a community outreach center with a single computer and an internet connection. He asked Marlon if he could spend some of his free time training a few former gang members on computer skills. He recalls, "There was no grand plan at the time, we just went into a class with these guys and asked: 'What do you know about computers?' and they replied: 'Marlon, the only thing we know about computers is how to steal them.'" This is where Brent met Marlon for the first time.

Like Brent, some of the youth in the class were dealers. Others were addicted to drugs or belonged to gangs. Most had dropped out of school and a few had children to support. They all shared an interest in turning their lives around, but also, like Brent, didn't know where to start. Marlon didn't have any tricks up his sleeves, but he did know about computers. So he started with what he knew and introduced them to basic computer skills.

Brent recalls the day they started, "The first time we ever opened up a laptop and tried to sign up to email, we were all so intimidated that our hands were shaking. Can you imagine that? A room full of hardened criminals who are all terrified of something as small as a computer!" With Marlon's help, however, they soon got the hang of it. Before long, they were looking for new ways to apply their skills, so Marlon introduced them to blogging and social media. Pretty soon, the former drug addicts and gang members had discovered a new addiction: technology.

Marlon wasn't surprised that technology was addictive—this he knew from his own experience. But he *was* surprised to discover the ways in which these young men and women were using technology. When surfing the internet, they found stories and blogs by others who had gone through similar situations—youth in other parts of the country, even the world, who were struggling with drugs, violence, and gangs. They gravitated toward a new South African social media platform called Mxit which gave them a chance to tell their personal stories, unfiltered, something they were hungry to do.

One day, Marlon, Brent, and some of the others were having a conversation about how technology was turning their lives around. Marlon realized that the young men and women were using social media to connect the dots, to make sense of their lives. The conversation turned to how they wished they had had access to social media at their previous points of crisis—Brent, for example, wished he could have talked to someone at the moment he was having his binge. As they were talking, they were getting excited. Would it be possible to create a mobile app that would give this opportunity to others who were in similar situations, to connect to people like them when they needed some help or just to share? They decided to give it a shot.

The mobile app was built on top of Mxit and they called it Jamiix. It was one of the first mobile counseling platforms in the world—designed by a group of ex-gangsters and drug dealers. The number of active users grew so quickly it caused the system to crash. By the end of 2013, Jamiix had been accessed 27 million times, by more than 4.5 million users, facilitating more than a billion messages. Marlon and his team decided to set up a nonprofit called Reconstructed Living Labs (RLabs) to formally manage the platform. However, they knew that the platform wasn't really the point—the app was just the channel. It was *what* they were channeling that was important: a sense of connection. Among those who had similar life experiences, they could recreate the feelings of belonging that gang membership and drug addiction had provided in the past. Upon this sense of unity, these youth could envision a path forward, a way to reconstruct their lives.

A New Web of Relationships

Philanthropy advisor Edgar Villanueva writes, "There's a reason why folks vow to stick together for better or for worse, for richer or for poorer, in sickness and in health. Real, complex relationships are necessary not only for whatever the present entails but also to face challenges in the future. Relationships create resilience; transactions don't."[3] While Villanueva reminds us that complex, large-scale, and deep issues require us to work together, RLabs illustrates that groups can be purpose-built to forge new relationships, building connections that nurture a new way of seeing the future.

In our research, we came to recognize a clear pattern: while many organizations (or their founders) started out trying to influence the behavior of individuals, they soon found themselves working in the other direction—intentionally creating new groups to connect individuals to one another. With RLabs, Marlon could have easily gone the first route, focusing on "heroic entrepreneurs" like many of the technology incubator programs that have sprouted up in recent years. While observing how Brent and others interacted with the Jamixx technology, however, Marlon stumbled upon a critical practice of systems work: building a new web of relationships that supports individual and collective change.

Collective organizing is nothing new—union organizers, community mobilizers, and social activists have been drawing upon collective strategies for more than a century. However, too often, social change practitioners, particularly those with an industrial approach to social change, are focused on the outcomes of the practice rather than the process itself. Activist and author Jonathan Smucker writes, "Yes, we come together with others because there is political strength in numbers, and we are aiming to accomplish instrumental goals. But we also come together with others because it feels good to do so—because we find a deep sense of community and belonging that accomplishes what could be described as 'therapeutic' purposes."[4]

When organizations forge a strong collective identity within groups, they are connecting those with lived experience of an issue as well as those with diverse or "outsider" views. Within these groups, individuals can explore new ways of seeing the current situation, challenging the status quo and considering new perspectives. This process requires time and trust, surfacing the mental models that drive our most deeply held beliefs and engaging in conversations that may feel uncomfortable, especially when awareness of an issue begins to shift to a new perspective. Once a new collective consciousness is borne, truly effective organizations can then harness this collective energy to engage with other groups—often across diverse geographies and cultures—building communities that stretch beyond the initial core collective. As we'll see in the subsequent chapters, this expansion is tricky, since it can move a group from the safe "fringe" to the center, but when done attentively, it can create the prospect of learning across many groups, triggering wholesale change in systems.

Building a "We"

At RLabs, it is easy to be distracted by the cutting-edge technology and sheer scale of what they have deployed and accomplished. Through their hub in Cape Town and multiple franchises, RLabs has trained 200,000 individuals, incubated 3,500 businesses, and created 90,000 job opportunities worldwide. Yet, these numbers and programs can obscure the true nature of the work. As we spent time with RLabs, we came to see the training and incubation platforms as a sophisticated yet underappreciated way of developing a new collective identity about how impoverished youth and their communities envision their futures.

When Brent joined a gang and started doing drugs, he did it because it was the normal thing to do. Growing up on the Cape Flats, this was what he saw everyone around him doing and he figured it was the right path for a kid like him. "Joining a gang felt like my only option; I thought it was just part of my culture. After a couple of years I realized that I had become someone I never wanted to be."[5] Brent's initial attempts to change his life were unsuccessful because the culture in which he grew up associated adulthood with gangsterhood. Another path was nearly inconceivable. The collective identity formed in his gangster life was so engrained that to diverge from this path was to be alone.

With Marlon and the rest of the RLabs founders, Brent found another identity that valued the skills of technology, entrepreneurship, and innovation, all of which gave him a way to spend his time in new and positive ways. Importantly, it was this sense of trust and togetherness that kept Brent coming back. If Marlon had merely provided him IT training, overlooking his need for a new sense of belonging, he never would have persisted in his newfound hobby. The technology was sticky, but the connection to the group was the true addiction.

Collectives are built on a common sense of identity, the traits and categories that we use to make sense of who we are in the world. *Collective identity* is different than a common vision or purpose; it is the sense of "we-ness" that emerges when a group of people develops a sense of belonging with one another over time. This common identity establishes a sense of trust where people—in many cases including those who have been previously marginalized—can explore common experiences as well as their differences. Together, groups probe current problems, often raising their awareness and seeing a situation in new ways. As sociologist Alberto Melucci theorized, out of this emerging awareness an *action system* is conceived for new possibilities to emerge.

Systems Work Terms 8: *Collective identity and action system*

collective identity	*a sense of 'we-ness' (group identification) that is forged by collectively seeing the current situation in a new way*
action system	*a system comprised of new relationships which creates a foundation for broader social change*

Importantly, the process of forging collective identity enables those with lived experience of a social issue to become primary actors in the change process. Often, those who are most affected by a social issue are isolated, with few opportunities to set the rules by which society operates. People who live in conditions of poverty, ill-health, or poor education are unlikely to be in the drivers' seats of economic, health, and education systems. Those who are young,

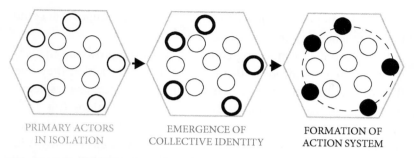

PRIMARY ACTORS
IN ISOLATION

EMERGENCE OF
COLLECTIVE IDENTITY

FORMATION OF
ACTION SYSTEM

Fig. 4.1 Collective identity and action systems
Source: Authors.

female, of color, or of different sexual orientations or gender preferences are often sidelined by decision-makers. When systems no
longer serve people, new collective identities can emerge at the
boundaries of social systems (see fig 4.1). People who no longer feel
that the status quo is working for them then migrate to these "fringe
groups" to consider new identities that serve them better.

In these boundary areas, individuals can connect with others
who are fully immersed in the context but with different perspectives. Through these new connections, they can process their
experiences and gain a fresh take on their situation, converting
their feelings of difference to a sense of dignity. Successful social
movements show examples of what happens when previously
unorganized groups of people develop a consciousness about who
they are as a collective. Consider the Black Power movement of the
1960s and 1970s, which aimed to recover a sense of pride among
African Americans and instigated a turning point for the Civil
Rights movement in the United States. In recent years, the #MeToo
movement has generated a sense of collective identity among those
who have experienced sexual harassment and violence, moving
from a place of shame and acceptance to resistance, spreading globally beyond the entertainment industry to include corporate, political, and academic spheres. And, most lately, the movements for
racial justice that have swept the world in the wake of COVID-19
are uniting previously disparate groups into a collective voice,

pushing for policing reform and far more radical changes that could have impacts for generations to come.

When groups form strong collective identities, evolving the way they see their situations and the environments in which they live, they can set in motion an action system that creates new trajectories for individual biographies and societal expectations (fig 4.1).[6] These shifts are mutually reinforcing: as groups change the way they see themselves and the way they live their lives, society changes its assumptions about what is acceptable and desirable. When societal perceptions shift, the conditions for these new norms and rules are reinforced. By forging collectives with strong identities, converting deep-seated isolation to connectedness, organizations can shift the structure of a social system and open up new terrain for what is possible.

From Stigma to Pride

Strong collectives can also shift the unjustified shame associated with a stigmatized identity into a source of pride.[7] We could see this shift quite dramatically in another one of the organizations we studied: mothers2mothers (m2m). When American obstetrician Mitch Besser began his work in the South African training hospital Groote Schuur in 2000, he could see that his words were simply not getting through to newly diagnosed pregnant women living with HIV. Stunned by their diagnosis, fearful for their future, and worried about disclosing to partners and family, these women were experiencing a trauma that made it very difficult to comprehend that there was hope for their baby. Yet, Mitch also saw that there was opportunity in these crucial moments. If he could find a way to turn these critical exchanges into meaningful conversations, they might change the trajectory of the mother's life—and that of her baby. In a world where more than 1.4 million women of reproductive age are diagnosed with HIV annually,[8] this change could be transformational.

However, Mitch and his medical colleagues at Groote Schuur were trapped in a certain type of relationship: trained experts delivering information to patients. Mitch knew that his expert information was falling on deaf ears, but stepping back from this role was not easy. Describing his former mindset, he said, "I'm a doctor. I tell people things to do, and I expect them to follow my guidance."[9] Over time, however, Mitch became aware that this particular relationship was unhelpful at that crucial moment. While imparting information was important, he first needed to shift things that were happening below the surface: personal feelings like shame and despair, as well as collective experiences like stigma. Yet, the very characteristics that made Mitch effective in the South African medical context—a Harvard-educated medical doctor, seeing dozens of patients each day—made it very difficult for him to build a relationship and have a different type of conversation.

As a physician devoted to preventing HIV infection in babies, Mitch could have chosen to double-down on the expert-driven approach. He might have set up a program to train more nurses and clinic staff or designed more comprehensive brochures and mobile-ready information for women to read and absorb on their own. He could have insisted that the information was already available for mothers to protect their babies. However, he chose to invest in a deceptively simple technology: a new relationship. To do this, he chose the very women who would most easily connect with his patients—women living with HIV who had already delivered healthy babies.

It was from this idea that Mitch started the m2m program. He recruited a few of the mothers who had successfully gone through prevention of mother-to-child transmission (PMTCT) in his hospital to return and speak to his new patients, both in one-on-one conversations and in support groups. He paid these mothers from his own pocket, believing that fair compensation for valuable work was an important principle for the program. Eventually, he received a small grant to expand the program and provide formal training to the women he now called "Mentor Mothers."

Since its founding, m2m has operated in ten African countries, employed more than eleven thousand Mentor Mothers, and reached 11 million women and children in sub-Saharan Africa with their services. Women enrolled in m2m's support program have a scant 1 in 60 chance of passing HIV to their babies, a rate of transmission that is far below the World Health Organization's predictions for transmission. The program has recently expanded to position Mentor Mothers in communities where they can have conversations about maternal health, infant care, and early childhood development, as well as coordinate prevention programs for adolescent girls and young women, in the living environments of their mentees.

Hosting Havens

In the initial years, both Marlon and Mitch discovered an important precursor to building collectives. Collectives require safe spaces in which to flourish. Identities, and the new perspectives that they inspire, need places of refuge or "havens" in which to germinate and grow. This is especially the case when emerging perspectives defy the status quo. Collective identity is not something that can be conjured up in a single meeting or consultation. It is constructed by the very process of being together, through repeated interaction, ongoing dialogue, and even conflict. Organizations can effectively support this process by providing spaces and structures for members of groups to come together and spend time with one another.

The most obvious type of havens is physical space. RLabs hosts innovation labs where community members can temporarily exit the day-to-day reality of Bridgetown and come together as a group of like-minded young and aspirational technophiles. m2m's Mentor Mothers meet their patients in public clinics, negotiating heavily for private spaces in crowded clinics and often making do with spare closets and storage rooms. Many of the other organizations that we studied actively curate physical spaces for groups to meet, learn, and grow together. Fundación Escuela Nueva (FEN) uses classrooms and teacher trainings as physical safe spaces where the new identities of community members as students and teachers are practiced. Nidan advocates for clean and functional areas in cities for informal workers to congregate, seek work, and conduct their trades. The Bertha Foundation, which funds the Bertha Centre, is currently developing retreat centers around the world where political negotiators, social justice activists, and dissidents can safely meet away from contested territories.

Havens can also be psychological, creating "containers" where members collectively get to know and trust one another.[10] We witnessed tools and methods for building trusting and protected emotional spaces in many of the organizations that we studied. m2m engages in a creative process called Body Mapping with its Mentor Mothers to enable them to get in touch with the deepest part of themselves and make that visible to themselves and each other. Each mother is invited to paint a life-size representation of her body onto a large surface using colors, pictures, symbols, and words to represent life experiences lived through the body. The process originated[11] as an art-therapy method for women living with HIV/AIDS and allows participants to rediscover their bodies as a source of strength, courage, and healing. Information about HIV, its treatment, and side effects are offered at key learning moments, preparing them for the work of counseling others.

Less on the creative end of the scale but no less impactful, Family Independence Initiative (FII) requires the practice of monthly journaling about financial decision-making which is then debriefed in support groups. While this serves as a practical tool to capture data, it also allows families to privately consider their decisions and then collectively discuss them with supportive friends. On a broader scale, Child and Youth Finance International (CYFI) hosts annual summits and award gatherings that recognize outstanding contributions by countries, organizations, and financial institutions toward financial literacy and inclusion for children. This recognition bolsters the sense of emotional wellbeing and camaraderie of participants in the network, providing incentives to stay together and to continue mobilizing.

Virtual havens are an emerging possibility that the COVID-19 pandemic has recently highlighted. During the lockdown period in South Africa, RLabs trainers, being from the same communities where their participants live, were able to quickly pivot their programs to the digital messaging platform WhatsApp. They chose to use the data-light platform since many trainers and participants are located in areas without ready access to laptops and high-speed connections. By sharing resources and meeting participants "where they are at," the virtual programs have been even more successful than they had hoped, ensuring that youth isolating at home are able to carry on their training and education despite the crisis.

In these havens—physical, psychological, and virtual—members are able to collectively see their experiences for what they are: a set of externally derived expectations forcing them into activities that they may not want for their lives, their communities, or their countries. At the heart of these activities is the common goal of reinterpreting what social change scholar Nancy Whittier describes as "one's individual experiences, seeing them as shaped by social forces and identifying as part of a group with shared experiences."[12] As collectives form and process their experiences together, they begin to translate these experiences into sources of value, worthiness, even anger. Ultimately, this creates a collective that is ripe for change.[13]

Pooling

While havens give room for connections to grow and life experiences to be processed, they also provide pathways for "pooling," a method for surfacing and sharing mental models while creating a new collective consciousness about what is possible. The term pooling comes from Kathie Sarachild, a feminist organizer who documented the method that became prolific in the Second Wave feminist movement.[14] The process was deceptively simple: women formed groups to get together and talk about predetermined topics, exploring how they felt about childhoods, jobs, motherhood, or more revealing or painful topics, such as sex, abortion, harassment, and rape. Initially derided as "group therapy" or "coffee klatches" for women, small group consciousness-raising rallied more than a hundred thousand American women in just four years,[15] paving the way for women's leadership in politics and activism. Since the 1960s, pooling has become a foundational practice for social movements across numerous issues and campaigns.

Pooling essentially involves practicing a new type of conversation—one that relies less on expertise and more on exploration. The late physicist David Bohm, who became fascinated by the role of conversations in the field of science, liked to distinguish between two types of conversations: discussion and dialogue. Discussion is a type of conversation to defend a position, where one person assumes a powerful, winning stance while the other becomes a passive recipient. By contrast, conversations based on dialogue are those where assumptions are suspended in order to create something new.[16] Dialogue serves an important purpose: it reveals the mental models used to make decisions. Mental models are the maps of assumptions that every person uses to assess new situations based on previous life experiences. No one person has the same set of mental models. However, in dialogue, we have an important opportunity to access other people's mental models and see a situation in a new way. When exposed to other mental models, we can choose to incorporate new ways of thinking into our own. This process can transform the way individuals and groups respond to day-to-day challenges.

Surfacing mental models is challenging since our human brains are designed to filter out information that does not conform to our expectations.[17] While these "defensive routines"[18] may serve us well in fight-or-flight situations, they are ill suited to complex situations where we need to be able to see beyond our own mental picture of a situation. Conversations to explore mental models require us to slow down long enough to listen and reflect. As systems scientist Peter Senge writes, "Skills of reflection concern slowing down our own thinking processes so that we can become more aware of how we form our mental models and the way we influence our actions."[19]

In many of our social systems—health, education, youth development—the ability to stop, listen, and reflect has become nearly impossible. Hosting these types of conversations requires organizations to actively manage spaces where pre-existing agendas do not exist. Often, this means creating a void rather than rushing in to fill a space with answers. The aim is to keep people with shared experiences, yet often with differing interpretations of the possible outcomes, in conversation with one another. Despite the significant time and energy involved, many of the organizations we studied are actively making the effort and employing the right people to open up significant time for transformational conversations.

In the m2m training, Mentor Mothers spend significant time sharing the life experiences they have had as women living with HIV as well as learning the basics of HIV and PMTCT. By telling their stories to each other, Mentor Mothers are able to "unfreeze" their own mental models about HIV, including the stigma and shame associated with the virus. These new mental models become an integral part of their conversations with newly diagnosed pregnant women, giving them a chance to open their minds to new ways of thinking. From these new models, they can make a new plan for their futures that will protect their babies and allow them to live healthy lives.[20]

When we visited m2m's programs across multiple countries, what surprised us was the quality and consistency of the conversations, despite the fact that these encounters are largely unscripted. Mentor Mothers are taught to first suspend any judgment about their clients and simply listen. In these moments, conversations are not between a clinic staff member and a patient, but rather between a mother and mother-to-be. Only when an m2m client feels emotionally ready to absorb new information about HIV and her baby is clinical information introduced. These conversations have tangible outcomes: mothers enrolled in m2m programs report feeling less alone in the world and less overwhelmed by problems than non-enrolled women.[21] Supported by Mentor Mothers, m2m enrollees have statistically significant lower rates of HIV transmission to babies and are also more likely to take care of their own health in the months following birth.[22]

RLabs also creates spaces for the sharing and telling of stories. Participants in RLabs' programs are invited to pool their experiences, challenges, ambitions, fears, and goals. For many, this is the first or only opportunity they have had to connect with their peers and air their innermost thoughts and feelings. Once they have mutually expressed and absorbed these experiences, they undertake a sense-making process where they reinterpret events, thoughts, and feelings in the context of the new information offered by the group. This process enables them to gain a new understanding and control over their perceived assumptions, which they can direct toward setting and reaching new goals.

Slowing Down

In contrast to traditional service delivery efforts, the practice of cultivating collectives at first can appear slow and meandering. Yet, these organizations seem to be "slowing down to go fast" engaging in what social innovation scholar Christian Seelos calls a "slow movement"[23]—using new collective identities to create action systems that facilitate broader change. MIT senior lecturer William Isaacs calls this process the "art of thinking together."[24] He writes, "Given the nature of global and institutional problems, thinking alone at whatever level of leadership is no longer adequate... Human beings everywhere are being forced to develop their capacity to think together—to develop collaborative thought and coordinated action."[25] To slow down, connect with one another, and reflect is part of the process.

m2m's trajectory is instructive, showcasing how "slow" conversations can result in outsized influence. Several years ago, by facilitating and participating in conversations across many public health systems, m2m was able to see that the conversation around PMTCT was shifting to become integrated into broader maternal and child health services. This meant that "stand-alone" programs like theirs were less likely to be funded. Rather than see this as a threat to its program, m2m expanded its work to employ mothers in many different health service areas, including HIV prevention, early childhood development, and adolescent treatment and care. Today, m2m has grown in scale—serving nearly 1.3 million clients in 2019 alone—as well as implementing a life-cycle approach reaching women, children, and adolescents. Its model of community health workers, especially the importance of paying Mentor Mothers rather than engaging them as volunteers—has normalized the professionalization of layworkers in health systems and displaced previous expectations of engaging unemployed people as volunteers.

The model is now largely accepted in the global public policy conversation and is being deployed by hundreds if not thousands of organizations across the world.

As these conversations progress, action systems develop so that lived experiences are integrated with full acknowledgement of the complex issues that they entail. Patterns of what works and what doesn't are revealed and integrated into the larger picture, including policies and frameworks that support people to step into positions of problem-solving. As new shared meanings develop and conversations proliferate, small actions can emerge in coordinated fashion even when top-down direction is not in place. One of the most effective ways to do this is detailed in the next practice: equipping problem-solvers.

Learning Notes: Cultivating collectives

A key role for organizations is to cultivate collectives comprised of people who are immersed in a social issue and who can stay together while learning. It is a seemingly innocuous role with profound consequences. The organizations we visited in our research are each doing this in different ways with similar objectives. Through peer groups, incubators, learning circles, committees, and numerous other structures, these organizations are:

- **Building a "We,"** or a collective identity, that creates a sense of belonging and keeps groups together while learning.
- **Shifting stigma to pride**, joining together primary actors—those who have lived experience of or are deeply immersed in a social issue—to reconsider and challenge deeply held beliefs, values, and assumptions.
- **Hosting havens**, where groups can temporarily exit their daily reality and explore alternatives to current assumptions.
- **Pooling**, merging experiences, ideas and feelings to develop shared understandings and new perspectives, while shifting mental models together.

These strategies to **cultivate collectives** enable individuals, families, and broader groups to gain new perspectives while learning together, ultimately creating an action system for broader change.

5
Equipping Problem-solvers

After starting the Family Independence Initiative (FII), Mauricio Lim Miller had to fire four employees for being helpful. One employee, Mathew, tried to hide the fact that he was helping families, but as his helpfulness grew, the hours that he was spending at work increased. The management at FII noticed the heightened workload and investigated. They discovered a pattern of Mathew assisting clients who were unfamiliar with computers, phoning them with reminders of important information, and filling out monthly data questionnaires on their behalf. Mauricio finally confronted him: FII would need to let him go. At FII, helping is a fireable offense.

Mauricio founded FII in 2001 on a belief that the traditional social service sector is doing the opposite of what it is meant to do. Rather than making poverty obsolete, he concludes that social services are simply making poverty tolerable. Even worse, he suspects that the sector actually exists to maintain and benefit those in positions of power and privilege, not to help the poor out of poverty.

Mauricio's revelation that he was harming instead of helping came slowly. In the late 1990s, Mauricio was running a program with over a hundred social service workers, annually serving two thousand youth and adults. But he felt like a fraud. He had crunched the numbers and he knew that most of the grant money he managed was going into the pockets of social workers and administrators. It felt like his programs were designed to increase benefits to those who were "helping" rather than to those who were being helped. Families cycled in and out of poverty programs while he and his team of social workers enjoyed steady employment and a secure future.

Mauricio was sensitive to issues of power and privilege because he had been born with neither. Mauricio grew up in poverty in California, the son of a single mother from Mexico. Equipped with just a third-grade education, his mother, Berta, had moved to California and worked two jobs to support Mauricio and his older sister. While he wasn't a "straight-A" student, Mauricio did well enough to get into the University of California, Berkeley, where he studied engineering at his mother's insistence. He was drafted into the Vietnam War and then took a job as a plant engineer with the Union Carbide Corporation in order to send money to his mother and sister. When his mother, whose health had deteriorated due to a life of stress, decided to take her own life, he grieved in the only way he knew how: by taking control of his future. He quit his job and moved into the nonprofit sector where he hoped he could begin to close the disparities he had experienced growing up. Over two decades, he steadily moved up the ladder, becoming the executive director of a large and well-funded program devoted to helping disadvantaged youth.

Mauricio's work began to be noticed at the highest levels. However, when President Bill Clinton's chief of staff invited him to be an honorary guest at the 1999 State of the Union Address, alongside activist Rosa Parks and baseball star Sammy Sosa, he was filled with doubts. In a private meeting with the president and First Lady Hillary Clinton, he accepted the congratulations for his work. But later, he noted, "I didn't have the courage to tell him that if he considered my anti-poverty work as among the best in the country, our national standards were too low."[1]

A few months later, Mauricio got a surprise call from the mayor of Oakland, Jerry Brown. Mayor Brown wanted an explanation for a proposal which planned to spend US$10.2 million in federal grant money to open three new youth centers in Oakland. The proposal had all of the qualities that Mauricio had quietly begun to question: full-time jobs for professionals, big construction developments for contractors, juicy projects for consultants. On the phone, the mayor got angry, describing the proposal as "poverty pimping." It was a harsh term, but Mauricio couldn't help but agree. Mayor Brown ended the phone call with a surprising offer: Could Mauricio come up with an alternative program, one that could actually make a difference? He gave Mauricio a month to make a plan.

Even after two decades of working in the field of social services, Mauricio didn't know where to begin. But he figured that the experience of his mother might be a good starting point. Berta had faced a lifetime of hardships and had managed to pull her son out of poverty. How had she done that? Mauricio recalled all of the times when his mother had watched and learned from her fellow immigrant friends, sought advice and help from neighbors and colleagues, and had single-mindedly pushed for him to attend school and then college. Inspired by his mother's story, he began to study mutual support approaches used by immigrant communities from across the country. He started to consider an alternative to the traditional social service model. What if they—the professionals—didn't help at all? What would it look like if they merely supported families as they lifted themselves up? And what if they shared this knowledge across groups and communities, letting them choose for themselves what might work or not?

With the backing of Mayor Brown, Mauricio launched FII in 2001. The concept is relatively straight-forward. Low-income families come together in groups chosen from their own personal networks and work together to set goals for savings, employment, and income generation that meet their individual family needs. The families are given a computer from FII and paid a small amount to keep a monthly journal detailing their activities to meet these goals. Groups meet at least monthly and provide support to each other, sometimes emotionally and other times tangibly, by offering childcare, sharing information, or making loans to each other. FII then provides additional monetary support when goals are reached and documented, but only as matching funds.

Sixteen years later, before Mauricio retired from FII, the initiative was showing results that most anti-poverty programs can only dream about. After being enrolled in FII for two years, families report an average 22 percent increase in income and a 55 percent decrease in government subsidies. Nearly two-thirds of families start new businesses, growing their liquid assets by nearly six times. By FII's calculations, in 2018, families enrolled in the program exchanged social capital to the value of nearly $11 million through activities such as lending money, watching each other's children, and cooking for each other.[2] FII's CEO, Jesús Gerena, who took over from Mauricio in 2017, describes it simply: "The essence of FII is putting people back in the place of power, investing in themselves and investing in their communities. We eliminate any direction— there is no right answer except the answer that is right for them. They are the leaders of their own lives."[3]

"Knowledge at the Edge"

In their break-away management book, *The Starfish and the Spider*, co-authors Ori Brafman and Rod Beckstrom note that "the best knowledge is often at the fringe of the organization."[4] Social systems are the same: the best knowledge is often found at the social "margins," the least likely place for traditional "experts" to situate themselves. Yet, as social change practitioners, we often try to solve social issues without the knowledge and continuous involvement of those who are closest to the problem. By relying too heavily on "experts," we lose our best chance at finding the most durable solutions. In our research, we found that several organizations were making rather extraordinary decisions to keep the source of expertise very close to the ground.

Poverty is often held up as a quintessential complex problem. With numerous root causes and issues, there are as many reasons for poverty as there are impoverished. Yet, Mauricio is impatient with complexity as an excuse for ineffective or slow responses to poverty. In a talk that he gave at the White House in 2016, he said, "The fact is… [poverty] is complex for us because every family is different. *It is not as complex for my mother.* She knew what she had to deal with. She knew if she wanted to get me into college she had to save this month, she had to take care of the car the next month. These are all of the things you will never know by any program that you have. The fact is that people have to build their lives in the way they have to build their lives and they are the only ones who know."[5]

FII—and now its international version, Community Independence Initiative (CII)—demonstrates what can happen when an organization recognizes the strengths of those who are fully immersed in the context of a social challenge. When Mayor Brown asked Mauricio to explore alternatives to the current social service sector, he first considered his own experience growing up in a poor family. His mother dealt with the complexity of her daily life in the best way she knew how: relying on family and friends and looking for examples of others who were achieving success in reaching goals she had identified as important. He knew that his mother had leaned heavily on her community, using their knowledge to inform her own steps. When she decided she wanted to learn bookkeeping, she asked a friend to teach her. As she navigated the American education system, she watched what other families were doing and realized that a home in a decent neighborhood would secure a good school for her kids.

Mauricio has seen this similar pattern play out in other families and communities. In one example at FII, a Salvadoran couple named Javier and Maria made the announcement that they would be purchasing their first home. Staff members were suspicious of the rates they had secured with their mortgage provider, but were careful to keep their suspicions to themselves. Within a few months, it was clear that the money lender was a loan shark and the couple were in danger of losing their home. FII staff continued to refrain from intervening and simply observed. Javier and Maria, together with the other families in their peer group, put together a plan. With the group's help, they renovated the house, utilizing the skills of each person to landscape, retile, and repaint the home. Ultimately, the increased value of the home allowed Javier and Maria to secure a refinanced loan with a more reasonable interest rate. The learnings within the group were exponential. Within eighteen months, every single family in the group purchased a home.

Many programs inadvertently stifle this process of knowledge-sharing by prescribing a path that people must follow. When people living close to a complex issue share knowledge with one another about what is working and what is not, a natural process of peer exchange and learning is fostered. By alternating between small, daily decisions and larger stories of success, people can navigate their own context—a concept that we call *contextual responsiveness*. As small behaviors coalesce into broader themes, entirely new trajectories—for families, communities, and even societies—emerge. Mauricio writes, "You can't 'program' that many people out of the cycle of poverty. There is no 'vaccine'. It must be a natural process that promotes the positive aspects of human nature."[6]

Systems Work Terms 9: *Contextual responsiveness*

---

contextual
responsiveness

small, positive adaptations that coalesce into broader patterns, made by people who are fully immersed in the context of a social issue

---

Circulating Data (Both Small and Big)

As we researched FII further, we came to realize that the organization equips problem-solvers to be *contextually responsive* with two types of knowledge. The first level of knowledge sharing is among family members, as feedback from the monthly journaling system. Mauricio describes the system: "As [families] enter changes in income, for instance, they can see a chart that shows the income line move up or down given what they entered over time. It is instant feedback."[7] The second level of knowledge sharing occurs across families and groups who are able to access a private online social network called UpTogether, allowing them to connect to other FII families and groups. Through this network, families share successes and failures and provide advice and support to each other online. The network also has the effect of "social signaling," a mechanism that shows avenues for reaching goals, while also providing motivation to FII families. FII has been able to use the data it collects to show how sharing indicators with families can change behavior.

For example, when FII started tracking "acts of kindness," or ways that families supported one another, these activities jumped by over 30 percent in six months.[8] Internationally, the online platform—called the Mutuality Platform—can be used by any community who also believes in the basic premises of this approach.

"Small data," (see fig 5.1) which captures the anecdotes, stories, and intelligence that are distributed from friend to friend, colleague to colleague, family to family, are essential to getting things done. Sociologists call these community resources "social capital."[9] Social capital, and the network ties that distribute it among communities, is a tangible resource that organizations engaged in systems work can use to take knowledge-sharing to scale. FII uses its peer family groups to create small data transfer across networks with a common identity, usually the cultural ties of an immigrant or community marginalized from the mainstream. This is a form of social capital called "bonding capital" which connects people who are alike and who share a strong sense of trust with one another.[10] This form of capital is useful for making the day-to-day decisions that lead to incremental change, an important pathway for change when dealing with wicked social problems.

Through its social network, the FII and CII approach also creates social capital *between* groups. This is particularly evident as the original model begins to flourish internationally with projects in Liberia, West Africa, Colombia, Mexico, and the Philippines. "Bridging capital" serves to form links among disparate groups that might not otherwise have a deep sense of trust. This type of social capital works across geographies, networks, and cultural backgrounds and is useful for leapfrog-style change, which happens when an individual or a group is able to see an opportunity that is far beyond their normal social network and incorporate it into their own behaviors. Both forms of social capital are critical to systems work: the first provides the ability to "get by," through incremental adaptations as responses to daily challenges, while the second provides the chance to "get ahead," as individuals and groups see transformative opportunities that they can leverage to improve their long-term trajectory.

Through the organizations we studied we were able to see how responsiveness can work in other scenarios too. In fact, many of the activities to build collectives can "grow" into mechanisms for knowledge sharing. For example, as we mentioned in the previous chapter, at RLabs, training and mobile apps provide a way to process themes and learnings, creating a sense of camaraderie and connection. However, they also serve as a very effective way to share knowledge across individuals and groups without building a cumbersome bureaucracy to do so. Similarly, m2m's one-on-one conversations and support groups allow pregnant women to see what is possible, building a common identity as resilient women living with HIV while also sharing the "small data" that drives their future as positive mothers.

While the small data generated across informal peer networks can have a significant impact on the way systems function, access to data generated across an entire system—so-called "big data" (see fig 5.1) presents a relatively new and untapped opportunity for organizations engaged in systems work. As data storage and computational power have soared, the ability to capture complex insights into behaviors across systems has increased as well. While there are still important questions to answer about disclosure, privacy, and ownership, some experimental initiatives have begun to demonstrate the potential opportunities that these data sets can provide. These include open data governance programs by cities,[11] social audits by "grassroots" organizations,[12] user-generated data maps for humanitarian aid and protest action,[13] and pandemic identification and tracking.[14] Larger initiatives to invest in data gathering and dissemination have been initiated by the OECD, the World Bank, and the United Nations. However, the public availability of these data sets has not always been at the forefront of initiatives, raising the question of who is being empowered and who is envisioned as the center of change efforts.

Several of the organizations we studied are using large-scale data sets to identify and share trends across groups. Importantly, we found that these initiatives are generally focused on sharing data widely rather than reserving it for elite decision-makers. FII has

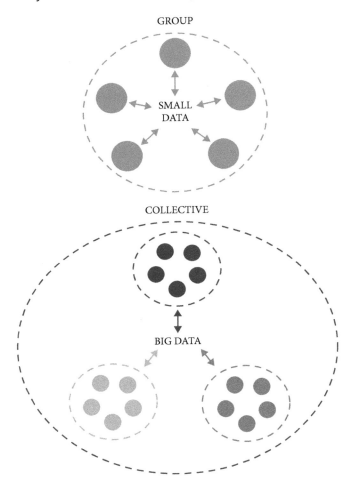

Fig. 5.1 Small data, big data
Source: Authors.

shown how this can work by providing families with real-time insights based on the network's activities, including successes and failures. Similarly, Slum Dwellers International (SDI) has created a large-scale initiative to make its "community-driven" data open to all. Through their Know Your City (KYC) website, anyone—citizens, policymakers, and funders included—can drill down into detailed statistics and information for 7,712 slums in 224 cities. The data are owned and have been collected through tireless efforts by community-based affiliates to catalog the structures and services in their own communities. Representing "alternative systems of knowledge" and the "largest repositories of informal settlement data in the world", the campaign has created a wealth of information to drive urban research and development that benefits rather than harms slumdwellers themselves.

Decentralizing Decision-making

Despite its success with lifting families out of poverty, FII has found it difficult to convince funders and policymakers that low-income families can make their own decisions. Jesús considers the mindset of philanthropists and development practitioners to be the fundamental difficulty in growing their approach. He says, "We have built a deficit-based approach when dealing with the challenges of society. Rather than investing in what is working, we have built an army of human services [professionals] going into communities to ask what is wrong."[15] In recent years, FII has decided that simply growing its model through replication is not enough. Rather, it needs to disrupt the belief system that drives most social service programs. FII is now partnering with cities, states, and even countries through Mauricio's international initiative, CII. The aim is to incorporate its strengths-based approach into philanthropic and public spending initiatives, demonstrating what is possible for families and communities when they are allowed to lead.

However, Jesús describes it as a "long and tedious road." Decentralizing decision-making and putting people in a position to solve their own problems is contrary to the industrial view of social change. Our industrial mindset says that there is a "right" way to do things regardless of the context in which people live. Experts are positioned at the top in decision-making roles, while people living close to a problem are relegated to "beneficiaries" or even "customers" of services and solutions. Organizations are encouraged to focus on scale and throughput, delivering evidence-based services to more clients at lower costs. This approach is built on the factory model, where raw materials and activities are fragmented into high and low value, delegated to the most efficient worker and coordinated by upper management.

While these assumptions may work well for the simple and complicated problems of assembling identical products or delivering transactional services, they break down when dealing with complex social issues. These assumptions also fail to capitalize on the intrinsic motivation and integrated feedback that people experience when they are able to solve their own problems.

Positioning Problem-solvers

One of the organizations that we studied, Buurtzorg, is also experimenting with how to keep expertise and decision-making in the hands of those who are best positioned to be contextually responsive. Based in the Netherlands, Buurtzorg is a home-based care organization working with aging populations. The Dutch system, like so many healthcare systems in developed countries, faces a challenge to meet the needs of a growing number of people who need long-term care. These patients, often based at home with family members providing daily care, have become a permanent feature in the country's health system—a feature that is growing across the world.[16]

In the 1980s and 1990s, Dutch insurers predicted this demographic turn and began to adopt new strategies. At the macro level, there was a clear starting point. Since the 1800s, neighborhood nurses have been a bedrock of the Dutch healthcare system, a role which appeared to have significant room for economies of scale. However, it seemed wasteful to have highly skilled, professional nurses attending to mundane tasks such as bathing and tidying-up. One neighborhood might experience a spike in demand while another might experience a lull, yet nurses were not able to take advantage of available resources in other neighborhoods. To optimize the use of resources, a new layer of professional management was created. Administrators planned the most efficient routes and schedules for nurses; call center agents responded to patient requests and routed them to appropriate staff levels; regional managers provided coordination across the system. Nurses were moved into higher-value roles, performing only highly skilled tasks and even becoming sales agents, selling products from company-based pharmacies to provide new avenues for "cost recovery." It seemed obvious that merging neighborhoods into larger organizations with efficient, highly functioning systems would create efficiencies for the Dutch model of healthcare.

Only it didn't work. Between 1990 and 1995, the number of home care organizations consolidated from 295 to 86. Within ten years, costs had doubled.[17] At the same time, quality of care and patient satisfaction declined. Patients receiving visits from multiple caregivers were unable to communicate their needs effectively, while caregivers were harried by the new work schedules and worried about their inability to provide continuous care to their patients. Employee satisfaction fell precipitously, exacerbating a situation that was already in a downward spiral.

In 2006, Jos de Blok was one of the community nurses who had risen to the managerial ranks of the new system. He saw first-hand the shift from the decentralized system of the 1980s to a far more centralized one in the 1990s. As a result, he, like so many of his colleagues, was disgruntled and disillusioned, feeling like he had lost the plot. He had entered the field of nursing to care for people and now felt like he had no contact with people at all. When he and his wife, Gonnie Kronenberg (also a community nurse) decided to quit their jobs, they had meagre savings and five children between the ages of twelve and twenty-one. They also had an idea germinating: Could they build a home care organization that would operate with the team-based structure of the original Dutch neighborhood model? Would they be able to do this while delivering superior care to patients as well as cost savings to insurers?

Jos dug deep into his experience as a community nurse to recall what inspired him about his career before shifting to the management ranks. Much of his motivation came from solving problems for patients, trying different things, and ultimately getting it right, feeling the satisfaction of helping someone through a hardship. As he describes his realization at the time, "The idea about good healthcare was that it should connect to the intrinsic motivation of the nurses, that it had to be inspiring to do this work so that the nurses themselves would be the carriers of the vision and the concepts."[18]

After extensive conversations with friends and colleagues, Jos and Gonnie set up an organization named Buurtzorg, meaning "neighborhood care" in Dutch. They started by recruiting community nurses in small teams, each serving a neighborhood. From the start, they envisioned a no-hierarchy structure with teams operating autonomously and making decisions collectively. Patients would be cared for by two nurses at most, giving them a chance to build deep relationships with their caregivers. There would be strictly no managers, either at the central or team levels. Rather than regional managers, teams would be able to access regional coaches whenever required, helping them make decisions as a collective rather than taking direction from a distant bureaucracy.

Early on, the Buurtzorg model was so strikingly different from the efficiency model that had become the norm that Jos was told his model would be unfeasible. It seemed impossible that the model could work, much less deliver savings.

Sustaining Motivation

Over the last thirteen years, Buurtzorg has been proving that the very opposite is true.[19] While many look at Buurtzorg as a poster-child for the "leaderless" movement, when we looked closer we saw a philosophy that went far beyond this management technique. At its core, Buurtzorg doesn't see itself in the business of delivering health services. It sees itself first and foremost as supporting problem-solvers. Rather than delivering individual services, Buurtzorg first asks, "How can we make ourselves redundant?" To do this, Buurtzorg nurses are highly focused on achieving the maximum degree of independence for patients possible. Jos explains, "I say you must look at it upside down, from the point of view of the client."[20] Like FII, Buurtzorg recognizes that people are the experts of their own lives. Rather than see patients as recipients of fragmented medical products and services, Buurtzorg recognizes that they are complex human beings, requiring unique and individualized approaches.

To engage patients as whole people, Buurtzorg has identified who they believe to be the very best people to come alongside patients and caregivers: highly qualified, self-motivated nurses. Nurses are encouraged to look closely at the entire care system for each client, taking into account the level of assistance they have at home and what other services they can access in their neighborhood. Rather than being hurried along with rigid schedules and the pressure to hand off to the next practitioner, nurses spend time with families and caregivers gathering essential information on the patient's support system. Over several visits, by getting to know a patient's household and situation, nurses are able to assess what type of care is best suited to the client. They then work closely with the patient and their family to create the best solution for the particular situation.

This level of attention comes with a hefty price tag. Buurtzorg nurses are paid higher hourly rates than competitors, making unit costs high. They spend far more time with clients, aiming for 61 percent of time in patient homes. Nurses also take care of fewer patients, sharing clients with just one other nurse and performing "menial" personal care tasks like washing and dressing in addition to their skilled duties. Moreover, nurses often stop to have a cup of coffee with patients and chat with family members and caregivers, and these conversations give important insights into the patient's situation. These small efforts add up, making each patient visit far more costly than other health providers.

To ensure this level of attention to patients, Buurtzorg removes nearly all of the administration and bureaucracy that one would normally find in a large organization. Nurses work in teams of ten to twelve and receive no supervision or direction from a head office. Teams meet regularly but are not led by any single nurse. Rather, they take turns to set agendas and collectively determine how to handle emerging issues. If nurses run into issues that cannot be resolved within the team setting, they engage a Buurtzorg coach who acts strictly in a facilitation role. At the same time, nurses keep all of their patient records and schedules, as well as access up-to-date clinical information, on a centralized Buurtzorgweb platform.

For Buurtzorg, the coordination of these activities does not need to come from a centralized management team because nurse teams are continuously building their shared identity through the conversational meetings that they hold on a regular basis. Groups who have built a common identity supported by shared meaning can act in response to daily challenges while still retaining a cohesiveness across the system. In the case of Buurtzorg, the common identity is that of the highly skilled nurse with a strong connection to a neighborhood community. As a result, patients on average recover faster and need fewer days of care—108 rather than 168—than with other organizations.[21] By stripping out all layers of management, Buurtzorg operates its entire Netherlands-based organization of ten thousand plus nurses with just fifty back-office personnel and a traveling group of twenty coaches. Administration costs are minimal, comprising only 8 percent of the total expenses of the organization compared to 25 percent for a typical care organization. Overall, Buurtzorg has consistently shown that higher quality care can be delivered at below-average costs when motivated teams of primary actors are able to unlock their problem-solving potential at the most dynamic point in the system.

When Jos founded Buurtzorg, he thought extensively about how this process works, as a key to the relationship between the nurse and the patient. When the capacity of a person is matched to their attitude and motivation, and when those two key components are aligned in the pursuit of a singular goal, the problem-solving nature of a person is unlocked. The ability to do what is necessary and right is not only possible (i.e., they have the competence to do it) but also intrinsic (i.e., they have the attitude to do it). Thirteen years later, across seven hundred teams in thirty-five countries, this approach still holds. Buurtzorg hires highly educated nurses and ensures they have the time and latitude to care for patients as whole people.

In a similar fashion, on our visits to m2m sites in multiple countries we were interested to see that the conversations between Mentor Mothers and patients are generally unscripted and unsupervised. Mentor Mothers often seem to operate semi-autonomously, guided by the quasi-managerial role of "site coordinator," but far from the hierarchy of a typical international NGO structure. The supervision of Mentor Mothers is designed to ensure proper case management, but is far more supportive than managerial. Mentor Mothers are directly supervised by site coordinators, who are often former Mentor Mothers. In addition, m2m uses case studies, role playing, and teach-back group learning to train and support Mentor Mothers, which prepares them with on-the-job experience to address a large variety of situations. This style of supportive supervision is even more surprising since Mentor Mothers are embedded within the strict hierarchy of clinics operating inside government health system hierarchies.

When we probed this in a conversation with m2m's current CEO, Frank Beadle de Palomo, he almost seemed to dismiss the observation, saying that "m2m operates an incredible recruitment engine, which means we hire exemplary staff and support their empowerment."[22] Later in the conversation, he noted that his "listening trips" to the field have strongly driven the changes in the organization to become more broad in their scope of maternal and child health. The bottom-up approach that m2m has been able to construct is largely due to the motivation that Mentor Mothers gain from their lived experience with HIV. While m2m may consider this a recruitment effort, it is designed in such a way that the organization can operate a relatively non-directed organization while responding intuitively to pregnant clients' needs.

Economies of Trust

Rather than operating through economies of scale, organizations like Buurtzorg, FII, RLabs, and m2m operate on "economies of trust." As we've seen, as organizations grow, too often learning becomes decoupled from the "grassroots." Authority moves to experts who are not living the problems they are trying to solve, to funders who sit far from the contexts they are funding, and to professional directors and managers who struggle to understand the lived experience of their clients. This decoupling happens with good intentions, particularly as organizations professionalize in an attempt to grow their operations beyond a single context. However, this professionalization can move the perceived source of expertise further and further from the actual context where the work is being done.

The organizations we studied have each, in their own way, gone against this path of professionalization, instead building organizational structures that maximize autonomy. These organizations maintain that when groups of people are supported with knowledge and skills, while motivated by their own attitude and capacity, they will make decisions that are useful for themselves and for those with whom they share a strong identity. Groups of primary actors with lived experience or full immersion in a context can more easily navigate their own complexity. The result is that these organizations do not need to always control outcomes—rather, they have built contextually responsive systems guided by a combination of self- and group-interest that naturally and creatively responds to problems in surprising and effective ways.

In these organizations, there is far less need for traditional hierarchies. Management structures are generally quite lean, with the greatest investment put into the groups of people at the "front lines" who make most of the decisions. Groups of people, cultivated with a strong sense of collective identity, are not supervised in the classic sense; groups are able to make decisions about their own families, neighborhoods, schools, and communities, reducing the need to micro-manage. While codified programs and standard operating procedures are useful, they are not the driving force behind quality and impact. When unintended consequences inevitably arise, they are dealt with on a scale that is manageable and a timeframe that is reasonable.

Since complex systems nearly always throw up unintended consequences, these organizations have positioned the people who are closest to complexity to respond confidently in times of uncertainty. These primary actors have the opportunity to draw upon their own lived experience as well as the collective intelligence of the group, seeing both the fine-grained detail and the big picture of the complex system in which they live. Bolstered by this knowledge and guided by shared meaning, groups and individuals can move into action and practice intuitive problem-solving, solving day-to-day challenges with a cohesion that is rarely found in a top-down, directed effort.

Learning Notes: Equipping problem-solvers

Organizations can create responsive and representative systems by positioning and equipping primary actors to be contextually responsive, positively adapting to situations as they evolve and change. These actors, when equipped with knowledge, skills, and "on-the-ground" expertise, are motivated to do what they do best: solve problems. Organizations are equipping problem-solvers—including families, nurses, community health workers, mothers, and numerous others—through:

- **Circulating data (both small and big)**, creating quick feedback cycles so that primary actors can learn about what is and is not working in their particular system.
- **Decentralizing decision-making**, so that primary actors can self-manage and make choices in real time based on the knowledge they are able to access.
- **Positioning problem-solvers**, to try new things based on what they are seeing, devise informed solutions, and feel the satisfaction of getting it right.
- **Sustaining motivation**, ensuring that skills are matched with intrinsic drive and primary actors are supported in their endeavors.

These strategies to **equip problem-solvers** allow organizations to operate with less hierarchy and reduced bureaucracy, setting them up for scale while addressing contextual variability. Most importantly, they give people agency over their own lives and workspaces while ensuring they feel motivated to experiment, learn, and succeed.

6
Promoting Platforms

In 2016,[1] residents of a waterfront fishing settlement outside Lagos alerted police officers to a clash among youths from a nearby community. When the police arrived, it quickly became clear they were not there to help.[2] Instead, they joined in, setting fire to homes and chasing out residents while fires raged through the shacks. That night the police officers returned, this time escorting a bulldozer which was set to work dismantling homes. Demolition continued through the night, ripping through tin roofs, scrap wood, and poles, tearing down more than eight hundred houses. As residents protested, police fired gunshots into the crowds, dispersing them to the nearby lagoon where they sheltered in boats and canoes, some jumping into the water although they couldn't swim. Resident Celestine Ahinsu described the aftermath: "After a couple of days we started seeing the bodies floating. I saw three—a man with a backpack and a pregnant woman with a baby on her back."[3]

Despite public outcry and two court restraining orders, evictions continued in Otodo-Gbame and nearby Ilubrin until all homes were demolished. The destruction, now complete, could be tallied: nine deaths, seventeen missing persons, five razed primary schools, and a total of thirty thousand displaced persons. Amnesty International reported, "All seven forced evictions in Ilubirin and Otodo-Gbame communities occurred without prior consultations with affected residents, without adequate prior notice, and without the provision of compensation...Alternative adequate housing for those who could not provide this for themselves was never offered."[4] A few months later, signboards appeared on the demolished sites marketing luxury developments. If you do an internet search for "Ilubirin Lagos" as of the writing of this chapter, you'll find a

Google ad for "a substantial and new exciting waterside district" on Lagos Island.[5]

Biologist and town planner Patrick Geddes wrote, "A city is more than a place in space, it is a drama in time."[6] We would guess that not even Geddes could have predicted the drama of a city like Lagos, Nigeria. No city in the world epitomizes urbanization like Lagos, which surpassed Cairo in 2012 as the largest city in Africa. While the official population of the city is 17.5 million, the population likely exceeds 20 million.[7] Lagos faces numerous challenges, but first and foremost is housing. The city has a housing gap estimated at 2 million units, with more than 70 percent of the population— 15 million people—living in informal areas, often in close proximity to high- and middle-income areas. As the pressure to "clean up" these districts intensifies, slum eradication schemes are often seen as a necessary step to accelerate urban development.

Yet, urbanization does not have to come at the expense of the poor. While violent evictions raged in Otodo-Gbame and Ilubirin, a far different process was unfolding in the very same city.[8] Inspired by a peer-to-peer exchange with a Kenyan federation of slum-dweller organizations, the Lagos State Urban Renewal Agency (LASURA) opened a dialogue with their Nigerian counterpart, the Nigerian Slum/Informal Settlement Federation. Together, the Nigerian federation and LASURA mapped out next steps for a plan to upgrade the existing community rather than resort to a large-scale eviction. Their first step would be a community-led data-gathering exercise.

The learning exchange which paved the way for this process was facilitated by Slum Dwellers International (SDI), an organization that connects slum communities around the world as part of a global movement of the urban poor. SDI was founded in 1996 by the late Jockin Arputham, a carpenter from outside Bangalore who relocated to Mumbai at the age of eighteen. With nowhere to live, he made his home on the streets and soon discovered a penchant for organizing his fellow pavement and slum dwellers to resist the Indian state's eviction efforts. Like many of the founders profiled in this book, Jockin received numerous international accolades for his work, including a nomination for a Nobel Peace Prize. But he shrugged off these awards with deference to the slum dwellers who make up SDI: "All these awards I accept on behalf of the slum dwellers who were my university, my teachers."[9] Until his death in 2018, Jockin continued to live and work in the slums of Mumbai, eschewing conventional markers of success and directing all of the funds he raised toward the activities of SDI and its partner organizations.

SDI is built on the concept of peer-to-peer learning through horizontal exchanges, where community-based coalitions of slum dwellers visit other coalitions in countries with more established operations. These seemingly simple exchanges serve multiple purposes. First, emerging groups learn practical strategies for how to organize as a counterweight to the elite interests and government initiatives that threaten to displace them. These strategies include participatory data collection, group savings schemes, and collective self-help approaches. Second, learning exchanges including government officials, such as the Nigerian example above, allow policy leaders to see what is possible and encourage pro-poor policies that integrate slum dwellers into the process of urban development. The aim is to ensure that slum dwellers themselves are part of the process, and, if displacement is necessary, to do it in a way that is minimally disruptive to families.[10]

Today, SDI creates solidarity among more than a million slum dwellers across thirty-two countries in Asia, Africa, Latin America, and the Caribbean. While it is a global nonprofit organization with a secretariat based in Cape Town, its structure and operations depart significantly from the traditional nonprofit or NGO model. Professor of geography at Durham University, Colin McFarlane, describes SDI as "a learning movement based around the structure of exchanges, involving small groups of the urban poor travelling from one settlement to another to share knowledge in what amounts to an informal learning process."[11] McFarlane's description calls to mind a vast network of urban slum groups, connecting and learning from one another, which is what we visualized when we first began to research SDI. Yet, McFarlane, who has studied SDI as part of his work on the experience and politics of cities, hesitates to even use the term "network" to describe SDI, feeling that the term does not truly represent the organization. Over time, as we dug deeper into SDI's activities, we began to agree. SDI seems to have found a way to sustain the critical balance between "grassroots" activities and "big picture" advocacy. Yet, as an organization, it looks very different to what we were used to seeing. In order to truly understand SDI, we realized we would have to overcome some critical blind spots.

Vertical *and* Horizontal

James Mwangi, executive director of development consultancy Dalberg Group reflects, "At a time of global crisis and urgency, one of the most interesting questions to ask is, 'how can we shape the next phase of making meaningful and urgent change in the world?'"[12] Mwangi, originally from Kenya with a sensitivity to solutions "imposed" from above, continues, "Part of what we need to figure out over the next ten years is how do we equip truly grassroots-based change-makers of different kinds with the tools to drive systemic change where they are. Because they're the ones who know best how to do it, and if they are successful, they are the ones who will have the legitimacy to build on that systemic change."

As an organization linking more than a million slum dwellers in 527 cities,[13] SDI epitomizes this concept of scale. Yet, at the beginning of our research, SDI seemed to contradict most of the nonprofit organizing strategies we knew. The organization takes participation to an extreme, shunning professionalization of any kind. Its structure calls up the image of a giant funnel, an inversion of the standard operational organogram. Governance structures start with thousands of local groups—slum dwellers who self-organize at the neighborhood level and then elect leaders to sit at city, regional, and national levels. "Mature" federations then appoint members to a transnational Council of Federations which selects the Management Committee. At each of these levels, different tactics prevail. In some neighborhoods and cities, groups engage in protracted policy negotiations with municipalities; in others, they are embroiled in protest action; in still others, groups are building private sector investment funds. All activities taken up at the national and transnational levels are driven by local needs, percolating through various governance structures if other localities are experiencing similar issues. If this sounds unwieldy, time-consuming, or even messy, that's because it is.

However, this inverted hierarchy is only part of the structure. Imagine an upside-down organizational chart that comes to life in three-dimensional form. Although SDI's groups are organized vertically, the learning exchanges in which they participate also link them to each other horizontally in a growing web of connections spanning cities, regions, and even continents. Ilda Lindell, a scholar of geography at the University of Stockholm who has studied informal social movements in several countries, describes this "multi-scalar" approach as neither local nor global, but both. "Action at one scale influences and shapes action at another…the argument runs counter to a tendency in the literature to focus on either transnational movements or on place-based resistance as the sufficient and adequate scale of analysis," says Lindell.[14]

This three-dimensional structure at first seemed confusing to us. How does anything get done? Over time, however, it became clear that we were looking at something more akin to a living system than a static organizational structure. The multiplication of efforts at the local level happens as the day-to-day political context unfolds, which is exactly what needs to happen for urban slum dwellers to pressure municipalities to work with them. However, when SDI groups meet others engaged in similar struggles across localities, regions, and countries, they are able to develop a "globalized" imagination about what is possible in their own setting. Rather than create a perfect strategic plan, SDI generates a proliferation of tactics that is then customized to the local context.

While the accumulation of tactics is vital for gaining momentum, these exchanges also exist to counteract the powerful forces which aim to keep the status quo. Activist and scholar Raj Patel describes the spaces for these exchanges as crucial, yet often requiring significant struggle. "In almost every case where alternatives are being practiced, there are spaces in which people are allowed to think for themselves. These spaces are fought for against the predations of poverty—particularly time poverty—and it is [here] where other possibilities are born. In these spaces, there is the freedom to become active scholars of their own struggle, not passive recipients of others' prescriptions," he said.[15]

At SDI, local groups experiment with possibilities and share them with other groups, refining them as ideas, strategies, and advocacy efforts to gain momentum through the organization. As groups gain political power in one locality or region, they use this momentum to "leapfrog" in another jurisdiction. Lindell writes about other transnational movements, "In situations of acute crisis, often triggered by government actors' actions, these groups are now able to mobilize considerable international solidarity through their international connections."[16] In the case of SDI, slum dwellers with very little positional power can exert considerable influence over political processes, inducing cities and states to work with them to upgrade their living conditions rather than resort to evictions. Through solidarity with more than a million slum dwellers across thousands of groups in thirty-two countries, those living in urban poverty have shifted their development agenda from a side-lined effort to a mainstream global movement. As an organization representing slum dwellers, SDI has built partnerships with local and national governments, as well as transnational institutions such as UN Habitat, Cities Alliance, and the United Cities and Local Governments Africa (UCLGA). Over the years, SDI has become an essential player in conversations about urbanization and city development, putting poverty at the top of the agenda for cities.

Linking Groups Together

In the previous practice, we explored what it looks like when organizations equip groups of problem-solvers at critical points in a system. Yet, to scale beyond local activities, organizations need to link these groups together across contexts and geographies. By linking groups into larger bodies, problem-solvers are able to see the proverbial trees ("context") *and* the forest (the "big picture"). This is a crucial balance that traditional organizational structures make difficult. In our research, we spent time with organizations that have built impressive local teams, but, when it comes to governance, strategy, and funding at the national and global levels, have resorted to professionals and experts to sign contracts, make decisions, and enforce policies. We have also witnessed activist organizations that are highly skilled at bringing people out into the streets to protest, generating power from grievances, but which make subsequent policy decisions behind closed doors between experts who have not lived through the pain. "Grassroots" problem-solvers are often acknowledged at the local level, but then excluded at higher levels by the very organizational structures that claim to "help" them.

SDI's unconventional way of organizing ensures that knowledge and experience travel horizontally *and* vertically, giving community-level groups a genuine pathway to interact with one another as well as participate at higher levels of decision-making. As we saw earlier, it is tempting to call SDI a "network," but this doesn't really capture the full extent of the approach. Networks are built of transactions and are generally agnostic as to who or how people participate. SDI is instead built of intentional relationships that enable participation by those who have been previously marginalized. Researcher Angelo Gasparre writes, "The basic idea within SDI is that the lack of participation by the urban poor has historically been one of the major obstacles to achieve real development: either the government or the donors' agencies, in fact, usually treat the poor as beneficiaries of someone else's actions, thus undervaluing their knowledge and skills. Radically opposing this view, SDI interprets its role not as an intermediary...but rather as an 'enabling tool' of direct negotiation between the urban poor and the public institutions."[17] Much more than a network, SDI acts as a *platform*: a space for learning and collaboration, giving representative groups the foundation and tools to engage in high-level political action while keeping expertise close to the ground.

Systems Work Terms 10: *Platforms*

platforms   *an intentional space for learning and collaboration, giving representative groups the foundation and tools to participate in high-level political action while keeping expertise close to the ground*

We realize that the term is a bit of a loaded one. Nowadays, it seems that every entrepreneur or business aspires to build or be a platform. "Platform strategy" is used to describe the business models deployed by high-growth and increasingly dominant companies such as Google, Amazon, Uber, and Airbnb. However, as businesses have rushed in to capitalize on these models, many have forgotten that platforms were originally an organizational model deployed by social activists. Some of the first platforms to gain international exposure were those that burst onto the activist scene during the 1999 World Trade Organization protests in Seattle, expanding to the anti-globalization movements of the late 1990s and early 2000s. Fueled by the ease of connecting across geographic boundaries that the growth of the internet facilitated, local activist groups—particularly the Independent Media Center (IMC) in the media sector[18]—developed platforms to share stories, methods, and strategies.[19] Similar platforms were later created by the commercial companies that now dominate the business landscape, including Google, Facebook, and Amazon.[20] In circular fashion, many of the founders of these companies are now promoting the concept of "societal platforms" as a means of providing "unified but not uniform" approaches to social challenges.[21]

Whether for commercial or social aims, enabled by technology or not, platforms provide an outlet for participation among groups who have differing strategies, structures, and even ideologies. They also offer a way to celebrate diversity, learning from a cacophony of different players. As with SDI, this type of organizational structure can appear messy and chaotic, particularly for those used to dealing with

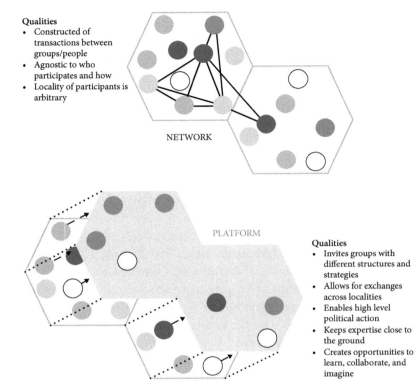

Qualities
- Constructed of transactions between groups/people
- Agnostic to who participates and how
- Locality of participants is arbitrary

NETWORK

PLATFORM

Qualities
- Invites groups with different structures and strategies
- Allows for exchanges across localities
- Enables high level political action
- Keeps expertise close to the ground
- Creates opportunities to learn, collaborate, and imagine

Fig. 6.1 Platforms vs. networks
Source: Authors.

traditional hierarchies where decision-makers deliver "best practices" and single programmatic models. Rather than offering easy solutions, platforms require participants to deeply engage with what is happening "on-the-ground," learn from the experiences of others, and then experiment with the application of these ideas in their own context (see fig 6.1). The learning process is fraught with trial and error. However, the opportunity to grow the imagination and acquire a clearer vision for what is possible is magnified exponentially.

Collaborating with Flexibility

While platforms offer the chance for learning and imagination, they also provide paths for shared activities while maintaining crucial flexibility for members. One of the organizations that we studied,

Child and Youth Finance International (CYFI), highlighted this to us in our research. The organization developed an approach that they call "collaborative systems change," which envisions a type of social change where teams and organizations working across the world come together, learn from each other's experiences, celebrate each other's successes, and return to adapt what works for their context. CYFI stresses that program models used by members are "offered simply as possibilities to local actors who can contextualize based on their own intimate knowledge of their context."[22] The approach is refreshingly open-source and unorthodox, just like the organization itself.

With an annual budget of less than US$2 million, a staff that never exceeded twenty-five full-time employees, and a contingent of student interns who spent anywhere from two to six months with the team, CYFI is a tiny organization by most global standards. Yet, in less than ten years, the organization changed the economic futures of 32 million children in 175 countries. In fact, the organization recently closed its doors and transferred key projects to other institutions, not because it ran out of funding or can't find support for its cause but rather because they believe their members have gained enough momentum for them to cease operations. Co-directors Lubna Shaban and Bram van Eijk had the unprecedented job of letting funders know that they did not need any further financing, saying that their mission has been accomplished. Lubna says, "It's so rare to hear of an organization shutting itself down that most people were quick to think we had run out of money or that this was a failure. We worked very hard to explain that the reality was the complete opposite: this was a success."[23]

Similar to SDI, CYFI was always an organization of contradictions. It was big yet small, influential while obscure, impactful but agile. While its ambitions were extraordinary—it aimed to impact 100 million children when it was first founded in 2010—it kept its management model very lean. And although the organization never hired a formal finance director or a human resources manager, its back operations were kept to an extremely high standard. It relied heavily on volunteers and interns to work alongside staff members and also on board members for their skills and expertise. CYFI's structure was part of its design, making closing down relatively simple compared to organizations with large bureaucracies.

From Outrageous to Acceptable

CYFI was founded in 2010 by serial social entrepreneur Jeroo Billimoria, who had the inspiration to grow a global movement for economic citizenship for children and youth. According to Jeroo, families and societies can break intergenerational poverty when children become full "economic citizens": educated about money and financial matters, with access to child-friendly bank accounts. But Jeroo is frank about the challenge that they faced in convincing countries and organizations to focus on financial inclusion for children: "It's not a sexy topic. It's not! It seems a pretty redundant, useless topic, if I can be honest. But if we can crack intergenerational poverty, we can crack related issues and ensure inclusion right at the beginning."[24]

CYFI grew as an idea out of Jeroo's experiences with three previous ventures: Aflatoun, an organization which develops financial curriculum for schools and extracurricular programs; Child Helpline International, a franchise community of 178 child hotlines in 146 countries; and MelJol, a children's rights program that brings together children from different backgrounds to learn from each other. Through these experiences, she developed a sort of "process model" for organizing. First, Jeroo has always utilized what she calls the "Indian wedding approach" to launching a new idea. Her initiatives start with a massive gathering, including community organizers, academics, financiers, youth, and sometimes even royalty. Through these gatherings, Jeroo seeks to put a "finger on the pulse" of a movement and gauge the readiness for leaders and organizations to take on a new challenge. At the outset, these challenges seem to border on the outrageous—providing toll-free hotlines for street kids in every country in the world or providing 100 million children with bank accounts. However, as groups get together and hash out the "impossible," practical ideas start to take root. Jeroo then organizes participants into working groups across functional areas and regions. These working groups may, for example, include academics who work together to gather evidence for a specific idea or engage with international agencies to build up a database of workable policies across the world. With a growing sense of possibility, country representatives then return to their regions and start to test the ideas within their local contexts. Representatives build in-country teams to launch local initiatives while working groups connect people across geographies and share ideas. Before long, an "outrageous" idea is not just acceptable, but commonplace.

In the case of CYFI, Jeroo and her team launched the first gathering under the auspices of Aflatoun, which already had strong connections with nonprofits delivering financial education curriculum to children in many countries. Realizing that curriculum was only a single aspect of empowering children as "economic citizens," they expanded the invitation list to include central bankers, finance executives, and national education ministers from around the world. At the launch, 120 stakeholders and experts from over forty countries came together to discuss what a financial movement for children could look like. The gathering took inclusivity to a new level: the team produced fifty versions of the agenda to accommodate more than sixty speakers on the podium. While many participants arrived at the event with little idea of what a financial system for children might look like, most left with a strong commitment to develop national initiatives when they returned back to their countries. These initiatives ranged from promoting policies for financial education in national curricula to working with banking authorities to ensure safe and appropriate banking products for children.

Similar to SDI's experience, CYFI's platform allows ideas to gain traction across multiple localities. When this happens, institutions and organizations emerge to provide structure for greater scale. By the end of 2019, when the organization closed its doors, seventy countries had shifted their policies to include more child-friendly financial goals, while sixty-three thousand organizations in 175 countries had taken action to improve children's financial literacy. Over nearly ten years, CYFI nurtured and grew these initiatives—rarely through financial grants, but rather by connecting representatives to each other when ideas or assistance was needed. They brought people together regularly, and importantly, celebrated progress at every milestone.

Observing Rituals

CYFI utilized one of the most fundamentally human ways to keep people together while learning: rituals. When CYFI hosted a gathering, celebration and play were a key component of the agenda, from video and social media competitions to traditional costumes and balloon releases. Beyond the initial gathering, CYFI kept the momentum going by hosting annual awards events and regional learning sessions to showcase country initiatives and highlight successes. Children and youth were often present at these events, turning the most staid financial conversations into opportunities to connect their professional work to future generations. CYFI also launched an annual "Global Money Week," now coordinated by the OECD, a financial awareness campaign that encourages children around the world to participate in activities where they can learn about money matters, livelihoods, and entrepreneurship. Activities are diverse, including visits to stock exchanges and central banks, seminars on budgeting and saving, and social media contests. While Global Money Week is exciting and informative for children and youth, its main purpose is to catalyze those organizations and decision-makers who can bring about more durable changes to national policies and practices, in a playful, positive way.

SDI also uses rituals, albeit in a much different style. For SDI, data-gathering is an essential ritual for building alignment among disparate groups. After organizing into savings communities, SDI groups are encouraged to start their activities around a process they call "enumeration." Co-founder and former chair, Sheela Patel, describes enumeration as "a range of rituals. It starts off with numbering every single structure so that every household is ensured that their house is included in the process."[25] Slum dwellers take charge of documenting their own communities, going from shack to shack and counting the structures, households, and people who are living in their settlement. Importantly, communities set their own priorities, agreeing on the questions and methods for data collection. Communities also retain ownership of data since control gives residents the ability to decide how, when, and for what purpose the information is used. For slum dwellers living in communities that have been marginalized, rarely acknowledged or "counted" by municipalities in official budgets and planning, this process can be deeply moving. This process is the first step to making their needs visible: first to each other, and then, to those in positions of formal authority.

It would be easy to dismiss these meetings, celebrations, and exercises as routine organizing activities. Yet, for platform-style organizations, rituals provide necessary structure in the absence of traditional hierarchy. Groups engaged in change efforts need to see that their efforts are delivering progress against a bigger picture of change. They also need to be encouraged and incentivized by similar groups engaged in the same efforts or struggle. Rituals create periodic breaks in time and space where milestones get recorded and counted. CYFI's celebrations are dramatic and colorful, creating friendly competition among country teams as they work toward financial inclusion for youth. For SDI, the onerous, sometimes dangerous, process of collecting, owning, and sharing data is just as important as what the data reveal. SDI's South African national coordinator Rose Molokoane describes the challenges that members go through to gather data: "I want [SDI members] to tell you about measuring shacks that are so close together you need to climb up on roofs to see what's what; about mapping settlement boundaries and trying not to fall in drainage channels lined with garbage; about going house to house and hearing stories that make you want to cry; and about being chased by dogs and even by people with weapons as you administer enumerations."[26] Through rituals, groups build solidarity in hardship, and by knowing that other groups have gone through the same process, this solidarity connects groups together across countries and the world.

Platforms for Power

While platforms offer significant opportunities for participation and collaboration, they also come with a unique set of challenges. Both at SDI and CYFI, as well as other organizations in our research, we found that the process of expanding beyond the core collective can trigger crises of identity and rupture. In particular, building bridges and partnerships with those in formal power can divide groups as they jockey for position or work to ensure that their needs are not subsumed by powerful players. Communities may have experiences with politicians who make empty promises, creating "tokenistic" relationships at the local level only to disappear when the election is over. These groups may also feel co-opted by corporate interests that have used community buy-in to "rubber stamp" access to resources and markets. Even more insidiously, well-meaning funders and investors may try to assert their own agendas into communities, inadvertently positioning their own needs as the needs of a community.

At SDI, discussions about partnering with impact investors to access capital for slum upgrading has required the organization to look deeply at the way they partner with powerful players. For investors, social impact is often positioned as inclusion, or delivering access to housing, electricity, water, and sanitation to those who have previously lacked access. Yet this largely assumes that the ways in which these goods and services have been historically developed and distributed are fair and right for all. As a result, SDI affiliates have engaged in serious conversations about who makes decisions and profits from their communities. In 2007, SDI launched the Urban Poor Fund International (UPFI), the purpose of which is to provide venture capital to federations to capitalize important urban improvement and housing projects. UPFI has proven to be a valuable means of giving funding directly to the urban poor across SDI's networks. SDI is now experimenting with other forms of innovative finance as "learning experiments" to see if new forms of finance in which slum dwellers are equity holders can generate much-needed capital while still retaining ownership by communities. The jury is still out on whether these new financial models will be a desirable way of partnering with impact investors and new and emerging players in city landscapes.[27]

Similarly, CYFI spent considerable effort in its early years collaborating with the formal banking industry to develop a set of child-friendly banking standards. The aim was to provide certification to institutions with accounts designed for kids and youth, ensuring that fees never exceeded revenue, that rates of interest were financially incentivizing, and that the privacy and identity concerns of children were addressed. However, financial institutions were wary of further regulation, even self-imposed, in the post-financial crisis environment. As they progressed with the project, CYFI began to realize that some financial institutions were eager to share in the goodwill generated by partnering with a youth-friendly organization, but not willing to sign up for a program that required certification and accountability. In order to progress with the certification program, CYFI realized it would need to compromise some of the standards that were critical to the initiative. After two years of development, CYFI decided to terminate the certificate in order to preserve the integrity of the project.

These crisis situations raise a critical issue for organizations, particularly those which are promoting platforms that amplify and elevate community actors. As co-authors and digital activists Jeremy Heimans and Henry Timms write in their book *New Power*, "How do you use institutional power without being institutionalized?"[28] Platforms provide significant momentum for participation and collaboration. But, as they grow in size, they accumulate power from two of their most critical assets: legitimacy and solidarity. These sources of power can be extremely attractive to those in upper positions of a hierarchy, since they can reinforce their own power. For example, UN Habitat capitalizes on SDI's legitimacy when it invites slum dwellers to sit in the front rows of their convenings. Similarly, financial institutions garner good feelings from their customers when they host groups of enthusiastic children at stock exchanges and central banks.

As organizations grow platforms that span geographies and ideologies, it is even more important to set up equal relationships with powerful players, going slowly and reconstituting collectives through the tactics discussed in the previous practices: creating a shared identity, building safe havens, pooling feelings, circulating knowledge, and decentralizing decision-making. Through these strategies, the truly important ways to reconfigure power—concerning access, distribution, and profit—became possible.

Learning Notes: Promoting platforms

To expand beyond local activities, organizations connect groups to one another, ensuring that knowledge-sharing, experience-gathering, and decision-making happen both vertically and horizontally. Organizations can promote platforms to enable this crucial balance between "on-the-ground" expertise and large-scale learning and action. To do this, organizations are:

- **Linking groups together**, building intentional relationships through horizontal exchanges, cross-country working groups, and inverted governance structures.
- **Encouraging collaboration with flexibility**, so that local groups can learn from the experiences of other groups and experiment with the application of these ideas in their own contexts.
- **Moving from outrageous to acceptable**, where groups draw on the successes and momentum of other localities to progress their own initiatives.
- **Observing rituals**, events and undertakings that celebrate milestones and deliver a sense of progress in playful and positive ways, providing necessary structure in the absence of traditional hierarchy.

By **promoting platforms**, organizations can maintain a local diversity of approaches while harnessing the shared learnings, legitimacy, and solidarity that comes from a large-scale web of relationships.

7

Disrupting Policies *and* Patterns

Bachan Mishra, a street vendor from the Meena Bazaar in Delhi, India, raked his fingers through his thick black hair as he remembered that day in February 2014. He and hundreds of his fellow street vendors had just entered their fourth day of an indefinite hunger strike. "It was do or die,"[1] he recalled. They were taking extreme measures to urge their Parliament to pass a crucial piece of legislation: the Protection of Livelihood and Regulation of Street Vending Act. Weeks earlier, they had flooded Congress President Sonia Gandhi's office with thousands of postcards and letters and marched to the house of her son, Vice President Rahul Gandhi, to demand his support. Now, thousands of vendors were leaving their livelihoods in cities across the country to join strikers in front of Parliament House. Still, the members of the Rajya Sabha—the Upper House of Congress—knew they had time on their side. In just two days, the final session would close, signaling a new general election and a change in power for the entire country. If the bill did not pass in forty-eight hours, the street vendors' efforts would be in vain.

Arbind Singh was among the hunger strikers, trying to keep his thoughts focused. He readily admits, "being hungry was very difficult...I was having serious headaches."[2] Arbind had been working with informal workers as an activist and community organizer since 1996. As he surveyed the thousands of street vendors assembled in front of Parliament, he reflected on their journey over the past two decades. The path to power had not been obvious. Informal workers couldn't rely on the same labor-organizing tactics that formal workers had in previous generations. In fact, many informal workers did not even identify as workers.[3] Street vendors, casual laborers, and wastepickers—many of them women—viewed their way of life as simply survival. Migrant laborers were far from home, a shadow workforce with little legal or social legitimacy. While workers could articulate their daily challenges—precarious income, insecure housing, police harassment, lack of protection when times got tough—these issues had no legally recognized connection to the broader system in which they operated.

When Arbind first began working with informal workers, the perception among labor experts was clear and linear: first, get people into formal employment, then governments will provide them with standard protections under formal labor laws. This perception was based on the widespread belief among labor economists that informal work is merely a temporary imbalance on the road to economic development. As long as countries followed the "proper" development path, informality would go away on its own. Arbind was not convinced. His mentor, Viji Srinivasan, who had worked with informal women workers since the 1960s, had pushed Arbind to see that, contrary to the experts' opinion, informality would likely persist and even increase as economies globalized and worker protections loosened. The solution was not integrating informal workers into the formal economy as formal workers, which could possibly leave them in worse circumstances. Rather, informal workers needed to claim their legitimate place in a globalizing economy, demanding the recognition and rights that this critical role deserved.

For organizers like Arbind, this meant that their work had to start from a more fundamental place, with informal workers staking a new and powerful identity for themselves. Arbind began this process in the mid-1990s when he established a nonprofit organization called Nidan (meaning "solution" in Hindi) to mobilize the street vendors in his hometown of Patna. Police across the country had recently stepped up their efforts to clear street vendors from traditional marketplaces, imposing heavy fines for vendors to retrieve their goods and equipment.[4] In response, internationally renowned activist Ela Bhatt set up an international coalition, StreetNet, issuing a declaration that called for street vendors to organize at the city and national levels.[5] Answering the call, Nidan performed an extensive data-collection process, interviewing more than six thousand vendors, while similar efforts were underway in major cities across India.

Based on these efforts, hundreds of street vendor associations across the country banded together to form the National Association of Street Vendors of India (NASVI) in 1998. Recognized for his work in Patna, Arbind was elected as national coordinator, using Nidan as an "incubator" for the new alliance. Bringing together the data from each of the major cities represented,[6] it was possible to see the contribution of street vendors to the economic life of the country for the first time. The data revealed that street vending was not a nuisance to ignore, or a temporary glitch, but rather a structural shift due to India's emerging place in the world economy. Urban consumers patronized street vendors because of convenience and affordability while street vendors responded as hardworking entrepreneurs pursuing viable livelihoods in a rapidly urbanizing country.[7] Bolstered by this research, NASVI's organizers realized that they needed to move beyond "fire-fighting" efforts, which only resulted in stopgap measures and temporary relief. Rather, they decided to fight for something far more durable: legal recognition and self-governance as vital contributors to India's emerging economy.

Using NASVI as their voice, organizers turned their attention to policymakers and city administrators. In 2001, NASVI presented their findings to the Ministry of Urban Development, emphasizing the need to develop a national policy that recognized street vending as a viable profession. NASVI then mobilized hundreds of leaders from nearly every street vending association in the country, inviting the minister of state to form a policy task force. Facing increasing pressure in 2004, the Indian cabinet adopted the National Policy on Urban Street Vendors. This policy was pivotal. As Arbind and his colleague Sachin Kumar explained, "for the first time in the history of India, street vendors were officially described as contributors to the urban economy and not as encroachers into public space, a paradigm shift in [the] true sense of [the] term."[8]

Ten years later, the energy and solidarity generated by NASVI culminated in an even greater victory. NASVI's members decided that to gain the upper hand with the government they had to put their lives on the line. With five hundred hungry strikers outside of Parliament, the street vendors' plight rose to the top of the news cycle, causing one of Arbind's friends to say, "you would think that nothing was happening in India except for the street vendors!"[9] Just one day before the close of Parliament, the Upper House succumbed to the intense pressure from the street vendors and the public support they had garnered, passing the Street Vendors (Protection of Livelihood and Regulation of Street Vending) Act, the first of its kind in the world.

The journey from the formation of NASVI to the Street Vendors Act was far from linear. Along the way, street vendors first needed to recognize their own contribution to the economic and cultural life of cities. Even when these contributions were legitimized by the national government, street vendors still faced significant resistance from their city and state governments who did not feel compelled to honor a policy without a law mandating their compliance. It took hunger strikes, protests, and petitions from thousands to overturn longstanding prejudice and apathy for their plight. The long fight for the Act is a symbol of the country's greatest political tension, which persists to this day: Can India modernize while ensuring that the poor and marginalized are meaningfully represented in the country's vision for growth?

Policies for Participation

For Arbind, the question of inclusion has never been a matter of "if" but "how." He states emphatically, "Cities require citizen participation. When you are in the speed of things, you don't always bring people along. It is important to bring people along."[10] When Arbind started Nidan, he embedded this philosophy into the organization, believing that the poor do not need charitable services but rather the power to create their own circumstances and new systems that exist "in perpetuity."[11] As he explained, organizations "come and go, and when organizations go away, people are left in the lurch." He knew that if he built an organization to serve as an alternative to the existing system, he could, inadvertently, remove "systems that feed, not just corruption, but also people." For street vendors, any solution had to start with shifting their powerlessness in the economic life of the city. Without effective policies that recognized street vending as an essential part of India's economy, street vendors would continue to live at the mercy of police officers, moneylenders, and consumers.

Yet, the NASVI experience emphasizes that policies are not enough to put people in a real position to change their circumstances. The Street Vendors Act is a prime example of how ensuring participation is essential to reconfiguring power. The Act not only protects street vendors from eviction, but also guarantees their direct participation through the establishment of Town Vending Committees (TVCs). These committees are made up of 40 percent street vendors with one-third of those seats reserved for women. Enshrined by law, but entirely new to city governance, street vendors require substantial support to secure meaningful participation in these committees. NASVI, guided by Nidan, has now shifted its efforts to assisting local governments to set up TVCs so that they are implemented not only within the legal framework, but also with the full intention of their movement, ensuring that street vendors who join the committees become full participants in city governance and decision-making.

Based on the NASVI experience, Nidan now works to incubate what they call "people's institutions," elevating informal workers into positions of political, economic, and cultural power alongside existing decision-makers. Over twenty years, Nidan has incubated twenty-two self-sustaining and independent organizations to realize the interests of different groups of informal workers. Each of the organizations uses a slightly different tack. Some, such as NASVI, exert political pressure on government to incorporate the rights of informal workers into policy and law. Others are built to create more consistent economic markets for goods and services provided by informal workers. Still others work to change the cultural perception of informal products and services through training and positive publicity.

These organizations take on numerous legal structures, including cooperatives, unions, membership associations, and even for-profit companies. For example, in 2008, Nidan set up a for-profit company called Nidan Swachh Dhara Pvt Ltd (NSPL) to provide contract garbage removal and cleaning services to corporations, hotels, apartment buildings, and private homes. More than four hundred informal wastepickers—workers who collect garbage and recycling from streets and refuse sites—are now employed by the company and own an equity stake as well as voting rights to elect members to the board of directors. The company serves 18,500 residences and 200 corporations. Another of Nidan's offshoots is Angana, a cooperative of home-based artisans that successfully advocates for identity cards for members, providing 1,400 mostly women members access to social benefits and financing while also creating opportunities for local and national contracts for their handicrafts.

In each of these "people's institutions," informal workers take on leadership and governance roles, ultimately becoming the decision-makers who set the agendas and goals of the organizations. When informal workers take up board and leadership seats, they learn the important skills of agenda-setting, voting, and decision-making. These leaders are also able to take up official capacity in municipal committees, unions, and workers' boards, solidifying new policies that provide security and benefits for informal workers. Consequently, those who have previously lacked the ability to make or influence decisions are able to officially step into formal positions of power. In this way, the institutions serve to realize Nidan's ultimate goal: informal workers gaining positions of power in the global economy to uplift their own situations in perpetuity.

Patterns for Perpetuity

Civic entrepreneur and activist Eric Liu explains, "Power compounds. Power begets more power, and so does powerlessness."[12] Liu reminds us that power is not just a thing that gets passed from one group to the next. It is recreated and reinforced in every situation in which we engage, whether we know it or not. As we discussed in Chapter 2, power—in particular, ideological power—circumscribes not only the ability to *change*, but even to *imagine change*. All of the organizations that we studied are working within existing power structures by necessity. They receive funding from private philanthropists and grantmakers, they recruit influential board members, and they align with government and corporate interests when expedient. However, we also discovered organizations striving to reconfigure those very same structures even while working in them. Some of these organizations are rewriting the political rules—*policies*—so that power moves to those who have been historically marginalized. Still others are going further, fundamentally disrupting norms and beliefs—our social *patterns*—to entrench that power in even more permanent ways.

Systems Work Terms 11: *Policies and patterns*

policies   *the official rules—laws, standards, and guidance—that make up social structures*

patterns   *the unofficial yet accepted ways of being—norms, beliefs, meanings, and values—that guide social behaviour*

The way this unfolds is often less dramatic than one might think. In fact, as research from the Kellogg School of Management has shown, "activism often succeeds by influencing quiet, incremental change, or through reforms that may start as symbolic gestures and grow into more profound reforms—a slow burn that becomes a larger flame."[13] While the research runs counter to the headlines about protests and sweeping political change, it is consistent with the conversations that we have had with systems work practitioners. Activism and advocacy most often act as "small wedges that push open a policy door, allowing a new pattern to squeeze its way in.

Importantly, as one of the organizations we studied emphasized to us, these new patterns can persist when policies fail to provide durable shifts. When we first heard about Fundación Escuela Nueva (FEN) in Colombia, we were intrigued by the story. FEN is an organization devoted to expanding an educational model called Escuela Nueva based on a concept promoted by UNESCO in the 1960s. Modified for the country context and implemented across the country with extreme fervor, the model then lost some of its momentum. As a story of scaling social change, Escuela Nueva seemed to illustrate some of the biggest challenges: fidelity to standards, reliance on donor funding, and dependence on political will. Yet, as we spent time with co-author of the Escuela Nueva model, Vicky Colbert, and her team at FEN, we realized that the conventional story about the model obscured the far more interesting one playing out in the classrooms it supported.

Micro, Meso, Macro

It is hard to imagine just how progressive UNESCO's schooling method, Escuela Unitaria,[14] must have appeared in rural Colombia in the 1960s. Starting in Pamplona, a small town nestled in the East Andes mountains, a talented and charismatic instructor by the name of Oscar Mogollón began training teachers, replicating the UNESCO-led training he had received, in a global initiative for multigrade schools. The method emphasized different learning rhythms, with teachers developing instructional cards to support more individualized learning.[15] Traditional schools, particularly in rural areas, focused exclusively on memorization, copying lessons from the blackboard, and repeating answers in unison.[16] When describing his efforts to convert traditional classrooms, he said, "It's easy; all we did was come in with a saw, cut up the blackboards, and give the small pieces to the children, with a piece of chalk. The children should be doing the writing, not the teachers."

At the same time, Vicky Colbert, the government's national coordinator for Unitary Schools and Rural Education, was seeking to build on the different existing experiences in the country and promote a national consensus among them. Vicky's vision was to impact national policy from the outset, thinking more systemically and introducing strategies into the educational system that would facilitate replicability, scalability, and cost-effectiveness. Her biggest challenge was to design and introduce a scalable intervention that was feasible in three critical areas—technically, politically, and financially. She expanded the experience Oscar was leading in Pamplona, yet introduced a systemic approach and went beyond just classroom organization and innovation. To reflect these and other changes, she gave the model a name: Escuela Nueva, meaning new school. In collaboration with the Department of Planning of the Ministry of Education and USAID, Vicky transitioned Escuela Unitaria to the Escuela Nueva program, initiating it in three regions of Colombia.

As Escuela Nueva's national coordinator, Vicky recruited Oscar and a team of rural teachers and researchers—non-traditional candidates for government positions. After all, she rationalized, they were the ones who knew best the educational context that was being served. The team worked hard to gain acceptance from government, international donors, and teachers' unions, but resistance was strong. Convincing high-level decision-makers that practitioners could serve in government was a crucial battle for Vicky, as well as working within the bureaucracy to "shield" the innovation and the team.[17]

Implemented with sound techniques and a support system, Vicky could see that the Escuela Nueva model had the potential to transform classrooms and schools—even entire education systems.[18] Together, she and her team considered how to address three important challenges: teachers' time and capacity, ongoing teaching support, and the relevance of the content. First, they decided to design a set of instructional materials for children which they called "learning guides." These materials were a sort of hybrid between a textbook and a worksheet, allowing students to guide themselves in pairs and small groups through the curriculum. They then developed a training and support system for teachers using the same participatory methods, which demonstrated how it felt to be an active student. Finally, they experimented with democratic school governance to engage students, parents, and communities, making the content relevant for citizenship building.

In 1983, Vicky was appointed as a vice minister of education, providing a position from which to champion the model. In this role, she managed to upgrade her team into high-level positions in the

Ministry. Long-standing civil servants were divided about the team's application of educational theory while teachers' unions were worried about sidelining teachers. Vicky and her colleagues pressed ahead, growing to eight thousand demonstration sites while gathering compelling evidence that Escuela Nueva schools were raising levels of literacy and numeracy.[19] The team's efforts were rewarded when the Ministry of Education adopted Escuela Nueva as national policy in conjunction with a US$100 million World Bank loan. By 1992, the Escuela Nueva model was being used in twenty thousand schools.

If this were a story about creating social change through policies alone, the narrative would end here. However, in the early 1990s, reforms to the Constitution promoted decentralization, creating administrative and implementation challenges to the national rollout of the Escuela Nueva program. Even in schools where Escuela Nueva was implemented faithfully it became difficult to provide continued support. Trained teachers were transferred to other schools and replaced by teachers with no training. Training and follow-up were put on the back burner and materials never replenished. By all accounts, it seemed as if Escuela Nueva would go the way of most educational reforms: celebrated for a time, then diminished by bureaucracies and administrative changes.

Yet, vestiges remained, and teachers' attitudes toward Escuela Nueva remained very positive. Vicky visited schools where Escuela Nueva learning guides were meticulously maintained with glue and tape, still in use by teachers and children. In some cases, students themselves "trained" teachers in the model when they arrived at Escuela Nueva schools. She began to receive calls from teachers and school principals who continued to use the model in the classroom. Vicky, who had already devoted more than twenty years of her life to Escuela Nueva, stepped down from her role in the Ministry to promote the model internationally. However, her heart remained with the teachers of Colombia. In 1987, Vicky tenaciously set up FEN to continue working to promote, innovate, and enhance Escuela Nueva in Colombia and abroad.

Outside of government, Vicky began to really look closely at what the Escuela Nueva model was doing—not just in schools but within the "micro" level of communities generally. Scholars Andy

Hargreaves and Michael T. O'Connor, who have visited many Escuela Nueva classrooms, write, "It's a highly cooperative environment—teachers supporting students and students of all ages assisting each other."[20] When implementing Escuela Nueva, multigrade classrooms provide an opportunity to transform conventional teaching practices, as children of different ages and abilities work in groups and pairs to reinforce learning. Teachers move from group to group as facilitators, assisting students with significant latitude and contextualizing the material for relevance. Parents and families become part of the school curriculum, contributing stories in journals that pass between children and teacher. In the rural communities where the model was first implemented, old patterns were disrupted and expectations of what a school looks like, how it functions, and what it is supposed to achieve necessarily shifted.

Old patterns were also disrupted at the district, or "meso," level. Rural teachers are usually isolated, working at long distances from each other and with few opportunities to interact with their peers. New Escuela Nueva teachers were invited into a community of practice, initially visiting demonstration sites to see the model in action. Then, during their first year, they attended three one-week teacher trainings which paralleled student learning activities. Teachers were matched with peer learning groups who met monthly to reflect and exchange on their practices, jointly problem-solve and collaborate. While these training and support methods acted as cost-saving measures, they also had the benefit of creating a highly collaborative community, driving teacher motivation and commitment to the Escuela Nueva model.[21] Most tellingly, even in schools where the model was implemented inconsistently due to decentralization, many teachers felt motivated to include the model's active learning and group approaches.[22]

Finally, Vicky had worked hard to disrupt patterns at the "macro" level, within the national education ministry. She fought against protocol to employ rural teachers on her team, arguing that the model required hands-on experience in order to be deployed effectively. Although there was opposition, the teachers she recruited proved exceptionally good at connecting with principals and training teachers. As "unlikely bureaucrats" with an insider-outsider status, they learned to be administratively and politically savvy, an important set of skills that they deployed in other countries when Colombia's ministry decided to de-emphasize the model.

These new patterns—students engaged in self-paced learning, communities as a source of curricular content, rural teachers supporting each other across schools, and teachers as civil leaders—were not just "feel-good" measures. They were highly effective. Studies showed that students in Escuela Nueva schools scored higher in language and math by the third and fifth grades than students from traditional rural schools.[23] They also reported higher measures of civic values and self-esteem. Out of these small changes, a "grassroots" movement grew. Several of her government colleagues who had helped to roll out the model moved on to education roles in other Latin American countries, enabling Vicky to position FEN to support Escuela Nueva as a regional and then a global model. FEN migrated to a new role as a "community connector," disseminating knowledge about the model and forging connections across schools and countries that want to fundamentally change their approach to education.

Today, FEN has expanded its reach as an advisor and technical supporter of the Escuela Nueva model, influencing national education systems that reach children in sixteen countries and counting. In the thousands of schools where Escuela Nueva has been introduced, an entire generation of children, along with their teachers, parents, and communities, have developed new expectations for what schooling should be like. While these new expectations have resulted in better learning outcomes, they have arguably also shifted patterns related to communication, teamwork, self-management, and even leadership—the so-called "twenty-first-century skills" that are prerequisite for flourishing political economies.[24]

An Iterative Effort

As Nidan and FEN illustrate, disrupting policies and patterns is an iterative effort. Policies—rules, laws, standards, or guidance—are often needed to create a "small wedge" so that primary actors can gain a seat at the table. From this officially sanctioned position, new patterns—expectations, values, and beliefs—begin to take root. Alternatively, organizations can work in the opposite direction: practicing new patterns internally, within management and govern-ance structures, to experiment with ideas for new policies. For sure, setbacks are inherent when political regimes change or programs reach their end date. Yet, the infinite symphony of social change plays on.

When policies are undone by political upheaval, organizations like FEN which have done pattern work will likely find that their changes endure in subtle yet important ways. Equally, organizations that have created official structures, such as Nidan's TVCs, will be able to use these policies to deepen their pattern work, pushing against engrained social patterns, such as caste and prejudice. Recent history is rich with examples of this type of iteration between patterns and policies. Legal successes for marriage equality around the world were preceded by cultural demonstrations that brought LGBTQ rights into public view, including parades, television series, and artistic expression.[25] The legal right to marry in twenty nations and counting has been followed by further mainstreaming of social norms in the media and public spaces. Similarly, the movement to compel political action against climate change, which has been largely led by youth, has challenged the legality of inaction through formal courts as well as the court of public opinion, using emo-tional tactics such as shame and guilt to force older generations of leaders toward commitments. The socio-political movement Extinction Rebellion uses cultural theatre to demand greenhouse gas reductions as well as a "Citizen's Assembly," a randomly selected body of "ordinary" people who will make recommendations for climate-related issues.

As these initiatives suggest, not all policies and patterns are equal. The aim is to reconfigure power toward greater participation by pri-mary actors in the pursuit of more responsive and representative systems. Two of our colleagues at the University of Cape Town Graduate School of Business, associate professor Warren Nilsson and PhD student Ella Scheepers, have developed a set of questions to explore specific types of power shifts in social systems which we

SYSTEMIC DIMENSION	POWER DETERMINANT
Roles and routines	*Who does what?*
Authority flows	*Who decides what?*
Resource flows	*Who gets what?*
Social identities	*Who connects to whom?/Who belongs to what?*
Meanings	*Why? What's it all about?/Who signifies what?*

Fig. 7.1 Questions to explore power in systems
Source: Nilsson (2019).

find highly instructive (see fig 7.1).[26] While these questions may sound obvious at first, we have found that the answers provoke new thinking about what types of policies and patterns may lead to durable change. Most importantly, the questions are designed to interrogate *who* is in the driver's seat of systems, more importantly than what or how systems are designed.

Nidan and FEN both tackle these questions through their political and programmatic efforts. Nidan's "people's institutions" create pathways for informal workers to insert themselves into new and powerful roles within municipal governments and corporate environments usually dominated by political and business elites. Informal workers then become decision-makers alongside established leaders, shaping cities and redirecting resources to suit their needs. FEN puts children at the center of the learning process, allowing them to advance at their own pace under the guidance of teachers and the support of fellow students. Teachers move into new roles as facilitators, children step into roles of active learning, and parents become providers of relevant learning content. Everyone shares decision-making responsibility of school administration, creating new connections to principals and government officials, and ultimately an environment where children learn and thrive.

What's It All About?

Finally, new policies and patterns can surface and confront deeper meanings for individuals and society as a whole. When working in systems, the organizations that we studied continue to go deeper, asking, "Why?" These changes are the hardest to detect yet the most transformative in practice. Escuela Nueva has been challenging the meaning of education for nearly fifty years but has only recently begun to gain international recognition for the crucial deeper work they are doing. Public policy professor David L. Kirp writes, "Escuela Nueva turns the schoolhouse into a laboratory for democracy. I'm convinced that the model can have a global impact on the lives of tens of millions of children—not just in the developing world but in the United States as well."[27] As "twenty-first-century skills," such as critical thinking, collaboration, and flexibility, have become desirable by government and corporate leadership, Escuela Nueva has fielded increasing requests from developed countries to apply the model in both under-resourced as well as resourced schools.

Similarly, when Nidan began its work with informal workers, the idea that economists and policymakers alike would embrace informality as a fundamental characteristic of modern economies was nonsensical. Now, as developed countries have looked inwardly at the precarity of their own workforces, the policies and patterns advocated by Nidan's offshoots are seen as relevant not just to India but to the global conversation regarding the "future of work." Arbind has embraced this conversation by setting up a new initiative he calls the "Self Worker Movement", an effort to assemble the needs of informal workers with those of the "precariat"—zero-hours contract workers who form an increasing percentage of the global workforce.[28] This movement has struck a chord with labor organizers who have witnessed the decline of the traditional worker movement and who see the potential to apply the policies and patterns from Nidan's India experience to a far greater audience.

The organizations we studied often started by experimenting with the more obvious patterns described earlier in this section. Over time, however, they have each come to articulate the deeper values and meanings they are shifting very clearly. Former gangsters and informal workers become social leaders rather than costs for society to bear; students are educators themselves rather than products of schools; communities turn into centers for healing rather than catchment areas for clinical services. Even slums and rural areas hollowed out by economic and environmental devastation become real places of possibility. When these shifts in perception are palpable and authentic, real change is occurring at the deepest levels. And nothing is the same as it was before.

Learning Notes: Disrupting policies *and* patterns

To uproot the deeply rooted structures that keep existing power dynamics in place, organizations can work to disrupt both the policies *and* patterns that make up these structures. Policies are the official rules—laws, standards, and guidance—that make up social structures; patterns are the unofficial yet accepted ways of being—norms, beliefs, means, and values—that guide social behaviour. To do this, organizations agitate and advocate for:

- **Policies for participation**, ensuring equal engagement for primary actors in key decision-making bodies, including committees, associations, working groups, and legislative groups.
- **Patterns for perpetuity**, using policies as "small wedges" to open doors so that long-term pattern changes can take root.
- **Changes at the micro, meso, and macro levels**, which shift roles, distribute decision-making, and channel resources toward primary actors and the structures that support them.
- **An iterative effort**, alternating between policy and pattern work, using approaches that will suit the current environment and have the greatest impact on both the short and long term.

By **disrupting policies *and* patterns**, organizations can work to change formal rules as well as deeper ways of being. Ultimately, these policies and patterns serve to reconfigure systems so that primary actors are able to take up positions of greater power, ensuring that systems are more representative of and responsive to the people who live in them.

PART III
REIMAGINING THE FUTURE

Systems work cannot be done in isolation. Organizations pursuing systems work are supported in their efforts by numerous funders, philanthropists, advisors, and government partners. To deal with complexity, scale, and depth, *supporting actors* from all sectors will need to reconsider their roles and approaches in measuring and funding social change. In Part III, we discuss what it will take to reimagine the future of social change—from those who work internally, as professional managers and advisors, to those who work externally, providing funding and resources. In these chapters, we explore how new roles and approaches to social change are moving from the fringe to the mainstream. Since systems work is far more about processes than outcomes, the ways in which these supporting actors approach their work is just as important as the ends. This shift is well underway and perhaps one of the most exciting aspects of systems work.

Measuring for Learning

Andrew Darnton is an ex-advertising professional turned independent researcher specializing in behavioral change and practice. Andrew Harrison is a social entrepreneur turned international organizational consultant and facilitator who leads the creation of learning systems through his consultancy, The Learning Studio. The two became unexpected collaborators in 2015 when a mutual contact working in Britain's National Health Service (NHS) reached out to them on a hunch that, together, they might be able to solve a problem that no one had yet managed to address on their own.

The challenge was to assess whether an initiative known as "Change Day"[1] was actually doing what its name claimed. As a "grassroots" movement within the NHS, Change Day encouraged staff and service users to take action aimed at improving patient care. In response to this call, everything from specialized training and skills development to taking thirty-minute computer breaks was put on the table.[2] The initiative seemed to be having a positive effect, becoming a source of renewed energy and improvement for many. Yet, neither the NHS nor the participating hospitals and clinics had any real way to measure this—there were just too many variables. No one was in charge and there were no budgets or set outcomes against which to track progress. Since Change Day didn't fit the commonly accepted paradigm of an internal improvement program, alarm bells were raised in some quarters. How could the NHS expect to learn from Change Day if it was not possible to measure or evaluate its impact?

Enter Andrew D and Andrew H, who at this point had never met each other before. They were tasked with the challenge to reimagine evaluation, essentially to measure the unmeasurable. To do this, they were given permission to experiment and trusted to "take the thing to where it wanted to go," as Andrew D put it. He says that it was a classic tale of learning through doing—a creative process that "welled up from the practice on the ground."

Over the course of nine months, they discovered just how important this exploratory process was to developing a new approach to measuring change. Recalling the early days of the project, Andrew D says, "Talking to each other was a hugely creative experience right from the start. Andrew talks differently, from a very different place, which I find fascinating. And he, in turn, found my stuff fascinating." They were drawing from a wide array of interests and theoretical knowledge, but they rapidly bonded over a shared skepticism for the way monitoring and evaluation is currently carried out in the mainstream. As they saw it, the prevailing paradigm for impact assessment is not designed for innovation, but rather to retrospectively determine whether an intervention had ticked a series of prescribed boxes. Because these assessments are entirely backward-looking, they have the cold and deadening qualities of a post-mortem analysis. These are not tools for change, but stasis. "If you get the outcomes you were told to purchase, then you are just an accountant," Andrew H says.

To imagine a better way forward, Andrew D and Andrew H decided they would *not* be accountants. Instead, they started in the middle with a novel approach. "When dealing with complexity, there are really only two things you can do: high level scenario modelling or participative processes—get everyone into a room and talk about it," says Andrew D. They chose the latter, deciding to highlight the question "what is going on?" rather than "what worked?" Then, they sat back, listened, and observed as the people engaged in Change Day activities explored that question for themselves through exchanging stories of their experience in the system. Their goal was to help the Change Day participants better understand the effectiveness of their actions and how their initiative unfolded in order to increase the positive impact of their interventions.

During the story exchanges, employees and users inevitably talked about value: the things that mattered most to people.

As Andrew D and Andrew H found, a conversation about what is important and useful brings people together and creates a common purpose. Suddenly people are empathetic with the needs and desires of others. "The discourse about value creates the conditions for all kinds of other things that are latent in the system to emerge," says Andrew H. "If we can find ways to reflect on and help each other make visible the discourse about value, we stand a chance to make change. So almost all of the most generative instances of our process lie in that social interaction in developing a sense of what we are creating together." Uncovering what is valued, as part of the evaluative process, is therefore valuable itself.

They have called this process "Revaluation" and since its emergence from the Change Day project, it has been applied to a range of developmental initiatives, including work on the natural environment, encouraging physical activity, and family nursing. And like any good practice of systems work, it is continuously evolving and adapting to suit the context of the problem.

The Pressure to Measure

The reason Revaluation's predecessors struggled to determine the efficacy of the Change Day project is steeped in the mental models for how things are measured and what constitutes a proper measurement tool.[3] The notion that "you can't manage what you can't measure," a mantra attributed to management scholar Peter Drucker, has become the guiding principle for evaluating efforts undertaken in nearly every aspect of life. Yet, through this managerial approach to measurement, outcomes are elevated over processes and metrics become synonymous with value judgments. We use these metrics daily. Individual metrics such as report cards, salaries, and key performance indicators (KPIs) provide useful feedback for their corresponding activities, but they also serve as proxies for the contributions and value of the activities and people behind them. This same mindset feeds into our organizations and institutions. We are conditioned to believe that the value of every project, effort, or action must be substantiated with numerical data and tied to a pre-defined outcome. The result is a dominant evaluation methodology across all sectors in which every activity must have a defined target and is only valid if attached to a corresponding metric.

The tendency for organizations to select quantitative methodologies for evaluating change work reflects a firm trust in numbers to address social issues, even within sectors and organizations that might otherwise reject the tenets of the industrial mindset in their work. Organizations are encouraged to set "North Star" goals that presuppose the anticipated outcome and to develop robust theories of change that will get them there. These tools and frameworks form part of a larger strategy to identify predictable rules to use as a basis for "rational" decision-making in the work of social change. Although there is merit to this technical approach, as we established in Part I, there are also clear limitations, particularly when employed to the exclusion of other, more emergent methods.

A simple and prominent example of these limitations comes from the primary measurement tool used to capture economic value across countries. Gross domestic product (GDP) was originally invented in the wake of the Great Depression as a metric for monitoring the economic development of the subsequent industrial boom. GDP provides a measure of the size of the economy and therefore, in the minds of many, serves as a proxy for the welfare of a country. While perfectly functional as a singular measure of economic growth, GDP has since become *the* central indicator for national development around the world, including other dimensions that shape a country's growth, such quality of life, health, education, or plain happiness.[4] Based on this metric, economic growth at all costs has become the coveted outcome of nearly all development efforts. Of course, this number excludes the many nuances and complexities of human life, pointed out by its own creator Simon Kuznets.[5] As the editor of the *Financial Times Africa*, David Pilling, puts it, "It squishes all of human activity into a couple of digits, like a frog jammed into a matchbox."[6]

To a large extent, the pressure to measure is self-justifying. If practitioners can demonstrate to clients, governments, or funders that their work served more people or surpassed improvement targets, they can carry on doing what they are doing. They will likely even get more money to do so. And as governments and funders seek to do more with less, the pressure to measure in this way is, if anything, increasing. As development researcher and practitioner Robert Chambers observes, "procedural demands by governments, lender and donor agencies, foundations, and other funders have tightened over the past three decades." According to Chambers, this has been done "in the name of efficiency, effectiveness, value for money, and accountability."[7] Harvard Business School economist Michael Porter goes so far as to say that the lack of effective measurement is the core issue preventing further progress in social change. Porter, who pioneered the concept of "shared value" and is chair of the advisory board for the Social Progress Imperative, has observed that "we have no standardized industrial classification here."[8] He advocates passionately that if we are ever to achieve our development goals, the same rigor applied to measuring business effectiveness should be brought to bear on social progress.

Porter's point is not entirely unfounded. Data and evidence create critical feedback mechanisms that enable self-regulation and adaptation within systems. Shared metrics can also align disparate activities into coherent strategies, similar to the way that the Sustainable Development Goals have channeled local initiatives into global trajectories. But the very way Porter talks about measurement also highlights its intrinsic challenges. If it were simply a matter of getting the right numbers in place to count and track social progress, we would already have an effective social impact assessment methodology. Alex Nicholls from the Skoll Centre of Social Entrepreneurship at Oxford University points out that the "how" of measurement is actually the easy part—there is no shortage of robust tools and frameworks available.[9] However, we have yet to fully engage with the deeper questions of measurement, starting with who, what, when, and, crucially, why?

Social change practitioners know that the complexity, scale, and depth of social issues make these questions especially tough to answer. The path to breaking free from unhelpful mental models to answer these questions is fraught with paradoxes and inconsistencies. Fortunately, this has not stopped a cohort of practitioners from actively engaging with these contradictions to imagine new approaches. By overturning some of the key assumptions that underpin traditional evaluation approaches, they reveal how the measurement and evaluation of systems work should reflect the same principles of systems work itself.

Supporting Self-evaluation

As with the principles and practices of systems work, measuring and evaluating change in complex systems must start with the question of "who." Rather than bringing in experts and outsiders, planning an evaluation approach should rather begin with primary actors—those most immersed in the system that is changing—as designers, participants, data collectors, and evaluators themselves. Efforts that fail to keep people most exposed to change at the center of the evaluation process can easily become skewed and the integrity of the work jeopardized.

Martin Burt, founder and CEO of the anti-poverty social enterprise Fundación Paraguaya, is one such practitioner who has experienced this acutely in the global fight against poverty. In over thirty years of fighting poverty himself, he has watched as fellow campaigners—all with the best of intentions—have made critical decisions on behalf of the poor, starting with the very definition of what it is to be "poor." His own daily encounters with people living in poverty showed him that the definition of a "poor person" as someone who lacks income, education, and access to essential services is reductive. It fails to capture the multidimensionality of lives which are rich in things like joy, generosity, creativity, problem-solving, and entrepreneurial spirit. Their lives are bigger than whether they live on one dollar or two dollars per day, he argues.

Over and above fraught terminology, Burt has observed that while there is an abundance of poverty data in the world, it does not appear to serve the needs of poor people themselves. As he explains, our unquestioning acceptance of expert-driven data has further marginalized the people we want to help, making them "passive recipients of someone else's poverty definition, someone else's poverty measurement. As a consequence, poor people are also locked out of the room where decisions get made about what our poverty solutions look like, unable to articulate their perspectives and priorities."[10] His words echo the concerns of the organizations we studied, who have often centered their organizational work around primary actors in response.

Burt has taken the issue one step further with a practical measurement tool that enables poor families to self-diagnose their level of poverty as a first step toward developing a personalized strategy to lift themselves out of it. Known as the Poverty Stoplight, this simple diagnostic tool uses traffic light colors and simple visuals, allowing families to rank themselves on fifty indicators of poverty. Through this process, families can literally see and understand for themselves the ways in which they are poor by self-evaluating their own situations. They are then able to devise their own maps to change this. Laura Berg, a sustainability researcher and practitioner who brought the Poverty Stoplight to South Africa, says that the tool is revolutionary because it gives people at the center of a systemic issue an internal locus of control. She says, "I've seen this get individuals and their families to a point where they have dignity and independence, which is everything."[11]

Supporting primary actors as the principal sources and evaluators of their own work was the key action that led to the Revaluation approach. During the Change Day project, with a mandate to determine if change had indeed followed from the activities, Andrew D and Andrew H went straight to the primary actors involved, but with a fundamentally different mindset than traditional methods would prescribe. Following the mainstream model, they would have assumed the roles of "external evaluators," approaching employees and service users as subjects and imposing their own pre-selected metrics on the data-collection process. Instead, Andrew D and Andrew H acted as instruments, supporting NHS employees to surface information they themselves deemed to be relevant and uncovering emerging patterns. By this approach, primary actors are treated as both sources and evaluators of information, while experts serve as supporting actors. This makes sense not just to elevate primary actors, but also to ensure data reliability since people most immersed in the process of social change can most accurately surface and interpret information about the quality and efficacy of that work. And because change may be experienced very differently from one person to another, a sense-making process that pools insights from different primary actors is a necessity.

Many of the organizations we studied are promoting primary actors as self-evaluators. SDI demonstrates this most vividly by engaging local slum residents to collect information about their neighborhoods as one of their core activities across the platform. This is coupled with a community-led monitoring framework that maps pathways to settlement, cities, and global systemic change for urban development. In terms of practicality, as SDI founder Jockin Arputham once remarked, "Slum dwellers can count huts better than any educated person or government official."[12] But on a deeper level, slum dwellers themselves are uniquely placed to make sense of the value that exists in their communities. Similarly, FII's UpTogether platform collates self-generated stories from across the national network of families and makes them available to the entire community. Families choose to tell stories reflecting their pressing challenges and proud successes while users can browse the stories to identify those that are most meaningful and useful for their own journey. These data-gathering exercises are designed to make sense of complexity for the very people who are navigating it, surfacing what is valuable to drive further change.

Surfacing Invisible Value

Systems work also requires a deeper look at the "what" of measuring social change. For Andrew D and Andrew H, one of the most exciting findings of the Change Day experiment was the way social interaction allowed the primary actors at the NHS to uncover different, less visible forms of value derived from their own activities. Out of this discovery, Revaluation developed its method to initiate conversations along three dimensions. They summarize these as the "3Cs": calculate (quantitative outputs and outcomes), calibrate

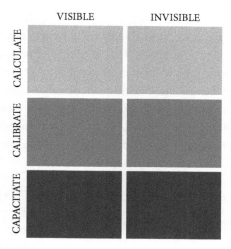

Fig. 8.1 Revaluation's 6-box dashboard
Source: Revaluation (https://www.revaluation.org.uk/).

(judgments about the relative merits of different actions and out-comes), and capacitate (the strengths and potential of a movement or network) (see fig 8.1). Along these three dimensions, Revaluation looks at two streams of data: *visible* (that which is evidenced today) and *invisible* (that which may be revealed over time). They believe that, like an iceberg, much of the value of systems work lies beneath the surface, requiring time and resources to emerge.

In the industrial model of social change, this *invisible value* can be overlooked when seemingly simple actions are not recognized as significant by those who commission, fund, or control an initiative. These actions are often relational, pertaining to the quality of inter-actions between people, and therefore difficult to quantify. An example of this might be the so-called "water cooler" effect, where unofficial time spent by people in informal conversations around the water cooler or other casual spaces can be more beneficial to productivity than official meetings or memos.[13] These types of rela-tional activities are widespread in the organizations that we studied: the camaraderie built in the "bull-pen" where Kisimbi and Salim sat with Kenya's community health managers, the trust developed among Buurtzorg's nurse teams through rotationally facilitated meetings, and the sense of efficacy developed by horizontal exchanges among SDI affiliates, to name a few. In traditional measurement and evaluation, invisible value is largely treated as positive yet secondary consequences that emerge from change work, assigned to a footnote with greater weight given to tangible outcomes that can be assigned a numerical value. Yet, these are the values which primary actors experience first-hand, often serving as the main value that they assign to a change initiative, unforeseen and unacknowledged by decision-makers and evaluators.

Systems Work Terms 12: *Visible and invisible value*

---

visible value   *the value that is evidenced today*

Invisible value   *the value that may be revealed over time), requiring time and resources to emerge*

Andrew D and Andrew H have observed that in systems that exhibit complexity and depth, invisible value is most evident at the deepest level of scale, at the "grassroots."[14] By this observation, many social change organizations are sitting on treasure troves of positive experiences, incremental improvements, and better-quality relationships that rarely register on current impact assessments. The inclusion of metrics in these assessments often has more to do with their ease of quantification rather than their value to those living through the change. This is not a minor issue. As mentioned earlier, the pressure to measure is increasing as public and philanthropic funders partner with private-sector capital and urge practitioners to do more with less.[15] The rise of impact investment structures—including traditional grants, debt, and equity as well as outcomes-based payment models such as social impact bonds—have brought return-seeking capital into the mix of funders, now totaling US$502 billion[16] and accompanied by a burgeoning field of social impact assessment. This new cohort of experts is tasked with building coherent metrics and indicators that serve as proxies for the intangible social change that can be so hard to quantify.[17] Metrics are often chosen because data are available and agreeable to investors within their chosen timeframes, rather than as a true reflection of the desired social change.

Measurement, therefore, challenges systems workers not only to surface invisible value but to restructure the power relationships that keep it hidden. Jeroo Billimoria, founder of CYFI, has often been quoted as saying, systems change requires "a major mindset shift" for social change. As a self-styled collaborative systems change broker, CYFI has been objectively successful in achieving its aims to financially empower children and youth. But they encountered real challenges in showcasing these achievements—which in turn impacted their support and funding. All-inclusive metrics such as number of children empowered and number of education interventions conducted were largely meaningless since they didn't capture the true extent to which a country had changed the policies guiding children's futures overall. Eventually, CYFI took things into their own hands and began an internal initiative to develop a diagnostic tool that could document change efforts across 132 of the countries in their network.

The study aimed to assess each country's progress on a CYFI diagnostic tool that charted ten key stages that policymakers in countries generally take in their journey toward ensuring economic citizenship for children and youth. These milestones were cross-referenced against correspondence and documentation of CYFI staff with each of the countries where they had worked. The study then assessed the potential relationship between the progress made by the country's policymakers on economic citizenship and the improvement along macroeconomic indicators of economic citizenship in that country. While the study was only able to measure correlation, the results were indicative, creating a greater level of comfort about the progress that countries were making in their work toward economic citizenship for children and youth. It also created an important feedback loop for the ongoing adaptation of their work and impact while allowing funders and stakeholders to understand how this change unfolds and the contribution that CYFI makes to this change process.[18]

This dual approach highlights what Tufts University public sector scholar Alnoor Ebrahim terms "multiple accountabilities," the need to identify data that bring primary actors together around what they deem valuable while ensuring that funders and stakeholders can also see the value that the work brings. Funders and stakeholders *as well as* primary actors have a role to play in demonstrating value in the world of messy problems. "Accountability as such is a relationship of power, it does not stand objectively apart from the expectations and demands of external actors which are sometimes in conflict," he points out, and concludes by saying that he hopes that those working in the sector will, as CYFI has tried to do, "ultimately have the courage to set their own terms of accountability."[19]

Shortening Feedback Loops

One of the additional barriers arising from the pressure to measure is the timeframe—the "when" in which reporting generally occurs. As nearly all practitioners can attest, it can take years, even generations for visionary social change to materialize. Periodic reporting cycles force organizations to probe for change that has not happened yet—change with uncertain arrival dates. Reporting horizons are largely stakeholder-imposed and—if we are honest—arbitrary, matched to investment timeframes and budgeting cycles rather than to the social change that is sought.

Many of the organizations that we studied are pushing back on these requirements with an interesting argument. Rather than fret that periodic timeframes are too compressed, they are arguing that these reporting cycles are too long. These organizations—including Buurtzorg, FII, SDI, and others—are cataloging change in real time, or nearly so, with ongoing data collection that guides learning and interim decision-making as well as meets stakeholder reporting needs.

The short feedback loop is a recurring theme among groups reimagining evaluation. Revaluation examines and describes the value that is emerging as it happens. Poverty Stoplight allows users to direct their own timeframes. Buurtzorg's self-managed nurse teams access real time insights from a centralized web platform. This is possible because under these approaches, evaluative activities are integrated into the work processes of primary actors. When measurement is seen as essential and valuable to everyday decisions, it is rarely relegated to the tasks of a single employee or as a quarterly or annual administrative effort.

The value of having timely, accurate, and trustworthy feedback about the value, experience, or quality of one's work is apparent for actors in any organization. The information empowers people to make appropriate decisions, change something, or to feel good about what they have done. But importantly for systems workers, the value of the short feedback loop is not just the information generated and received, but the process itself. There is evidence that even the act of feeling involved in evaluative practices changes the way people think about their work and makes them more open to ongoing innovation, thus further driving the systems work of the organization in important and tangible ways.

Measuring for Meaning

Finally, systems work requires a deeper look at the "why" of measurement and evaluation. Andrew H's scornful description of traditional evaluation as mere "accounting" highlights that most programs are currently assessed by a post hoc tallying of predefined indicators and outcomes, rather than on their broader transformative potential. All too often, evaluators focus narrowly on the question of whether the organization or program is working effectively rather than lifting their eyes to see what is happening at the system level. Inevitably, this approach causes evaluators to focus on some factors and ignore others. It also creates an overwhelming temptation for evaluators and participants to leave out the bad stuff and seek only the good bits that will impress and secure ongoing support. Theories of change aim to force-fit this anticipated vision into milestones that can be conclusively reported upon. This model over-assigns value to metrics that reassure us we are doing the right things, yet, as Michael Quinn Patton, former president of the American Evaluation Association, says, "It takes courage to face the possibility that one is deluding oneself."[20] By failing to learn from the past—both our miss-steps and our victories—the utility inherent in social change work is irretrievably lost.

Patton was one of the first people to identify this paradox. He became increasingly uncomfortable with what he saw as the sacrifice of vital learning at the altar of accountability and the market mantra of "value for money." Out of this discomfort he developed the concept of "developmental evaluation," which seeks to refocus evaluation on helping and supporting those who do the work rather than just serving the funder.[21] This is especially important, he says, when it comes to evaluating initiatives working in uncertain territory where social change practitioners have no blueprint laid out for what they want to achieve. In these circumstances, strategies are developed and tested as they proceed, in real time. The need to learn quickly and change course if necessary is critical.

Very often social change practitioners are "ahead of the evidence and in front of the science,"[22] Patton points out, so it is impossible to have a yardstick by which to measure their progress. What they need more than anything are ways to learn from their work in real time and to disseminate what they are learning. Developmental evaluation enshrines the idea that evaluation itself is a learning process. At its core, as the name suggests, is a sense of purpose: to develop rather than to sum up and judge. The approach is primarily focused on internal teams as a means of staying close to their commitments and values. Measurements and tracking mechanisms are created quickly, as outcomes emerge. Feedback is made as user-friendly as possible and passed quickly to those who are driving change. Instead of evaluating a program to determine whether resources are being spent on what they're supposed to be spent on, developmental evaluation strives to answer questions such as, "Are we being true to our vision? Are we dealing with reality? Are we connecting the dots between here-and-now reality and our vision? And how do we know? What are we observing that's different, that's emerging?"[23]

Following similar principles to developmental evaluation, Revaluation manages to answer these questions by continuously examining change work as it happens, rather than assessing compliance with a questionably relevant target as a once-off, post-mortem effort, when it is too late to adjust behavior. This approach directs the purpose of evaluation toward making work more effective and relevant—toward learning and creating more change. It is therefore both an approach for measuring change in a complex system and for making change in that system.

When tools like Revaluation, Project Stoplight, and developmental evaluation are placed firmly in the hands of primary actors and used for continuous learning, they become more than just measuring instruments or add-ons to the core work of systems change. They become an integrated part of systems work, inseparable from the other value-adding practices. This is a common theme among almost all of the systems workers we have profiled. Each of the organizations that we studied have data collection practices—often designed and led by primary actors—deeply embedded in their work as part of their change efforts. Most importantly, these measurement and evaluation processes are integrated into organizational processes, keeping their work aligned with their values, even as they evolve over time.

Deepening the Data

Once we embrace the deeper questions of measuring as systems work, there is still the practical question of how and where to use the measurement tools and methods available. Sophisticated data-gathering and analytic techniques have become accessible to even the most inexperienced of technology users over the past ten years and are currently allowing social practitioners to identify patterns and "see" systems like never before. This is creating exciting possibilities for monitoring, evaluating, and learning in the social sector.[24] And yet, the staggering profusion of data, frameworks, tools, and analytics can make it extremely challenging to know how to effectively integrate information into organizational decision-making.

Adding to this challenge is the age-old problem of attribution, which, in the era of big data, is even more demanding. The degree of interconnectedness between events and actors in complex systems makes it nearly impossible to assign credit for causes and effects. Alexander Krauss from the London School of Economics has demonstrated that even for the most advanced statistician, the ability to assess the relationship between complex phenomena, such as democracy and inequality, is much more limited than recognized in existing literature.[25] He argues that the limitations of analytical methods call for greater caution and humility in approaching complex issues. This is particularly the case in systems work, where misguided claims of causal relationships can easily be accepted and applied within public policy to harmful effect, even bringing about adverse social outcomes.

While data science can offer direction, we need to be wary of methods which claim to offer indisputable evidence of "what works." The enthusiasm for impact evaluation and evidence-based policymaking (including the "gold standard" of evaluations—randomized controlled trials—which has recently culminated in a Nobel Prize)[26] is largely predicated on a belief that we can isolate interventions and test their efficacy, thereby proving their effectiveness in "real world" conditions. Methodologies that mimic cause and effect can be beneficial by giving practitioners and policymakers guidance for strategies that work within a narrowly circumscribed set of conditions. However, as we have seen earlier, the ability to replicate within different contexts is fraught with issues. Even worse, these methods do not allow for the conditions themselves to be altered: by focusing on surface problems well, we may largely fail to address the deeper ones.

According to Dave Snowden, director of the Centre for Applied Complexity at the University of Wales, the danger of a reductive, number-chasing approach is that it can, in fact, block the positive change that we seek. Like Andrew D and Andrew H, Snowden believes proper evaluation of systems work requires us to explore the experiences of primary actors. Rather than isolating and interpreting individual actions on behalf of those living through change, he believes that primary actors should explain and deepen their own data. To do this, he has developed SenseMaker as "a tool for decision-making in a new world." The simple premise of SenseMaker is that the primary actors in the system must be engaged and empowered to tell and interpret their own stories. People are tired of surveys and focus groups, believes Snowden. Opinion polls aren't trusted anymore and the biased interpretations of experts just get in the way. Instead, people should become their own ethnographers in the system. Using SenseMaker's data visualization tools, hundreds and even thousands of stories are self-interpreted and aggregated to give a bigger picture of what is happening in complex and dynamic systems. By combining human-level storytelling with system-level data science, Snowden's approach provides primary actors with a way to make sense of their own circumstances while giving direction for where they want to go.

This "deep data" can reveal the nuance of each context while also tapping into a human desire for purpose. When people pursue explicit, externally driven targets, Snowden says, it destroys their intrinsic motivation. However, as we have seen earlier, it is intrinsic motivation that unlocks innovation, change, and value.[27] An intense focus on externally driven metrics actively disrupts the processes that are so critical to creating change. It is why organizations like Buurtzorg have focused on designing processes to let nurses and patients figure out their own targets as they go, prioritizing the value of intrinsic motivation in their employees,. Similarly, it is why FII and Fundación Paraguaya have created mechanisms for families to set their own goals to contribute to the organizational goal of eradicating poverty.

When organizations focus on capturing the day-to-day anecdotes and raw stories of people's existence—the fragmented narratives, the water-cooler conversations—a fuller, richer data set emerges. These "deep data" have many advantages for those engaged in systems work. Primary actors can instead explore their experiences, and in the process develop a better understanding of the way their actions play out in the system. As more experiences are added, a bigger picture materializes, allowing actors to see process and outcomes as they emerge. By oscillating between individual experiences and the big picture, decisions can be made about how to move forward—informed by current reality and the emerging future.

Learning Notes: Measuring for learning

Measuring systems change raises the fundamental questions of systems work: namely, who, what, and when are we measuring, and why? Measurement should be embedded in systems work as a practice, not just to prove successful outcomes but as part of the overall learning process of organizations and broader collectives. This kind of measurement puts primary actors in charge of their own data, revealing a deeper under-standing of what is valued by those who are immersed in the context of a social issue. To measure systems work more effectively, organizations and their supporting actors are:

- **Supporting self-evaluation**, ensuring that primary actors are the drivers of the entire measurement lifecycle, from design to data collection to analysis.
- **Surfacing invisible value**, identifying value that may be realized over time, including the quality of relationships and experiences. Organizations may need to confront powerful players who do not recognize this value as part of their own measurement processes.
- **Shortening feedback loops**, so that measurement happens in real time, with data quickly cycled back to primary actors who are posi-tioned as problem-solvers.
- **Measuring for meaning**, with activities fully integrated into the process, rather than as "bookends" to catalog the outcomes of a project or program.

When **measuring for learning**, organizations are able to ask different ques-tions, recognizing that the primary aim is to determine "what is happen-ing" rather than "what worked." Organizations and primary actors are also able to access "deep data" that capture the richness of individual experiences while visualizing the bigger picture as it emerges.

9

Funding for Partnership

"Nobody ever asks me why I started using drugs in the first place!"[1] The comment landed awkwardly in the room as a nervous young man addressed an audience of diverse community role-players from Greater Manchester in the United Kingdom. These participants ranged from government decision-makers and community workers to citizens like himself battling drug addiction and homelessness. They had all gathered in 2016 to engage in the simple act of having a conversation. But in a world where those living with systemic disadvantages feel largely unheard by those making political and economic decisions, this was a radical departure from the way most public outreach programs begin. "We need support not ultimatums," remarked another young citizen. They all hoped that this conversation was a first step toward achieving that. "It's not helpful to hear that the only way I can keep my accommodation is to stop smoking spice and just pay my rent!"

This carefully crafted "container" was designed as an experiment: could a diverse group of individuals and organizations come together to collectively tackle the causes of inequality in their city? Colloquially known as the "Elephants Project," as it sought to allow people to talk honestly about the "elephant in the room," this experiment quite literally allowed citizens struggling with drug addiction and homelessness to sit down with people at the forefront of policy decisions in an act of "co-production." The hope was that by combining the knowledge and lived experiences of citizens with the professional knowledge and budgets of decision-makers, better solutions might emerge.

The Elephants Project was an inspiring—even obvious—idea on paper. However, in practice, putting together these two groups of people in conversation was immediately unsettling for everyone in the room. Participant Christopher Woodward was already familiar with the challenges of "co-production" from his own work at Petrus Community, where his job was to ensure that the users of their housing and support services were involved in planning and delivery processes. Writing about his experiences with the Elephants Project, he recalled, "In our conversations, the notion of power kept cropping up. Who has power? Who is likely to give it up or even be willing to share some?" He observed that these comments often felt confrontational to those who had dedicated their careers to solving these problems. As a senior decision-maker from the public sector in the conversation put it, "People who are used to power want to believe they have all the solutions."[2]

The feelings of discomfort and helplessness were persistent even amongst those decision-makers who strongly believed in distributing power. When Big Lottery Fund portfolio manager Hannah Paterson—a self-described advocate of "co-production" processes—reflected on the surprisingly hard work involved in initiatives like the Elephants Project, she found it simultaneously gratifying and frustrating. "It allowed me the opportunity and time to…recognize that my approaches, although well meaning, were perhaps not breaking down the power structures I was hoping they would. Instead, in some ways I was holding them up," she wrote.[3]

Very few funders choose to start with an analysis of their own power before jumping into the fray. For those who are used to actively solving problems, it can seem rather revolutionary to step back, admit ignorance, and ask so-called "beneficiaries" what they might think. But this was precisely the starting point for Alice Evans, deputy chief executive of Lankelly Chase, one of the funders of the Elephants Project.

After years of working with various charities and organizations targeting homelessness in the United Kingdom, Alice had become increasingly frustrated with the half-successes of their projects. By 2013, she was facing the depressing reality that things were not getting any better for the people she was trying to serve. As a result, Alice began to think about new approaches. When she started talking more with the people she was trying to help, she began to identify the barriers they were experiencing when trying to access that help. Although there were plenty of interventions designed to help people experiencing homelessness, Alice could now see that they were often working at cross purposes, targeting mental health, drug addiction, and homelessness on separate fronts. More critically, the people themselves were not always aware of the opportunities supposedly created for them and frequently felt disempowered by the very systems designed to uplift them.

She concluded that addressing homelessness requires a "cast of thousands"[4] and that the different initiatives needed to be "joined up." One-off approaches from funders and organizations were creating problems rather than solving them. She realized that the whole system needed reforming, starting with the needs of individuals and their families. Most importantly, she felt that bringing the voices of the people experiencing homelessness themselves into the debate, foregrounding their concerns and giving them power to make decisions, would start to connect the dots in a more fundamental way.

That she was doing systems work did not occur to Alice at that point: "I wouldn't have felt I had the right to apply that description."[5] But when she saw a job for "systems change director" advertised at Lankelly Chase, she felt drawn to the role. She saw it as an opportunity to extend her work as a connector of the various role players in the system so that all voices could be heard. She was, however, accepting the role with very little idea of what systems change really meant. Thrown into the deep end, Alice set about trying to figure out what the term meant for herself, for Lankelly Chase, and for the sector more broadly. According to Alice, during the beginning phases of their work, many looked upon Lankelly Chase as being "a little weird." However, the subsequent journey of discovery has placed Lankelly Chase at the forefront of those thinking about the role of philanthropy and private capital in systems work. Today, they are one of several foundations confronting their own power and considering how they can shift some of this power to primary actors in their systems of influence.

The Fox in Charge

While funding for social change comes from many sources, philanthropy and private capital have an outsized influence on the trajectory of this largesse. With burgeoning issues of inequality, systemic racism, climate breakdown, and the exaggerated influence of business and technology in democratic processes, there is growing discomfort about the way funds are channeled toward the public good. It is impossible to ignore the fact that the fortunes of the world's billionaires now grow at more than double the pace of everyone else's and that the top 10 percent of humanity hold 80 percent of the planet's wealth.[6] At the same time, the ideology that drives the distribution of that wealth—the capitalist system itself—is being held up for scrutiny like never before.

Significantly, philanthropy now far outstrips official development aid in scale and magnitude. In 2018, developing countries received about $160 billion in overseas financial assistance.[7] In the same year, American foundations, charities, and philanthropists gave almost $427 billion to charitable causes.[8] At the same time, a growing number of "social investors" largely with private capital—have put $502 billion of grants and return-seeking funds into the new asset class of impact investments, which we discussed in terms of impact measurement in Chapter 8.[9] These funds are spent at the near sole discretion of private individuals, often with strong economic and political interests. They are also often used as "leverage," through private–public partnerships and pooled funding structures, to incentivize and shape government-led initiatives, the largest source of public aid.[10] These numbers are striking and point to an unnerving trend: philanthropists are arguably becoming more powerful than political leaders.

The industry of social change that we explored in Chapter 1 is booming like never before. In this version, philanthropists, socially minded businesses and investors are lauded for their generosity without being questioned as to where the money came from in the first place. However, recently this has begun to change, starting within philanthropy's innermost circle. In 2013, Peter Buffett—mega-philanthropist and son of billionaire Warren Buffett—made a splash with a *New York Times* op-ed that equated the "charitable-industrial complex" to "conscience laundering— feeling better about accumulating more than any one person could possibly need to live on by sprinkling a little around as an act of charity."[11] More recently, former *New York Times* journalist Anand Giridharadas brought wider attention to the issue with his 2018 book *Winners Take All: The Elite Charade of Changing the World*, where he excoriates the world of private philanthropy for these very contradictions. He explains how philanthropy has effectively taken over the role of public servant, making choices about where funding and resources should be spent at the expense of citizens. The fox, he says, is now in charge of the hen house.

Thus far, as Giridharadas and other critics have pointed out, the response to this evolving crisis of inequality and power imbalance has mostly been a kind of doubling down. Giridharadas coined the term "The Aspen Consensus" to capture this zeitgeist. This consensus holds that, yes, "capitalism's rough edges must be sanded and its surplus fruit shared, but the underlying system must never be questioned."[12] Market-driven solutions are enshrined as the only route out of the crisis, even as they take the form of impact investing, social entrepreneurship, sustainable capitalism, or philanthrocapitalism. The winners of our age are comfortable with being challenged to do more good, but not with being told to do less harm.

But not everyone is buying into this view blindly. Increasingly, social change practitioners—and funders themselves—are calling for a review of who makes the decisions about funding, and how. In our research, we observed an emerging inclination on the part of organizational leaders to challenge the power of the funders who held their purse strings. And in our conversations with funders across the world—from New York to New Delhi and Adelaide to London—we noticed a new and growing level of introspection.

Some forward-thinking funders are approaching systemic issues with depth and sensitivity as they confront the power they hold and their lack of proximity to the lives of the people and organizations they seek to support. We have witnessed funders wrestling with how to address the fundamental power relationships and systemic biases in funding. As part of this reflective work, a growing group of funders are beginning to experiment with new philanthropic practices and forms of grantmaking that are taking the sector into unknown and unexplored territory. In other words, like the organizations we have profiled, they are taking on real systems work. By coming alongside as true partners, they are embracing the same principles that guide systems work within the organizations they support: fostering connection, embracing context, and reconfiguring power across their portfolios.

Starting with Questions

In Part II, we saw how organizations are using the practices of systems work to create systems that are more responsive and representative of the people who live in them. For funders, the logical progression of this idea is to find ways to give greater expression to this work—spreading it across geographies and sectors, or "taking it to scale" in the sector parlance. But as discussed earlier, scale can be an illusion that removes the work of social change from its context and nullifies its potential. We have found that funders must therefore reframe their view of themselves and their role in the system. Adopting a systems work mindset, the job of funders is to come alongside social change organizations as supporting actors. Many of the funders that we studied are doing this in ways that create a fertile environment for systems work: *seeding, nurturing, and propagating* this work as it emerges and grows. However, before they can do this, funders often need to unlearn the very ideas and practices that brought them to their philanthropic roles in the first place.

Systems Work Terms 13: *Seeding, nurturing, and propagating*

seeding	*creating 'containers' where unlikely partners can come togetherand learn from each other*
nurturing	*trusting partner organizations by shifting decision-making to primary actors and by lessening restrictions and lengthening timeframes for partners to receive support*
propagating	*bringing together organizations that are already working along a common trajectory and aligning their work more concretely against funding opportunities.*

Unlearning most often starts with asking questions—real questions, not the ones funders assume they already have the answers to. Late in 2018, we found ourselves doing this alongside funders and social purpose organizations at a convening in Adelaide, Australia. Hosted by the Fay Fuller Foundation and the Social Innovation Exchange (SIX) Funders Node, it was one of several such dialogues convened in recent years to build a sense of solidarity amongst funders and increase the flow of funding to social innovation and systems change work. SIX believes that collectively embracing the concept of systems change requires different actors to come together and learn from each other in order to understand more about themselves and the consequences of their actions. As a report from the Adelaide convening declares, this is a space that "starts with questions."[13]

Specifically, SIX invites funders to probe an important question: Are we truly positioned, equipped, and prepared to engage in systems change? As SIX explains, even as many funders talk the talk of systems change, it can be difficult to grasp just how much they themselves will need to shift both organizationally and individually to enact this change. For example, when Lankelly Chase began its work in 2004, they saw themselves as being somehow separate from the system "on" which they were acting. "We thought we could fund some stuff and foreshadow change, and that systems change was one part of this...And if we published a theory of change that people would come to us and radical stuff would just come up," says Alice. "Believe it or not, that did not happen!" she says with a heavy dose of irony.

When well-intentioned funders see themselves as removed partners channeling resources to people doing work "on-the-ground," they fail to support organizations in the ways that matter. This process of unlearning does not suggest that funders must set out to mimic their partner organizations. However, if the structures, makeup, and processes of funder organizations are fundamentally different than those of change organizations, funders should not hide behind these differences to justify the power imbalances in their relationships with grantees. In order to be true supporting actors of social change, funders must humble themselves, joining primary actors in their day-to-day learning and relinquishing much of their power to set the terms of the relationship.

SIX is not the only group encouraging funders to engage with difficult questions. Similar dialogues are being curated by Catalyst 2030, a membership network of social change practitioners and organizations which encourages funders to choose their approach alongside the organizations they want to fund. In their 2020 report "Embracing Complexity"—a co-creative publication with large systems change funders—Catalyst 2030 synthesized a set of five principles for funders to optimize their funding of systems change.[14] Their first principle, "embrace a systems mindset," reflects the need for a preliminary stage of questioning assumptions and identifying partner organizations. They write, "Keep in mind that the range of systems change leaders you are able to connect with might be biased by your existing network, power dynamics, and even your own assumptions of what a systems change leader looks like. Actively work against these potential biases by...connecting with people that are outside your comfort zone. Moreover, consider defining objective criteria for identifying systems change leaders whose theories of change align with your goals, ideally in collaboration with practitioners on the ground."

Their third principle to "work in true partnership" emphasizes the importance of systems work in the early stages of collaboration. Referring to the types of funders who are able to work systemically, they write, "these funders listen with empathy and humility, engage in conversations with curiosity, and recognize their own biases and assumptions. This allows systems change leaders to be more open about the challenges they face, articulate their needs (which are often not just monetary), and drive their own agendas."

As we have discussed earlier, complexity, scale, and depth require us to learn how to work together and to stay together while learning. This applies equally to supporting actors as it does to primary actors in social change organizations. In other words, to use Catalyst 2030's fourth principle of funding systems change, "prepare for long-term engagement." We believe that groups like SIX and Catalyst 2030 are a reflection of the growing appetite to unlearn some of the funding practices that have constrained true systems work. By fostering connection and learning among funders themselves, they are able to participate in the new roles of seeding, nurturing, and propagating systems work.

Seeding Systems Work

One of the biggest shifts for funders involves undoing the sector-wide conditioning to "get things done" and to focus instead on bringing in the voices of different actors. By creating what philanthropy advisor John Kania has dubbed "radical containers"[15]— intentional ways for people to work together that transform dialogue, learning, and collective potential—funders are able to *seed systems work*. This is precisely what Lankelly Chase was doing when they convened the Elephants Project as one of their "place action inquiry" projects. When Alice came on board with Lankelly Chase, the deep unease she and her team were feeling about their power and wealth—and the sneaking suspicion that they were actually in some way part of the problem—led them on an unexpected trajectory. This move took them away from the traditional role of a funder toward something wholly different. Following a process of deep self-reflection, Lankelly Chase increasingly found itself drawn to a role that supports the health of the system: the nodal organizations and actors, and the relationships between them. Now, their goal is to create and maintain the conditions for primary actors to drive the activities of change while Lankelly Chase itself stays out of the way as much as possible.

Think about this for a moment: In a sector that is used to laying and enforcing the ground rules for engagement, here is a foundation that has frankly admitted it has no real idea what those rules should be. They have acknowledged that they can't go it alone because of the complex and messy nature of systems. And they have also seen that everyone within a system holds a different perspective of its nature, purpose, and boundaries. No one person holds the whole truth. "Depending on where you are in that system, you have such a blinkered view of it you can only see what you are coming at from your cultural point, positional point, power point. Then how do you understand how to change that?" says Alice.

For this reason, Lankelly Chase breaks its work into different forms of "action inquiry" where voices from different slices of the system are heard: cross-cultural, cross-positional, and cross-professional. The aim of this approach is not to substitute the voices of the marginalized for those who have traditionally held power, but rather to join them together in the spirit of genuine co-creation. Here, systems work is seeded as different actors bring approaches that reflect a plurality of experiences, knowledge, and capabilities. Importantly, achieving this unity is not just a matter of getting everyone in the same room, but of driving commitment to a deeply engaged process that brings together these myriad views. Funders must be willing to go on a journey with primary actors to places they may not recognize or fully understand.

We observed this commitment between systemic actors in the wake of the COVID-19 crisis in Cape Town. Community Action Networks (CANs)—coalitions of organizations and individuals from across the private, public, nonprofit, and social sectors—spontaneously emerged in the greater municipal region under the unified banner of Cape Town Together (CTT).[16] Within and between each CAN, participants engaged in unlikely partnerships with astonishing speed to address the hyper-local social catastrophes that arose as knock-on effects of the nationwide lockdown, including food insecurity, unemployment, and insufficient sanitation.[17] Of course, similar to the experiences of the Elephants' participants, the act of bringing together a diverse group of well-intentioned actors to respond to such immediate social needs brought with it great challenges and significant discomfort, all while dealing with much deeper social ills.

As in other parts of the world, increased vulnerability in terms of social, economic, and physical welfare during and following the COVID-19 shutdowns disproportionately affected Cape Town's most marginalized citizens. The structural barriers between Cape Town's citizens living in conditions of disadvantage and those living in conditions of privilege are defined by near insurmountable geographic, economic, and experiential gaps. As well-intentioned donors sprang into action with support for vulnerable communities, local community organizers who had been doing the slow, grinding work of social change for decades were overwhelmed, overlooked, and sometimes overridden by incoming change efforts. Our colleague Ella Scheepers was an early organizer with CTT and a leading member of her local CAN. Even as an activist, systems change practitioner, and long-time community organizer, she was still not prepared for the magnitude of the crisis: "You're seeing the politics of place, the politics of identity, the politics of money, and the politics of power play out in ways that silence people, in ways that are violent. Getting caught up in that and feeling complicit in that was really difficult."[18]

In those communities closest to the problems, there were many primary actors who had years of experience responding to community needs, yet the power differential introduced by inexperienced but wealthy actors was a clear artifact of longstanding apartheid-era imbalances that have not yet been rectified. As Ella explained it, "These [community organizers], who don't consider themselves activists at all but have been working most closely with communities, are not powerless at all. They are power-*full*. But in the middle-class circles, they are seen as powerless. So how do you *not* allow that narrative to play out?" For Ella's local CAN, their answer was to try to be as humble as possible and cognizant of the people and work that existed before them. They did this, in part, by using multiple communication platforms and approaches to ensure that the most important voices were heard. When digital platforms like WhatsApp proved insufficient, the group committed to more intensive phone and in-person conversations with the people providing work directly for communities. In doing this, they also began engaging in intentional forms of systems work. "The deepest thing we've done is try to build trust. Trying to recognize that connections are built one-on-one—not over platforms and grand statements but in the day-to-day small moments, even when we feel scared. This is the work of systems change."

Philanthropy advisor Edgar Villanueva, who specializes in the work of supporting Indigenous communities, describes the act of following primary actors into their own spaces as the single most important thing a funder can do. He beseeches funders: "Go and sit in a community. Participate in a feast day…By funding, you're opening yourself up to receive, so it becomes reciprocal."[19] His call to action is grounded in the need for funders to show up differently—starting by showing up at all—not seeking to become experts themselves, but rather to learn from the lived experiences with primary actors. As Mauricio Lim Miller, founder of FII, says, "We need to become part of *their* process," rather than just assume that our processes are the most valid and useful.

This is the simple yet difficult act of facilitating dialogue between actors in the system in order to learn together in the way that physicist and philosopher David Bohm envisaged when he began exploring dialogue as a way for people to conduct humble, non-defensive exchanges of ideas. This simple act has been largely overlooked and underfunded—much like the practices we discussed in Part II. And yet, since deciding to engage in systems work more authentically, Lankelly Chase has found dialogue initiatives like the Elephants Project to be the most transformative work they can do. For Lankelly Chase, the choice is therefore very simple: If no one else in the system is funding these efforts, they will. At the same time, they decided to stop funding social programs, which they felt did not square with their approach to systems change. In fact, Alice says they probably will never fund programs again. Alice says, "I think in the future our role will no longer be that we are the guardians of the money, but the guardians of system behaviors and how these are enabled to flourish."

Lankelly Chase's decision in this regard should not be seen as a rejection of the traditional funding of social projects. Rather, the decision signals that they have looked closely at the system in which they work and made a deliberate choice to focus their energy and resources on activities that reconfigure the system in a new way. Based on traditional funding metrics, the direct benefits of initiatives such as these—in the form of knowledge about the problem and new relationships—are intangible. But from a systems perspective, they are concrete. By creating "containers" that hold people in new and unlikely relationships to facilitate dialogue and learning, funders like Lankelly Chase are actively seeding systems work.

Nurturing Systems Work

In addition to seeding systems work, we have seen that funders can *nurture systems work* by developing partnerships based on trust. The decision of funders to trust their partner organizations manifests in two ways. First, it impacts who they choose to fund, by shifting decision-making to include unlikely or unrepresented primary actors. Secondly, it influences how money is distributed, by lessening restrictions and lengthening timeframes for partners to receive support. Trust, and the decision of funders to listen to the direct experience of organizations, is an essential part of transforming the relationship between primary and supporting actors.

Many of the funders we met are nurturing systems work by moving decision-making closer to the primary actors in systems. This often involves trusting primary actors as systems experts. For example, Lankelly Chase has fully shifted its grantmaking decisions from the trustees to the executive team. The executive team now works within a strategic framework agreed on by the Board, and has the freedom to work as collaboratively as possible with a growing network of partners. As the Lankelly Chase website states, "This feels like a more realistic response to a situation of high complexity, and one that exploits the independence, longevity, and flexibility of a foundation." And the plan is to not stop there. Alice says they are now figuring out how to transition decision-making to partners (which is their preferred term for grantees) so that "the people who know what is going on are the people who are delivering the work," as she says.

The transfer of decision-making power to organizations does more than ensure that the right projects and work are funded. It feeds into a reinforcing feedback loop of trust between funder and organization. This is particularly essential for systems work given the complex and uncertain pathways involved in tackling systemic problems. As we discussed in Chapter 8, the trajectory of social change is uncertain and comes with indefinite time horizons. This means that organizations require funders to be flexible with their expectations and to commit to nurturing the relationship over an extended timeframe—another expression of trust. We found this at the Fay Fuller Foundation in Australia, under the leadership of Stacey Thomas, which has transitioned to channel all of its available resources and skills to partner, commission, and influence health outcomes in the South Australian community.[20] Fay Fuller's approach to systems work parallels that of the Family Independence Initiative (FII). Rather than funding programs or services, Fay Fuller focuses fully on increasing the capacity of organizations that are closest to healthcare work and best positioned to respond to emergent needs. As a funder, they direct their energy and resources to supporting the skills and processes that these organizations require to do their work. Consequently, most of their partnerships are large, long-term grants that stretch over multiple years (sometimes up to a decade), reflecting a high degree of trust between grantor and grantee.

Beyond shifting decision-making power and committing to long-term partnerships, funders can further nurture systems work by evolving the ways in which they interact with organizations. "Trust-based philanthropy," a practice initiated by the Whitman Institute,[21] is an approach that foundations like the Bertha Foundation (our funder at the Bertha Centre for Social Innovation at the University of Cape Town) have deployed. This approach is based on the simple notion that relationships are stronger and more effective when they are built on a foundation of trust. In our case, the Bertha Foundation provided us with unrestricted, multi-year funding that essentially put decision-making power into our hands, similar to Lankelly Chase and Fay Fuller. The Bertha Foundation then carried this trust-based approach into our operational communication and learning processes. They didn't burden us with endless bureaucracy and reporting requirements, preferring instead to receive a short two-pager once a year explaining what we had learned during the process of doing our work. They also created a space for real conversations between us to surface roadblocks. This enabled us, as educators, researchers, and practitioners, to focus on our core work: opening a traditional business school to hundreds of social purpose organizations, acting as a trusted advisor between government and civil society on issues of access and equity, bringing unlikely and non-elite students into programs, and opening a campus in the historically under-resourced community of Philippi. We believe that this approach was instrumental in helping the Bertha Centre to flourish, becoming one of fastest growing centers of excellence within the University of Cape Town and building communities of practice that stretched outside the university, into its surrounding communities and across the African continent.[22]

The most progressive permutation of the trust-based approach emerges when primary actors become funders themselves. The Red Umbrella Fund is a community-led, participatory grantmaking fund and the only international fund for sex workers' rights.[23] The project was years in the making and the product of an extended trust-building exercise between primary and supporting actors. In 2006, the Open Society Foundation and Mama Cash initiated a dialogue with key stakeholders in the field of sex work—the first of many designed to understand the needs and rights of sex workers. After six years of planning and learning, the Red Umbrella Fund was set up to support sex worker rights groups fighting violence, stigma, and criminalization in an environment with little accessible funding. All grantees are sex worker-led and selected by an international committee which is itself led by sex workers. The Red

Umbrella Fund now acts as a mechanism for sex workers to set their own priorities and, quite literally, to claim power. Whereas our industrial funding mindset focuses intently on the monetary transaction between funders and organizations, a systems work mindset requires funders to focus on trust as the critical resource they give to partners. Funders who choose to follow these examples and approaches of facilitating co-creation between primary and secondary actors are continuously working to build trust between organizations in order to enable effective systems work. Without trust, funders may consider themselves "patrons" of a certain kind of social change, but only with trust can they nurture systems work, and in the process become systems workers themselves.

Propagating Systems Work

There is yet a third way in which we have seen funders supporting systems work, but at a different level of the system. If the work of seeding and nurturing allows funders to directly engage with systems work through funding primary actors, *propagating systems work* allows funders to work across systems to tackle a complex problem on multiple fronts. Funders who are well positioned— either due to their size, composition, resources, or context—to access, connect, and resource large groups of organizations and primary actors have the capacity to assemble the work of these organizations for greater, more targeted impact. They also have the influence to practice and uphold the principles of system work in their own processes.

This approach commonly takes the form of "collaborative philanthropy," where groups of prominent funders band together for collective action. In recent years, several large coalitions of funders have come together to aggregate their decisions, choosing to design and fund initiatives comprised of many coordinated players rather than single organizations. Their aim is to bring together organizations already working along a common trajectory and align their work more concretely against a funding opportunity. This is not scaling impact in the traditional sense, replicating "program-in-a-box" solutions, but rather bringing together organizations as a learning community with a substantial amount of funding to push activities that are widespread and coordinated, yet contextualized.

A forerunner of this integrated approach is Co-Impact, launched in 2017 as "a new global model for collaborative philanthropy and social change at scale" by a group of the world's leading philanthropists.[24] The model for Co-Impact grew out of the experiences and research of Olivia Leland, the founding director of the Giving Pledge, which highlighted key gaps in the current philanthropic and social change landscape amongst donors and social change-makers. Simply put, there was a mismatch between the demands of particular social issues and the size and timing of investments. Focusing its efforts in the Global South, Co-Impact attempts to fill those gaps with "system change grants," large-scale, long-term funding opportunities that cover large geographies and bring together a wide representation of organizations and primary actors as partners. To do this, they use an aggregation approach so that resources are pooled from multiple foundations to make large grants that target specific initiatives.

Beyond these "system change grants", Co-Impact has a second goal of advancing a model for other funders to adopt. They believe that collaborative funds like theirs are a viable model for providing long-term, flexible funding to unlock deeper levels of change. They therefore endeavor to lead by example as they elevate systems work in their own practices by focusing on supportive and non-directive grantmaking, promoting strong organizational capacity, and listening, learning, and adapting to partners.

Funders who seek to propagate systems work can also avoid one-off, tokenistic acts of inclusion and instead choose to strategically fund entire ecosystems of under-represented organizations and people. The McConnell Foundation in Canada shows how even small philanthropic organizations can adopt an integrated approach to this effect. Since 2011, this family-led foundation has launched several new projects to address the country's legacy of exploiting and oppressing Indigenous peoples. Director Nicole McDonald says these projects have been part of the foundation's intention to play a more systemic role in society by addressing the gap in social and economic wellbeing between Indigenous and non-Indigenous peoples.[25]

Today, this intention has coalesced under their Reconciliation Initiative which aims to create a "reconciliation economy" in which "wealth and resources are equitably shared and sustainably managed." Through this initiative, McConnell serves as a conduit for organizations throughout the country to work in collaboration with other local groups toward different reconciliation goals. McConnell does this by connecting with Indigenous communities and other stakeholders through a combination of three activities: (1) collaborative funding, which allows the coordination of resources through shared administration; (2) innovative platforms for change, which bring together stakeholders from diverse backgrounds to test new ways to solve problems; and (3) solutions finance, which includes responsible investing, granting, impact investing, and financial innovation.

When funders propagate systems work, their choices can also bring forth new patterns in their own policies and practices, particularly around *who* is heard and included. Echoing Green in the United States is an organization that emphasizes the "who" of funding decisions as a strategy for promoting and expanding the impact of social innovations. They are committed to increasing representation of people who are Black, Indigenous, and People of Color (BIPOC) in the field of social change and dismantling racism—both as part of their long-running operational activities and their response in the wake of the June 2020 racial justice protests in the United States. They embody the power of funders to create new norms through their own policies, becoming practitioners of systems work in their own right. As an international nonprofit whose primary activity is providing social change fellowships, Echoing Green focuses on developing individual social innovators through a two-year program that nurtures their ideas for addressing systemic issues of climate change, education, health, human rights, poverty, and racial justice. Through these emerging leaders, Echoing Green is building a network of diverse actors across systems who can pool resources and fuel each other's work. As part and parcel of this process, Echoing Green has been a steady advocate for equitable representation, consistently investing in individuals and ideas that both tackle systemic issues of racial injustice and come from individuals with lived experience of racial injustice.

In the wake of widespread activism and protest following the brutal murder of George Floyd by a police officer in May 2020 in the United States, Echoing Green issued a call to action for other funders to invest in black leaders and black-led organizations, not just as a reaction to current events but as part of a long-term commitment to racial equity.[26] They wrote, "The emerging leaders and social innovators of tomorrow are among those marching in the streets of Minneapolis, St. Louis, Brooklyn, Tulsa, and so many other communities... These future leaders deserve our support and we need to connect them to the broader field of social innovation." Connection—and by extension, the integration of systems work—is the practice embedded in each of the five strategies they propose for intentionally seeking change. Like the other funders propagating systems work, Echoing Green sees the capacity of funders to connect with partners and to facilitate connection between other partners as imperative to systems change. Their call to action, therefore, focuses on the ways funders must connect with BIPOC communities everywhere. These strategies include changing "the way you support black-led organizations" by eliminating arbitrarily burdensome processes and trusting partners to make decisions, supporting "collective mourning and healing" actions to help people deal with the trauma of injustice, and connecting local "work to dismantle structural racism to larger global movements." This is an elevation of process over outcomes, a call for supporting actors to think about *how* they fund change as much as *what* they fund, and to take immediate action accordingly.

Connecting the Dots

The three approaches of seeding, nurturing, and propagating systems work allow funders to "connect the dots" with systems work. By using their influence to facilitate, identify, and actively build connections within the system, funders can redistribute their power to enable greater expression of systems work. This is true for funders of small, local initiatives, as well as funders who aggregate global initiatives. In both cases, amplifying systems work does not necessarily imply investing in organizational scale, as is so often assumed, but rather investing in *systemic* scale. This means funders must look across funding portfolios to make connections that individual organizations may not be able to identify. By doing this, funders can resource the difficult and somewhat intangible efforts to build relationships, networks, and coalitions between all actors, including themselves.

Learning Notes: Funding for Partnership

Funders are best positioned to play a supporting actor role: *seeding*, *nurturing*, and *propagating* systems work through their funding processes and activities. To play this role, funders should use the same principles as their grantees, investees and partner organizations while at the same time committing to a learning journey together with them. Funders and investors must also analyze the power that they bring into the relationship and actively redistribute this power to primary actors. Funders support systems work by:

- **Starting with *unlearning*,** understanding the power dynamics that funders bring into the room and actively shifting power and influence to those with lived experience and deeply immersive knowledge of the issues and their context.
- **Seeding systems work,** bringing together unlikely participants— including primary actors and decision-makers—in "radical containers" that keep people together while learning.
- **Nurturing systems work,** reimagining the grantor–grantee relationship and basing it on trust rather than power and control. Practically, this is done by shifting decision-making to primary actors and creating less restrictive, long-term funding structures.
- **Propagating systems work,** bringing together organizations that are already working along a common trajectory and aligning their work more concretely against funding opportunities.

When **funding is a partnership** built on trust, it facilitates a process of unlearning and relearning, with power reconfigured toward those with lived experience and deep immersion in the context of social problems. Many "traditional" funder activities are then co-created or even ceded to organizations and primary actors as trust becomes a key component of the relationship.

10

The Principles and Practices in Action

As we finalized this manuscript in 2020, a singular crisis began to sweep the planet: the pandemic caused by SARS-CoV-2, otherwise known as COVID-19. We, like so many others, scrambled to make sense of what was happening, quickly feeling overwhelmed by the scale and complexity of the situation. Hundreds of millions of people have been infected and almost four million people have died—in a matter of mere months. Millions around the world are losing jobs and livelihoods, while hundreds of millions more are predicted to fall into hunger and poverty, reversing the trends of the last few decades. Earlier in the pandemic, it was possible to think that certain countries or communities would be spared from the virus. Now, the interconnectedness of our global society is laid bare: no corner of the earth will be untouched.

These statistics, while staggering, seem less surprising when placed on historical scales. Plagues and wars throughout history have killed tens and hundreds of millions of people, often decimating entire populations.[1] Economies have crashed and reemerged with higher trajectories, thwarting the most dire predictions. Yet, as we learned in our research, statistics often fail to tell the true story of social change. When something happens to change the societal psyche, when the narratives that we live by are exposed as fallacy, a challenge is no longer just big or perplexing: it is *deep*.

Much of the political and media discourse over the last few months has focused on predicting when the current situation will stabilize. Trillions of dollars are being poured into the global economy to prevent total collapse. Frontline healthcare workers are working around the clock to buttress failing health systems while factories have been repurposed to manufacture personal protective equipment and essential goods. Meanwhile, billions of people are enduring recurrent lockdowns and social distancing, waiting to return to work or school, while hoping that their jobs, small businesses, and institutions will be resuscitated when the world re-opens.

However, in the midst of this frenetic activity, as researchers and practitioners we have been absorbed by what is happening beneath the surface to the values and beliefs that guide our everyday existence. Even as we stay close to home, going about our routines, the shift in these norms is palpable. What it means to be a worker, a teacher, a leader, and a friend is fluctuating before our very eyes. More crucially, the divide of the experiences between the poor and the rich, the powerful and powerless, has been brought into sharp focus.

One particular video, filmed not too far from where we live, has haunted us.[2] Produced by the BBC, the video shows footage just outside of Johannesburg, where tens of thousands of people are standing in a queue possibly miles long. NGO workers are directing people to maintain their distance, but the fear of being left behind is apparent. By the end of the day, ten thousand food parcels were distributed, likely enough for some of the families to scrape through a few more weeks. In South Africa, the country with the highest wealth disparity in the world,[3] COVID-19 has lifted the already-thin veil that covered the precariousness of more than half the population. Yet this is just one glimpse from a city close to home. Images from around the world—from the United Kingdom to South Africa, the United States to Brazil and India—tell a similar yet false story that some lives are worth more than others. Simply put, we have constructed a world where the safety and security of the privileged few serve a higher priority than the lives and livelihoods of the many.

This pandemic has proven to be an odd catalyst as it pulls us away from each other rather than brings us together. We, like so many, have been frustrated by posturing at the political level which seems to entrench this dynamic rather than mitigate it. Yet, our conversations with social change practitioners leave us encouraged. Each of the organizations profiled in our research—and many more beyond—are using this time to pivot to necessary response measures while continuing to pursue the deeper systems work that will take us into a better future. This global crisis, which has physically kept individuals and communities apart, has created optimal conditions for us to become more aware of what binds us together as human beings.

These social change leaders are asking critical questions, such as: How do we ensure that this pandemic confronts and reverses, rather than entrenches, the systemic inequalities that have been laid bare? What are the ways that this experience will shift our relationships with each other and the environment? How will we choose the course that leads us toward a more regenerative future, rather than an apocalyptic one? And finally, how do we use this finite window of time to fundamentally alter the norms, beliefs, and values that no longer serve, rather than simply return to a previous state that was never natural or healthy for us or our planet?

Going Deep

In Part I, we emphasized that social challenges share three characteristics—complexity, scale, and depth—that produce bewildering results when we try to solve them. Complexity arises when there are many variables interacting in unpredictable ways, and scale means that our problems become bigger as we try to solve them across larger geographies and populations. While each of these features gives rise to confounding consequences, the third feature is the hardest of all. Social challenges have depth when they arise from deeply held beliefs, values, and assumptions that no longer serve us well. These norms manifest in the power structures that influence relationships and channel resources, impacting the agency that individuals and communities hold to choose their own futures.[4]

We then outlined two different approaches to social change: technical and transformative. The technical approach is seductive, since it leads us to believe that a perfect solution—a technology, an intervention, or a program—will solve the problem. On the other hand, the transformative approach is disruptive, mandating a radical overhaul or replacement of society's institutions in order to build anew. While both of these approaches have their uses, each is insufficient. By prioritizing lofty outcomes over the process of change itself, we can easily overlook the deeper work that social change requires.

The urge to default to one approach or the other is strong. Many are already seeing the COVID-19 pandemic as a technical problem, something that a vaccine will "fix" so that we can all go back to our normal lives. Others are quickly leaping to the conclusion that the challenge is power-based—the result of systemic inequality, off-balance geopolitics, and partisan decision-making—and therefore, only a transformative solution will work. Both of these analyses are correct but incomplete. A technical solution like a vaccine or treatment regimen will need to be coupled with a process that engenders trust and solidarity between public health systems and patients. And a transformational solution, such as policies to defund departments that refuse to reform, reduce the precarity of workers, or ensure broader distribution of wealth, will need to be accompanied by a process that brings many parties to the table and heals partisan fractures. Technical and transformational approaches are helpful to set a strong vision of change, while systems work ensures that the necessary day-to-day measures are sustained in order to get us there.

The Principles in a Pandemic

In the preceding chapters, we detailed three principles that comprise systems work. Fundamentally, these principles describe how primary actors—those who are immersed in the context of a social problem, who live it every day—become the key agents of change. Working with these principles, organizations act as catalysts, ensuring that the necessary conditions are present for systems to be more responsive and representative. First, they create enduring connections between primary actors, building a strong collective identity that keeps groups together while learning. They then equip these actors to become contextually responsive, so that they can adapt to complex dynamics as necessary. Finally, they ensure that the power of making decisions and directing resources is firmly put in the hands of primary actors, creating long-term mechanisms for change.

These principles were revealed to us over several years of spending time with social change practitioners, many of whom were pursuing this work instinctually, with very little validation or support for these particular elements of their work. Many of these organizations have been lauded for their innovative programs and the ability to scale up exponentially, but the actual work that drives their most profound impact is rarely articulated in marketing materials or funding proposals. Rather, it is beneath the surface, providing strong foundations for the more visible activities that win accolades. For this deeper work to become more widespread, it needs to be seeded, nurtured, and propagated in an intentional way by committed funders and leaders.

Fostering Connection

As we discovered in our research, systems work is less about ambitious outcomes and more about the process that enables people and organizations to become responsive and adaptive as the situation requires. This starts with a strong sense of connection among those who are living through an issue—creating a group that stays together while learning. By creating a collective identity that binds groups together, organizations build an action system for further change.

Creating this action system is not just a "feel good" process. Among the organizations that we studied, this has been readily apparent during the COVID-19 crisis. For the organizations that have fostered a strong sense of collective identity among their constituents, there has been significant opportunity to guide intentional social change amidst the chaos. For example, at m2m, Mentor Mothers have been able to build upon the trust that has been developed and nurtured with clinic staff and clients, helping mothers and children avoid misinformation and stigma while dealing with the immediate crisis. Mentor Mothers have been designated "essential workers" during country lockdown periods of the pandemic. CEO Frank Beadle de Palomo writes that Mentor Mothers are: "Bolstering the capacity of understaffed health centres, so that doctors and nurses can focus on more urgent and acute medical needs. Mentor Mothers are working at health centres every day to provide vital information and support on COVID-19, HIV, and other health issues—a critical first line of defense."[5]

Similarly, RLabs has quickly pivoted its activities from in-person trainings to virtual learning spaces while supporting its 200 staff members at a distance, many of whom live in challenging circumstances. While many NGOs have struggled to migrate their training programs online quickly—canceling or postponing immediate programing—RLabs has used its deep, family-like relationships among constituents to ramp up their activities. Most importantly, based on a strong sense of solidarity with their members, they have made a conscious decision to design their virtual programs to their lowest-access participants, believing that they have to meet people where they are during this time. As Marlon Parker, founder of RLabs, describes, "We lead with love. Leading with love means that if I love someone, I'm willing to change because of my love for that person. If I love that person, I'm willing to change my program just so that the person with the least resources can engage and participate. And that has always been fundamental to our approach. Look at the individual that has the biggest barriers and let's see if we can remove those barriers for that individual so that they, too, can participate."[6]

These case studies show that collective identities and action systems can be fostered at many different levels: family, community, and country. Each of these levels serve an important purpose, contributing to individual and collective wellbeing. However, as the scale of our challenges increases, the scale of our action system also needs to grow. As we head into the next decade, we face an urgent collective action problem at a global level. Many of our pressing social challenges cannot be solved by communities, cities, or even nations alone. Yet we are operating with an action system built for another era, one that is rapidly fracturing as its strictures prove incompatible with justice and wellbeing for all. To expand our action system at this scale requires a global collective identity—a sense of interdependence that keeps us together while learning.

While this may sound far-fetched given the many differences that divide the world, a global collective identity is already emerging. COVID-19 has provided a devastating, yet opportune backdrop to see this collective identity form, albeit in small pockets. When people across the world watch in solidarity as Italians sing from balconies, and students in South Africa join free online classes alongside children in the United Kingdom, and even when humorous memes, games, and videos spread messages of hope and empathy across the globe, we are experiencing the birth of a global awareness of our shared experience.

Prior to this crisis and now, in the midst of a global pandemic, a global collective identity to tackle the urgent issues of climate change has also been building, particularly among youth. Starting in 2018, Swedish activist Greta Thunberg staged weekly protests which have grown to include nearly ten million students in 261 countries.[7] Thunberg's unconventional leadership captured the imagination of the world when she sailed to New York on a no-emissions yacht to attend a United Nations climate conference. While Thunberg's activism has received the most high-profile media attention, she is emblematic of a growing global movement that emphasizes climate action as an issue of social justice rather than just an environmental one. She is joined by activists from around the globe who are foreseeing and actively protesting the effects of global warming on their own lives. By connecting individuals and communities across the world—largely through social media—these waves of social protest and collective action are showing what a larger "we" might look like in the post-globalization era.

Embracing Context

The second principle of systems work is to embrace context and celebrate the myriad manifestations of social change rather than try to arrive at a standardized approach. When groups are bound by a strong sense of collective identity, they can appreciate the differences that arise when people try out new things and learn from these experiences. By equipping problem-solvers to respond rapidly to emerging issues, organizations can promote social change that is imaginative and adaptive rather than rigid—an imperative for rapidly changing, complex issues. Moreover, these problem-solvers are able to circulate this information quickly—and widely, where there are strong platforms to do so—taking what is useful for their own context and adapting as their own needs require.

Perhaps no organization has exemplified this principle of systems work more readily during the COVID crisis than Buurtzorg. As an organization with global affiliates in Asia, Buurtzorg's leadership had a sense by early 2020—earlier than most—of what was to come. Predicting that the virus would have an outsized impact on their elderly clients, the Buurtzorg team began to think about how they could communicate in a way that kept them closely connected, even if they could not be together.[8] While leaders of many other organizations were emphasizing a "command and control" approach, Buurtzorg's founder and CEO, Jos De Blok, realized that this was the time to "listen and be sensitive." They instituted more frequent communications, assembling a crisis group with a network structure that met daily and was available twenty-four hours a day to neighborhood teams. According to Jos, there were "days when hundreds of nurses were calling," and the organization's primary aim was to ensure that nurses felt "safe and supported."

With this outpouring of communication, the Buurtzorg crisis group was able to quickly develop a strong sense of on-the-ground needs. By the time more centralized groups, including the Dutch health system, were aware of these needs, Buurtzorg had already set up supply chains and protocols to provide nurses with what they urgently needed: personal protective equipment, tests, and patient protocols. Jos explains, "What I see happening at the ministry and the government level is the want of centralizing things and I think it's more the reflex of an average manager...to want to have control. [But] you don't have control, so you should accept that you don't have control [and] think about what are the ways to build networks...I'm convinced that decentralized networks will develop themselves."

This approach is not limited to the health sector. FEN has also used the COVID-19 crisis to deepen its engagement with teachers and families and creatively use its strategies to support flexible ways of continuing education at home even in resource-limited contexts. Since the Escuela Nueva model is already geared toward students working autonomously and at their own pace, it is uniquely suited to the current challenge of educating outside of the classroom. The organization is finding, however, that even more consistent and rapid communication with educators and families is critical during this time, while the tools they use for engagement with displaced communities are particularly relevant. In a recent newsletter, FEN writes that in the cities where the Escuela Nueva Learning Circles program is operating, "Tutors, pedagogical, and psychosocial advisors...give feedback and evaluate the progress of each student through cell phone calls, WhatsApp groups, and video, audio, and text messages. The interaction between tutors, parents, and children is constant, reaffirming ties and bonds."[9] This constant engagement allows teachers and families to rapidly respond to the emerging situation and tailor interactions with students to daily needs.

It is likely that chaotic conditions such as these will become more frequent and enduring over the next decade as we live through the repercussions of economic and social choices from the last two centuries. These conditions will necessitate new ways of working, mirroring the "agile" ways of working that technology companies have been embracing for two decades. Already, organizations and movements across a range of sectors are pivoting to decentralized methods, tapping into the self-organizing potential of social technologies. Virtual working is rapidly normalizing as companies conclude that large-scale office spaces are not as necessary as they once believed. Self-organizing teams, decentralized decision-making, and circulation of data is quickly becoming key as managers realize that this is the most effective and efficient way to get things done in a virtual working environment. Even more telling, for those who are organizing social movements, emergent and agile tactics are blending the seamlessness of social media with the gritty "on-the-ground" tactics of protest-style change. Rapid adoption of technology tools will cement these ways of working into the future. As these ways of working become internalized, they will shift the ethos of organizing itself.

Reconfiguring Power

There is a strong instinct in the midst of chaos to look for heroes. As Margaret Wheatley writes, "Heroic leadership rests on the illusion that someone can be in control. Yet we live in a world of complex systems whose very existence means they are inherently uncontrollable."[10] As we head into a future with more frequent and recurring crises, many political and economic leaders will try to force a Faustian bargain where citizens give up their sovereignty in exchange for security. This choice is a false one. Systems work tells a different story: that complex, large-scale, and deep issues require a broader vision of leadership, one in which citizens and communities take on greater decision-making and resource direction, ensuring that social systems fully represent the people who live in them.

The current crisis of COVID-19 has forced the world to confront a harrowing truth. The political, social, and economic arrangements that prop up the status quo are not only grossly unjust, but also devastatingly insufficient as we head into an uncertain future. The prevailing ideology of sacrificing humanity and mutuality for individual gain has sown the seeds of our collective crisis—a perfect storm of social vulnerability, civic rage, and environmental degradation. At the same time, the most important counterbalance to this ideology—a robust and muscular civil society—has been weakened, even subverted, over the last half century. For many social change practitioners, this time has revealed not just complexity but complicity. In a raw email following the George Floyd protests that erupted in the United States amidst the pandemic, Mauricio Miller, the founder of FII who now runs CII, puts it bluntly, "By continually boasting about our importance, our innovations, and then portraying communities of color as needy recipients, we perpetuate the stereotypes, the racism, the denigration that sets the stage for three police officers to stand and watch as one of their own slowly murders a black man."[11]

The hollowing out of civil society has been a slow but steady march toward professionalization and paternalization, moving the source of power and leadership from those who have lived experience of social issues to those who are in service to the very elites they are meant to hold in check. As civic campaigner and legal scholar K. Sabeel Rhaman writes, "Too often grassroots communities are either ignored or engaged with as 'end users' or 'clients'—funded to execute specific initiatives and projects... but not to build durable grassroots capacity and infrastructure that cuts across specific policy fights and issue campaigns." This insipid version of civil society is destructive since it prevents citizens from amassing the knowledge and imagination to drive positive change in times of crisis.

However, for those organizations that are built to harness this extraordinary capacity, the time is ripe. In a webinar focused on the reconstruction of cities in a post-COVID world, co-founder and former chair of SDI, Sheela Patel, emphasized, "Wherever communities are organized, they have information about themselves, they know how to talk to their governments––things flow there." She continued, "We need to have courage to enter the spaces that were hallowed—where we had no right to knock on those doors—to ask simple but very difficult questions. [These things] cannot be manufactured just at the time of emergency... Let COVID change that to the new normal."[12] In low-income areas where SDI and its affiliated groups have already built strong relationships with local governments and officials, emergency measures such as food parcel distribution and health information distribution have been "hugely effective," preventing the upheavals and shortages that other areas are experiencing.[13]

Other organizations, such as Nidan and the National Association of Street Vendors of India (NASVI), are using this time to amplify demands that have long been on the table, but which are proving urgent in the wake of COVID-19. As street markets have re-opened following long periods of lockdown, the need for dedicated vending spaces is apparent as customers attract large crowds and queues.[14] Nidan, with its ready access to vendor communities and their needs, is using previous initiatives—such as identification drives and data collection—to negotiate policies and directives with a collective voice.[15]

These organizations are showing how the current crisis can serve as the impetus for a new balance of power—both politically and economically. However, this rebalancing will not occur without the organizational capacity to reimagine and assemble broad constituencies that challenge the status quo. In a piece on reclaiming civil society, Harvard scholar Marshall Ganz and organizer Art Reyes III write, "The promise of equal voice means little in the absence of a capacity to combine voices economically and politically to challenge the power of private wealth to capture government for its own ends."

The "In Between" Normal

Although partisan posturing is rife, one of the most interesting impulses during this time has been the instinct to assemble new collaborations to counter the complexity, scale, and depth of the crisis.[16] Countries with leaders who have fostered a sense of mutuality among their citizens, while utilizing compassionate and inclusive decision-making, are now showing better containment of the virus and lower death rates.[17] Moreover, businesses are being called upon to demonstrate their "social relevance" and create a culture of "collective action" in order to emerge from this crisis in a stronger rather than weaker position.[18] It seems prescient that while many authoritarian leaders are using this opportunity to intensify their political apparatus, it is the leaders who have taken the opposite approach who have captured the public's imagination. Amanda Taub from the *New York Times* writes, "Eventually [this] could change perceptions of what strong leadership looks like."[19]

The drive for mutuality and collaboration is a natural response to issues that are larger than any one leader or organization can solve—a recognition of humility and the insufficiency to act with a solo view of a problem. While collaborations are often seen as a strategy for scale, they are more fundamentally an opportunity to learn across entrenched silos. As Devi Sridhar, chair of Global Health at the University of Edinburgh Medical School warns, "All models are limited by the assumptions that they make...No discipline has all the answers, and the only way to avoid 'groupthink' and blind spots is to ensure representatives with diverse backgrounds and expertise are at the table when major decisions are made."[20]

In the social change sector, a number of collaborations have emerged during the pandemic, signaling a newfound awareness of interconnectedness and collective responsibility. In March 2020, the Schwab Foundation and the World Economic Forum launched the COVID Response Alliance, a coalition of over eighty global organizations who collectively support more than one hundred thousand social entrepreneurs working in over 190 countries. The aim of the alliance is to coordinate the work of social change supporting actors so that resources and activities are channeled effectively, acting as a hub of information and access to capital. Similarly, the Global Impact Investing Network (GIIN) has created the "R3 Coalition," which stands for Response, Recovery, and Resilience, in an effort to streamline and accelerate impact investing efforts and fill financing gaps during the COVID-19 crisis. Supported by prominent foundations and investor conveners, the coalition serves as a "meta-collaboration," aggregating efforts of existing networks to share information and reduce duplication.

While these high-profile collaborations are making headlines, a proliferation of local collectives around the world are creating immediate relief and regeneration for communities. Many of these collaborations, such as the Cape Town Together's CANs which we described in the previous chapter, have emerged organically, knitting together existing initiatives with newfound supporters.[21] Importantly, these local initiatives are building upon a sense of mutuality derived from a local collective identity activated by crisis. Mauricio has seen this sense of mutuality materialize in the communities where they work, explaining, "The character of this pandemic is somewhat different. It is not just a sense of charity as you will see after a hurricane, but it is a sense of how interdependent and caring we are. In our neighborhoods people are showing they care about the survivability of the mom and pop restaurants, the families of their gardeners, or domestic work services. We are appreciating the medical staff at hospitals, but more than that, we are finally recognizing the janitors there, the poorly paid staff at nursing homes as well as the grocery store clerks that we depend on. We must continue to recognize that we need one another and that no one is expendable. We cannot let this sense of community dissipate as we have after other disasters."[22]

The Window of Now

We started this research by asking a rather bold question: "How do organizations create systemic social change?" Over five years of research and writing, we have seen this question only grow in importance, becoming part of the strategic conversation for all types of organizations, not just those specifically focused on social change. Leaders of businesses—both large and small—as well as politicians, educators, employees, and parents are grappling with the realization that complex social change can rapidly impact their everyday lives. On our crowded and warming planet, teeming with individuals and communities with little choice but to live and work with one another, we believe there is no more urgent question.

Windows of opportunity can be years in the making and are often only visible in hindsight. The inflection point that we wrote about in Chapter 1 encompassed two World Wars and the Great

Depression, decades which involved massive deaths and upheaval followed by a dramatic reimagining of the social contract between citizens and government. As we face possible years of economic malaise, social unrest and climate change, it is difficult to see what may materialize. What is clear is that if we want to evolve into a more *just* social, economic, and environmental arrangement, while avoiding conflict at a global scale, we must do better than defaulting to autocracy or hard power as blunt tools to address uncertainty.

Reimagining a just future is within our reach, but it will force us to face our societal shortcomings as well as reckon with our personal demons. In a recent conversation, social innovator and technologist Anand Arkalgud, who is a partner at social consultancy Socion Advisors, explained that social change of this magnitude requires a certain "rewiring of the brain," creating significant personal upheaval—a process which he calls the "right kind of ugly."[23] But he is adamant that to genuinely achieve a meaningful change, we have to go through this discomfort. This reckoning is certainly happening at both the individual and societal level, creating significant turmoil and mental strain across the globe. Change, however, is coming at a more rapid pace than anticipated. Indeed, some of the very things that we wrote in this manuscript just a couple of years ago (which seemed radical at the time) suddenly feel "mainstream" in a matter of months.

Our colleague at the Bertha Centre, Ncedisa Nkonyeni, writes, "This positive re-imagining is at the core of systems change work. As frustration at the slow pace of change grows, and the world's wicked problems—such as climate change and wealth inequality—proliferate, people are increasingly recognizing that we need to find ways to tackle the root causes of these issues rather than just addressing the symptoms...But social systems are complex and many of them are resilient—for good or bad—and difficult to change...Most of us in the Global South know this from our lived experience."

She continues, "It is vital that those who understand the context and who appreciate most what needs to shift, are involved in bringing about this shift. This does not necessarily mean disregarding other voices. Systems work does not seek to merely tear down everything and disregard all ideas that we didn't come up with ourselves. Rather we are identifying what is not useful and replacing it with what might be."[24]

As we head into a new decade, we face unforeseen challenges that are materializing with speed and unpredictability as we experience more frequent and intense natural disasters, escalating drought and food insecurity, and the greater movement of people. In the face of these challenges, it will be easy to default to our more traditional views of leadership and problem-solving, which celebrate an us-versus-them mentality, top-down decision-making, and aggressive power stances. Systems work—with its focus on our day-to-day actions and relationships—may feel counterintuitive in this rapidly emerging future. Yet, as our research has shown us, the future is demanding a different kind of leadership, one that emphasizes the *ways we work* as much as the outcomes we pursue. The organizations profiled in this book have given us glimpses of what that can look like, and we must be ready to follow their lead.

Organizational Practices and Tactics of Systems Work

Cultivate Collectives
    RLabs   180
    mothers2mothers   182

Equip Problem-solvers
    Family Independence Initiative   184
    Buurtzorg   186

Promote Platforms
    Slum Dwellers International   188
    Child and Youth Finance International   190

Disrupt Polices and Patterns
    Nidan   192
    Fundacion Escuela Nueva   194

RLabs

www.rlabs.org
Founding: 2008 in South Africa
Core organization: Bridgetown, South Africa
Geographic scope: Franchises in twenty-three countries

SURFACE WORK	RLabs hosts technical training, entrepreneurship, and innovation programs that unite at-risk youth around their life experiences and passion for technology. Since 2008, RLabs has trained 200,000 individuals and incubated 3,500 businesses. Through their different programs, RLabs has created 90,000 job opportunities globally.
CONTEXT	**STATE OF STIGMA** *Racialized geographic, economic, and social exclusion of communities* The apartheid system in South Africa has left a legacy of disconnection between historically marginalized communities and privileged centers of economic activity. This racialized disconnection is epitomized in the Cape Flats region on the outskirts of Cape Town. Here, access to education, jobs, and opportunities is limited: too often, kids drop out of school, get involved with gangs, and become drug addicts and dealers. Adolescents in these communities often cannot conceive of alternatives even when they seek different paths.
SYSTEMS WORK	**PRACTICE: CULTIVATE COLLECTIVES** *Enabling a collectively constructed identity with technology-based platforms* Reconstructed Living Labs (RLabs) was initially formed as a nonprofit for managing the mobile app Jamiix—a mobile counseling platform designed by a group of people who were formerly gang members and drug dealers. The core team realized that the app was not the point of their emerging organization; it was just the channel. Rather, it was *what* they were channeling that was important: a sense of connection among those who had similar life experiences that could displace the feelings of

belonging that gang membership and drug use had provided in the past. Upon this sense of unity, vulnerable youth could construct a new path forward and reconstruct their lives. RLabs differentiates itself from other technology upskilling programs that influence the behavior of individuals by focusing its activities on creating a new web of relationships. By connecting those with lived experience of an issue with one another, individuals can explore new ways of seeing their current situation. From within the safety of their collective identity, they can then challenge the status quo and create new life pathways.

TACTIC: BUILD A "WE"

RLabs' training and incubation platforms are a sophisticated way of developing a new collective identity for youth and communities. Technology and knowledge are a draw for young people, but not sufficient to sustain their commitment to new ways of thinking and living. With its activities, RLabs creates trust and togetherness that lead to a collective identity. This sense of "we-ness" stems from shared life experiences and orientation to the future. Empowered by their collective identity, individuals stay connected through their learning journey and into new life pathways.

TACTIC: POOL EXPERIENCES

At RLabs, collective identity is formed through "pooling" participants' experiences, challenges, ambitions, fears, and goals. Pooling is a different type of conversation that relies less on expertise and more on the exploration of mental models. For many, RLabs provides a unique opportunity to connect with peers and air their innermost thoughts and feelings. Through this process, participants are able to reinterpret events, thoughts, and feelings in the context of new information offered by the group. This process gives them a new understanding which they can direct towards new goals.

DEEP WORK

GROWING ACTION SYSTEMS

In contrast to traditional service delivery programming, the practice of cultivating collectives can appear slow and meandering. Yet, organizations like RLabs are "slowing down to go fast," using new collective identities to create action systems that facilitate broader change. To connect with one another and reflect is part of the process of "thinking together." As these conversations progress, grassroots issues can be brought to higher-level conversations with full acknowledgement of the complex issues that they entail. By facilitating conversations at multiple levels, organizations can create collectives and shift mental models at increasing levels of a system.

mothers2mothers

m2m.org
Founding: 2001 in South Africa
Core organization: 2,000+ mentor mothers, headquarters in Cape Town, South Africa
Geographic scope: 11.5 million mothers and their children supported across ten
countries in sub-Saharan Africa

SURFACE WORK	mothers2mothers (m2m) employs mothers living with HIV as "mentor mothers" who support pregnant women in the prevention of mother-to-child transmission (PMTCT) of HIV. Since 2014, m2m has consistently surpassed the UN's 5 percent target for reduced transmission rates in sub-Saharan Africa for enrolled participant mothers.
CONTEXT	**STATE OF TRAUMA** *Emotional isolation of HIV-positive mothers* Mothers living with HIV are 15–45 percent more likely to transmit the virus to their child without PMTCT treatment and education. For women living in regions with limited healthcare infrastructure, the social stigma following an HIV diagnosis is exacerbated by social and emotional distance between them and their doctors. Stunned by their diagnosis, fearful for their future, and worried about disclosing to partners and family, these women experience trauma that makes it very difficult to comprehend that there is hope for their baby and their own future.
SYSTEMS WORK	**PRACTICE: CULTIVATE COLLECTIVES** *Recruiting women with lived experience of HIV to form a community of mother-practitioners* When American obstetrician Mitch Besser began his work in South African training hospital Groote Schuur in 2000, he could see that his words were simply not getting through to newly diagnosed pregnant women living with HIV. His solution was to invest in a deceptively simple technology: a new relationship. To do this, he chose the very women who would most easily connect with his patients: new mothers living with HIV. m2m employs and trains "mentor mothers" to share their personal experiences as they provide vital PMTCT information. m2m's role is to bring together mothers in a safe and accessible environment where they can freely share their experiences of fear and stigma following from HIV diagnosis. In the process of sharing, mothers connect and form a collective identity around their shared experiences that becomes a source of pride as they successfully manage their own health and that of their children.

TACTIC: SHIFT STIGMA TO PRIDE

Strong collectives can shift the shame associated with a stigmatized identity into a source of pride. When mothers with personal PMTCT experience and technical knowledge are brought together with newly diagnosed mothers, both participants are able to see themselves in a new and positive light. Mentor mothers take on expert status that gives them a unique ability to help others. Meanwhile, new mothers are given knowledge and support to prevent transmission of the virus to their child while building a relationship with a peer mentor who inspires pride and trust.

TACTIC: HOST SAFE HAVENS

Collective identities need "havens" in which to grow. New identities cannot be conjured up in a single meeting or consultation; they must be constructed through the process of being together with repeated interaction, ongoing dialogue, and even conflict. m2m supports this by providing the physical and psychological "containers" for mothers to come together and spend time with one another. Physically, mentor mothers are situated in clinics so that they can be fully integrated into government health teams. Psychologically, m2m uses creative processes and trainings to enable mentor mothers to prepare for the work of counseling others.

DEEP WORK

TRANSFORMING MENTAL MODELS

In many social systems—health, education, youth development—the ability to stop, listen, and reflect has become nearly impossible. Despite the significant time and energy involved, organizations like m2m actively employ the right people and open up significant time for transformational conversations. By sharing life experiences, mentor mothers are able to "unfreeze" their own mental models about HIV, including the stigma and shame associated with the virus. These new mental models become an integral part of their conversations with newly diagnosed pregnant women, giving them a chance to open their minds to new ways of thinking.

Family Independence Initiative

www.fii.org
Founding: 2001 in Oakland, California
Core organization: 3,500+ family partners across United States
Geographic scope: Sites in eight US cities

SURFACE WORK	Family Independence Initiative (FII) offers an alternative to the standard social service model, providing groups of families with a platform for mutuality: tracking goals, accessing resources, and sharing knowledge. Families have reported an average 22 percent increase in income and a 55 percent decrease in government subsidies over two years.
CONTEXT	**POLICY FAILURES** *Funding programs instead of people* In the United States, multi-million-dollar government-funded programs too often fail to keep individuals out of poverty over the long term. By design, the bulk of funding is allocated to program running costs, supporting an ecosystem of full-time professionals, contractors, and consultants. In the late 1990s, social program manager Mauricio Lim Miller observed that these social services, rather than eliminating poverty, only make poverty more tolerable. Even worse, he suspected that the sector actually existed to maintain and benefit those in positions of power and privilege, not to help the poor out of poverty. Even as he was himself managing a program with over a hundred social workers serving thousands of troubled youth, he felt like a fraud. Families cycled in and out of poverty programs while he and his team of social workers enjoyed steady employment.
SYSTEMS WORK	**PRACTICE: EQUIP PROBLEM-SOLVERS** *Trusting and investing in families to fulfill their own goals* Drawing on his own experience as the son of an immigrant mother, Mauricio studied the mutual support approaches used by immigrant communities. Mauricio wondered, "What if professionals didn't help at all? What would it look like if they merely supported families as they lifted themselves up? And what if they shared this knowledge across groups and communities, and let them choose for themselves what might work or not?" In 2001, Mauricio founded the FII to experiment with this alternative approach. It was a simple concept: low-income families come together in groups chosen from their own personal networks and work together to set goals for savings, employment, and income generation that meet their individual family needs. FII's role is to provide the tools and structures for families to solve their own problems.

TACTIC: CIRCULATE DATA

FII equips families with two types of data: (1) data from family members, generated from a monthly journaling system for tracking income management; and (2) data from across families and groups through an internal social network called UpTogether. Through this network, families share successes and failures, and provide advice and support to each other online. The network has the effect of "social signaling," a mechanism that shows avenues for reaching goals, while also providing motivation to FII families.

TACTIC: DECENTRALIZE DECISION-MAKING

FII realized that problems which are complex at the system level are less complex at the individual level. For this reason, the power to choose a course of action should be decentralized. FII is therefore focused on sharing data widely rather than reserving it for elite decision-makers. FII provides families with real-time insights to empower them to make their own decisions. By alternating between small, daily decisions and larger stories of success, people can navigate their own context.

DEEP WORK

USING ECONOMIES OF TRUST

Organizations like FII operate with "economies of trust." FII maintains that when groups of people are supported with knowledge and skills, they make decisions that are useful for themselves and for those with whom they share a strong identity. Groups with lived experience or full immersion in a context can more easily navigate their own complexity. Consequently, FII does not need to control outcomes—rather, they build responsive systems guided by a combination of self- and group-interest that naturally and creatively respond to problems in surprising and effective ways.

Buurtzorg

www.buurtzorg.com
Founding: 2006 in the Netherlands
Core organization: 10,000+ nurses serving 70,000 patients in the Netherlands
Geographic scope: 700 teams across thirty-five countries

SURFACE WORK	Buurtzorg provides home-based healthcare by positioning teams of highly skilled nurses in neighborhoods to deliver care to patients. On average, Buurtzorg patients recover faster and need fewer days of care. The organization's administrative costs comprise only 8 percent of total expenses compared to the 25 percent industry average.
CONTEXT	**BROKEN STRUCTURES** *An expensive and ineffective system for nurses and patients* The Dutch healthcare system, like many health systems across the world, faces a challenge to meet the needs of a growing number of people who need long-term care. To optimize the use of resources, in the 1990s, a layer of professional management was added to the system, while nurses were allocated to higher-value roles, performing only highly skilled tasks. Merging neighborhoods into larger organizations was expected to create efficiencies, however the opposite has occurred. Quality of care, patient satisfaction, and employee satisfaction declined, while costs increased precipitously.
SYSTEMS WORK	**PRACTICE: EQUIP PROBLEM-SOLVERS** *Distributing action and decision-making to the people closest to the work* In 2006, Jos de Blok was one of the community nurses who had risen to the managerial ranks of the new system. Like many of his colleagues, he was disgruntled and disillusioned. Digging deep into his own experience, he realized much of his motivation came from solving problems for patients and feeling the satisfaction of helping someone through a hardship. Collaborating with friends and colleagues, Jos and his wife Gonnie Kronenberg founded Buurtzorg to "connect to the intrinsic motivation of the nurses . . . so that they would be the carriers of the vision and the concepts," as Jos described it. Buurtzorg means "neighborhood care" and has a no-hierarchy structure with teams operating autonomously and making decisions collectively. At its core, Buurtzorg does not see itself in the business of delivering health services; it sees itself first and foremost as supporting problem-solvers.

TACTIC: POSITION PROBLEM-SOLVERS

Buurtzorg nurses are highly qualified, self-motivated professionals who focus on achieving the maximum degree of independence for patients as possible. They do this by working in teams of ten to twelve without supervision from a head office. There are no managers, either at the central or team levels. Teams meet regularly, taking turns to set agendas and collectively determine how to handle emerging issues. If they run into issues, they can access regional coaches who act strictly as facilitators. This independence allows them to come up with unique and individualized approaches for their patients.

TACTIC: SUSTAIN MOTIVATION

Buurtzorg has consistently shown that higher-quality care can be delivered at below-average costs when motivated teams are able to unlock their problem-solving potential on the ground. Buurtzorg believes this comes from two sources: capacity and motivation. When the capacity of a person is matched to their attitude and motivation, and aligned in the pursuit of a singular goal, the problem-solving nature of a person is unlocked. Buurtzorg hires highly educated nurses, supports them with upskilling opportunities as they grow, and ensures that they have the time and latitude to care for patients as whole people.

DEEP
WORK

UNLOCKING CONTEXTUAL RESPONSIVENESS

Buurtzorg maintains that when groups of people are motivated by their own attitude and capacity, traditional hierarchies are far less necessary. Management structures are lean, with the greatest investment put into the "front lines." Teams of frontline workers are not supervised in the classic sense; they are able to make decisions about their own teams, patients, and neighborhoods. Codified programs and standard operating procedures are useful, but not the driving force behind quality and impact. When unintended consequences inevitably arise, Buurtzorg is equipped to deal with them on a scale that is manageable and within a timeframe that is reasonable.

Slum Dwellers International (SDI)

www.knowyourcity.info
Founding: 1996 in India
Core organization: Headquarters in Cape Town, South Africa
Geographic scope: Active partners in more than fifteen countries across Asia, Africa, and Latin America

SURFACE WORK	Slum Dwellers International (SDI) is an organization that connects slum communities around the world as part of a global movement of the urban poor to ensure that they are part of the planning process for urban development. The SDI platform links more than a million slum dwellers in 527 cities globally.
CONTEXT	**DISPLACEMENT OF PEOPLE AND LIVES** *Urbanization at the expense of the poor* In cities around the world, economic growth and a rise in inequality result in large portions of the population living in informal areas, often in close proximity to high- and middle-income areas. Slum eradication schemes are often seen as a necessary step to accelerate urban development. The demolition of the waterfront fishing settlement of Otodo-Gbame by police outside of Lagos, Nigeria, in 2016 stands as a stark example of these often-violent schemes. The destruction in this case amounted to nine deaths, seventeen missing persons, five razed primary schools, and thirty thousand displaced persons.
SYSTEMS WORK	**PRACTICE: PROMOTE PLATFORMS** *Balancing grassroots activities and big-picture advocacy* SDI was founded in 1996 by the late Jockin Arputham, a carpenter from outside Bangalore who moved to Mumbai at the age of eighteen. He soon discovered a penchant for organizing his fellow slum and pavement dwellers to resist the Indian state's eviction efforts. Jockin built SDI on the concept of peer-to-peer learning through horizontal exchanges, where community-based coalitions of slum dwellers visit other coalitions in countries with more established operations. These seemingly simple exchanges serve multiple purposes. First, emerging groups learn practical strategies for organizing, including participatory data collection, group savings schemes, and collective self-help approaches. Second, learning exchanges allow policy leaders to see what is possible and encourage pro-poor policies that integrate slum dwellers into the process of urban development. More than a network, SDI acts as a *platform*: a space for learning and collaboration, giving representative groups the foundation and tools to engage in high-level political action while keeping expertise close to the ground.

TACTIC: LINK GROUPS TOGETHER

SDI is more than a "network." Networks are built of transactions and are generally agnostic as to who participates or how. SDI is instead built of intentional relationships that enable participation from those who have been previously marginalized. SDI's unconventional way of organizing ensures that knowledge and experience travel horizontally *and* vertically, giving grassroots groups a genuine pathway to interact with one another as well as participate at higher levels of decision-making.

TACTIC: ENABLE PARTICIPATION

SDI's structure is like a giant funnel, an inversion of the standard operational organogram. Governance structures start with thousands of local groups—slum dwellers who self-organize at the neighborhood level and then elect leaders to sit at city, regional, and national levels. Fifteen national federations then appoint members to a transnational Council of Federations, which selects the Management Committee. At each of these levels, different tactics prevail, including protest action, policy negotiations, and even private sector investment funds.

DEEP WORK

THREE-DIMENSIONAL CHANGE

SDI's structure allows it to integrate the work of slum dwellers vertically and horizontally to achieve a kind of multi-scalar impact. Local efforts are driven by the day-to-day political context, while national and transnational affiliation enables slum dwellers to develop a "globalized" imagination about what is possible in their own setting. Rather than offering easy solutions, platforms require participants to deeply engage with what is happening on the ground, learn from the experiences of others, and then experiment with the application of these ideas in their own context.

Child and Youth Finance International (CYFI)

www.childfinanceinternational.org
Founding: 2010
Core organization: Netherlands
Geographic scope: Collaborations with people and organizations in 175 countries

SURFACE WORK	Child and Youth Finance International (CYFI) convened stakeholders from around the world to empower children as "economic citizens." When it closed its doors at the end of 2019, seventy countries had adopted child-friendly policies and 63,000 organizations in 175 countries were mobilized to improve children's financial literacy.
CONTEXT	**POVERTY AT SCALE** *Intergenerational poverty across countries* Children in families burdened by the stress of severe financial difficulties often face vulnerabilities including hunger, poor health, sexual and emotional abuse, and bullying. These vulnerabilities are likely to persist into adulthood if children are not prepared for the economic challenges they will face as adults. Children's financial education reflects their parents' knowledge and access and may be limited in these circumstances. They do not have their own money, bank accounts, or financial instruments to start saving for their future. And as children, they have even less access to people, resources, and platforms for voicing their concerns, learning and developing, and getting support than an adult in their position. Children in these circumstances become part of a cycle of intergenerational poverty and are likely to end up in the same position as their parents.
SYSTEMS WORK	**PRACTICE: PROMOTE PLATFORMS** *Harnessing the power and expertise of different primary actors for collective learning* CYFI was founded by Jeroo Billimoria to empower children to become full "economic citizens": educated about money and financial matters with access to child-friendly bank accounts. Through her previous enterprises, Jeroo developed a "process model" for organizing that became the basis for CYFI. "Collaborative systems change" envisions a type of social change where teams and organizations working across the world come together, learn from each other's experiences, celebrate each other's successes, and return to adapt what works for their context. The organization was small by design with never more than twenty-five full-time employees and a

budget of less than US$2 million. Its core activities positioned it as an "honest broker" to bring actors together. In 2019, the organization closed its doors and transferred key projects to other institutions because they believed their members had gained enough momentum for them to cease operations.

TACTIC: ENCOURAGE COLLABORATION

CYFI's process model includes five ways to flexibly collaborate with diverse groups of stakeholders, including convening, connecting, co-creating, celebrating, and calibrating. The movement was launched with a convening that brought together 120 stakeholders and experts from over forty countries. This event was followed by long-term engagement through issue-based working groups and regional convenings. Throughout, CYFI extensively documented country-level policy changes and circulated these learnings for country representatives to monitor and chart their progress.

TACTIC: OBSERVE RITUALS

For platform-style organizations, rituals provide necessary structure in the absence of traditional hierarchy. CYFI hosted gatherings, such as annual awards events and regional learning sessions, where celebration and play were a key component of the agenda. CYFI's celebrations were dramatic and colourful, with children and youth often present, turning financial conversations into a chance to connect professional work to future generations. The main purpose of these events was to catalyze decision-makers to bring about durable changes to policies and practices in a playful, positive way.

DEEP WORK

KEEPING PEOPLE TOGETHER

Groups engaged in change efforts need to see that their efforts are delivering progress against a bigger picture of change. They also need to be encouraged and incentivized by similar groups engaged in the same efforts. CYFI created numerous configurations for collaboration—annual events, working groups, regional convenings—creating positive peer pressure among country teams as they worked toward financial inclusion for youth. These experiences encouraged participants to stay together while learning over many years and changing conditions.

Nidan

www.nidan.in
Founding: 1996 in India
Core organization: New Delhi, India
Geographic scope: 400,000 informal workers across twenty-five states in India

SURFACE WORK	Nidan advances the rights and status of informal workers by elevating informal workers into positions of political, economic, and cultural power alongside existing decision-makers. Nidan estimates this work has served a million people and fifty thousand families across the country.
CONTEXT	**INSTITUTIONAL EXCLUSION** *Lack of protection for workers in the informal economy* A dominant belief among labour economists is that informal work is merely a temporary imbalance on the road to economic development. Based on this belief, developing countries such as India often view formal employment as the first step to standard protections under formal labour laws. Seeing informal workers as a scourge, local police in Indian cities often clear street vendors from traditional marketplaces, imposing heavy fines for vendors to retrieve their goods and equipment. One event that has come to epitomize the government overstep was "Operation Sunshine," where police in Kolkata took to clearing the pavements of major streets around the city to prepare for a visit from the UK prime minister. In the process, they destroyed the livelihoods of a hundred thousand vendors.
SYSTEMS WORK	**PRACTICE: DISRUPT POLICIES AND PATTERNS** *Using policy to re-shape the dominant attitudes toward informal workers* Nidan was one of many organizations that emerged in the 1990s to combat the actions against street vendors. Founder Arbind Singh realized that he needed to start with shifting street vendors' powerlessness in the economic life of the city. Nidan decided to fight for legal recognition and self-governance as vital contributors to India's emerging economy. Nidan works to incubate what they call "people's institutions." Over twenty years, Nidan has incubated twenty-two self-sustaining and independent organizations to realize the interests of different groups of informal workers. Each of the organizations uses a slightly different tack. Some exert political pressure on government to incorporate the rights of informal workers into policy and law. Others create more consistent economic markets for goods and services provided by informal workers. Still others work to change the cultural perception of informal products and services through training and positive publicity. These organizations take on numerous legal structures: cooperatives, unions, membership associations, and even for-profit companies.

TACTIC: ADVOCATE FOR PARTICIPATORY POLICIES

Under the Street Vendors Act that Nidan fought for, street vendors were granted direct participation in governance through Town Vending Committees (TVCs), for which street vendors were guaranteed 40 percent of the seats. The process required to secure this legislation—widespread protest, petitions, and hunger strikes—was an important part of creating change after the victory as it unified vendors around a shared understanding of their value. For this reason, the participatory policies became gateways to new patterns of behavior throughout the various "people's institutions."

TACTIC: CREATE NEW MEANINGS AND VALUES

Nidan's tactics were born out of a survey conducted by the National Association of Street Vendors (NASVI) which revealed that street vending was not a nuisance to ignore, but rather an important and valued service in the urban economy. Consumers patronized street vendors for convenience and affordability; street vendors responded as hardworking entrepreneurs to meet these needs. Nidan decided to shift the value assigned to street vendors, highlighting their vital contribution to Indian life and culture. To do this, they host food festivals and hygiene training that celebrate and professionalize the role of street vendors.

DEEP WORK

SHIFTING MEANINGS ACROSS CONTEXTS

As the nature of work has changed across the world, Nidan's promoted policies and patterns are considered relevant not just in India but globally. In response, Nidan has launched a new initiative called the "Self Worker Movement" to relate the needs of informal workers with those of the "precariat"— zero-hours contract workers who form an increasing percentage of the global workforce. This movement has struck a chord with labour organizers, who have witnessed the decline of the traditional worker movement and has the potential to apply the policies and patterns from Nidan's India experience to a far greater audience.

Fundación Escuela Nueva

www.escuelanueva.org
Founding: 1987 in Colombia
Core organization: Bogotá, Colombia
Geographic scope: Model implemented in sixteen countries across Latin America and Asia

---

SURFACE WORK	Fundación Escuela Nueva (FEN) promotes a school model with students as active learners and teachers as facilitators. The model has inspired educational reforms worldwide. Students at these schools perform better and have lower grade repetition and drop-out rates compared to national averages.
CONTEXT	**DOMESTIC DIVIDES** *Inequities in rural school systems* In the 1980s, the Colombian school system was buckling under the strain induced by armed conflict and lack of state presence. People living in rural areas bore the brunt of this turmoil, with stark inequities between cities and rural regions persisting to this day. The adverse impacts on rural communities meant that teachers had limited educational resources and no support system, resulting in three major challenges for rural schools: guaranteeing complete basic primary education, training and ongoing teaching support, and relevance of curricular content.
SYSTEMS WORK	**PRACTICE: DISRUPT POLICIES AND PATTERNS** *Reconfiguring power by shifting roles, routines, and responsibilities* Escuela Nueva is a model of education which promotes children as active creators of knowledge through exploration, discussion, and self-expression. As Colombia's National Coordinator for Unitary Schools and Rural Education, Vicky co-authored Escuela Nueva in the mid 1970s by introducing a systemic approach to the curriculum, teacher training, and community participation; accompanied by instructional materials for teachers and students. She also developed an experiential training strategy and support system for teachers and engaged students, parents, and communities to make the content relevant. The model was ultimately rolled out as a national policy to twenty thousand Colombian schools. However, in the late 1990s, the national rollout was disrupted by the decentralization process of the entire educational system. In the rural communities where the model was implemented, old patterns were disrupted and expectations of how a school functions shifted. The success of the model, and its vulnerability to

political and administrative changes, led Vicky to establish FEN to promote the model more widely. FEN disseminates knowledge and forges connections across schools and countries that want to fundamentally change their approach to education.

TACTIC: DRIVE SMALL WEDGES	TACTIC: PRACTICE NEW PATTERNS AT ALL LEVELS
Policies—rules, laws, standards, or guidance—are often needed to "drive small wedges" so that new patterns can emerge. When policies create space for new activities, new patterns— expectations, values, and beliefs—can take root. Escuela Nueva was implemented across an entire country with extreme fervor, then lost its momentum. However, teachers, parents, and students maintained many of Escuela Nueva's features, ensuring that the changes that the model introduced were durable over the long term.	FEN promotes new patterns at the micro, meso, and macro levels of the system. Escuela Nueva puts children in charge of their own learning, allowing them to set their own pace under the guidance of the teacher and the support of fellow students. Teachers move into new roles as facilitators, children step into roles of active, learning, and parents are engaged to make learning content relevant. Everyone shares the responsibility of school administration, creating new connections to principals and government officials, as well as an environment where children learn and thrive.

DEEP
WORK

SHIFTING PATTERNS ACROSS SCALES

When policies are undone by political and administrative changes, organizations like FEN that have done pattern work will likely find that their changes endure in subtle yet important ways. In the thousands of schools where Escuela Nueva has been introduced, an entire generation of children, along with their teachers, parents, and communities, have developed new expectations for what schooling should be like. Escuela Nueva has been challenging the meaning of education for nearly forty years and has gained international recognition for the crucial deeper work that they are doing. Today, FEN has expanded its reach as an advisor and technical supporter of the Escuela Nueva model, influencing national education systems that reach children in sixteen countries and counting.

Endnotes

Epigraph

1. Max-Neef, M. A. (2009). From knowledge to understanding—Navigation and returns. *What Next Volume II*. Retrieved from https://whatnext.org/research_pubs/what-next-volume-ii-the-case-for-pluralism/.

Introduction

1. The phrase "freedom from want" comes from Franklin D Roosevelt's "Four Freedoms speech" delivered on January 6, 1941, which proposed four fundamental freedoms that people "everywhere in the world" should enjoy.
2. Paul Hawken's *Blessed Unrest* unifies the varied and disparate social activist work of the past sixty years under the singular banner of a "movement" characterized by shared values, sensitivity, pragmatism, diversity, and scale. At the time of writing in 2007, Hawken estimated there were some two million organizations across the world with the purpose of social justice and environmental sustainability. And yet, the movement as a whole is leaderless, driven by the self-organization of tens of millions of people who have consciously taken action in service of a goal that is bigger than their individual material needs.

    Hawken, P. (2007). *Blessed unrest: How the largest movement in the world came into being, and why no one saw it coming*. New York: Penguin.
3. The claim of declining global poverty rates is sometimes disputed on the basis of the appallingly low poverty line used to determine who is poor and who is not—World Bank uses a threshold of just $1.90 per day for extreme poverty. The World Bank data on global poverty up to 2013 show poverty rates have been falling across various poverty lines (daily consumption of $10.00, $3.10, $1.90, and $1.25) for a decade. This suggests extreme global poverty is genuinely declining in real terms with the increase in income for those at the bottom, and not as a consequence of artificially low poverty lines.

    Ortiz-Ospina, E., and Diana Beltekian (2018). Extreme poverty is falling: How is poverty changing for higher poverty lines? *Our World in Data*. Retrieved from https://ourworldindata.org/poverty-at-higher-poverty-lines.
4. Data from the United Nations, the OECD, and the World Bank, analyzed and presented by *Our World in Data* show dramatic advances in global health over the last two hundred years.

Roser, M., Ortiz-Ospina, E., and Ritchie, H. (2019). Life Expectancy. *Our World in Data*. Retrieved from https://ourworldindata.org/life-expectancy.

Roser, M. (2019). Child Mortality. *Our World in Data*. Retrieved from https://ourworldindata.org/child-mortality.

5. Based on World Bank's poverty line of $1.90 per day, extreme poverty around the world, adjusting for inflation and price differences between countries, has decreased from 89 percent in 1820 to 10 percent in 2015.

Roser, M. (2018). The short history of global living conditions and why it matters that we know it. *Our World in Data*. Retrieved from https://ourworldindata.org/a-history-of-global-living-conditions-in-5-charts.

6. Undernourishment, or the percent of the population whose caloric intake is insufficient to meet their energy requirements, is the UN's key hunger indicator. Data on global undernourishment prior to 1990 are limited. Although reports from the UN Food and Agriculture Organization (FAO) differ on exact figures, they place the undernourishment rate for 1970 between 32.5 percent (http://www.fao.org/3/a0750e/a0750e00.htm) and 37 percent (http://www.fao.org/3/i1683e/i1683e.pdf) for developing nations.

Roser, M., and Ritchie, H. (2019). Hunger and undernourishment. *Our World in Data*. Retrieved from https://ourworldindata.org/hunger-and-undernourishment.

7. A 2016 survey of 23,000 people across twenty-one countries showed that on average, even if people felt 2016 had been a good year for themselves, their families, and their countries, that they felt it had been a bad year for the world as a whole.
   https://yougov.co.uk/topics/international/articles-reports/2016/12/30/global-survey-2016-has-been-bad-year-world.

8. Hans Rosling's viral TED talk used jarring data visualization to demonstrate the extreme improvements in global developments over the past century. The presentation was emblematic of the work of the Gapminder Foundation, a nonprofit organization he co-founded to produce and promote accurate analysis of global development indicators. Gapminder echoes Hawken in its assessment of the current landscape: "More people than ever care about global development! The world has never been less bad. Which doesn't mean it's perfect."
   https://www.gapminder.org/about/ and https://www.ted.com/talks/hans_rosling_shows_the_best_stats_you_ve_ever_seen.

9. The "wickedness" of the problems Horst Rittel and Melvin Webber described in their pivotal research on social planning and design comes from their refusal to be tamed by analytical problem-solving approaches. Recognizing the complexity of social, political, and environmental systems, a facet which had come into relief with the waves of activism in the United States in the late 1960s, they went on to reject the utility of closed-system scientific methods in favor of more open-system, communication-oriented, feedback-based approaches. At the

time, the researchers did not anticipate the relevance of their concept to issues of global development. But in the twenty-first century, their insights about wicked problems have been applied to everything where collective action is prized, from climate change to economic policy.

Crowley, K., and Head, B. W. (2017). The enduring challenge of "wicked problems": revisiting Rittel and Webber. *Policy Sciences*, 50: 539–47.

Rittel, H. W., and Webber, M. M. (1973). Dilemmas in a general theory of planning. *Policy Sciences*, 4(2): 155–69.

10. In his 2008 text *Common Wealth*, Jeffrey Sachs observes we are now in a phase of tapered growth that requires us to recognize that our previous trajectory—where individual nation states competed and controlled to secure their own prosperity—is not sustainable for ensuring the health of the planet, reducing inequality, and eliminating extreme poverty. He surmises the fates of all humans, countries, and all possible groupings of people on planet Earth, are bound and inextricable, and that our global systems and values should reflect this.

Sachs, J. (2008). *Common wealth: Economics for a crowded planet*. New York: Penguin.

11. Rittel, H. W., and Webber, M. M. (1973). Dilemmas in a general theory of planning. *Policy Sciences*, 4(2): 155–69.

12. We use this term with some trepidation, but acknowledge the lack of mean-ingful alternatives. The *Global South* has emerged as an alternative term to *Third World*, *developing countries*, or *emerging economies*, terms which have political and hegemonic connotations. The Global South generally refers to countries in Africa, Asia, and Latin America. Of course, the questionable boundaries of the "south" and vast inequality within many southern hemi-sphere countries has invited criticism of the term and suggested that the descriptors of "north" and "south" do not connote geography but the degree of wealth and power.

13. François joined the Schwab Foundation of Social Entrepreneurship as director in 2019.

14. The definitions of systems change that we draw on come from a diverse set of players who are doing global development work at different levels and in dif-ferent systems. London Funders is a charitable company that creates effective pathways to city-level development by uniting different stakeholders under the same project roofs. They draw on principles of systems change as a new way of working to understand the efficacy of their funding processes.

Wharton, R., and Evans, A. (2015). Systems change: What it is and how to do it. *London Funders*.

15. The Canadian initiative Social Innovation Generation, a collaboration between university, nonprofit, and private foundation partners, grounds systems change within the core of social innovation. Their focus is on shifting full-picture eco-nomic, cultural, and political context so that innovation can flourish.

Kania, J., Kramer, M., and Senge, P. (2018). The water of systems change. *FSG*.

16. The Schwab Foundation looks at systems change with social entrepreneurs who design and develop interventions across different sectors and geographies in mind. Their definition helps them elide organizational scale in favor of systemic scale to replicate outcomes of system change without prescribing the model for achieving those outcomes.

World Economic Forum. (2016). Beyond organizational scale: How social entrepreneurs create systems change. https://www.weforum.org/reports/beyond-organizational-scale-how-social-entrepreneurs-create-systems-change.

17. Social change consultants Srik Gopal and John Kania are particularly interested in how the foundation, as an organizational archetype that has broadly embraced notions of "systemic change" in name, can effectively apply the principles in practice. Their definition is broad to match the different scales, impact areas, and goals of foundations that nevertheless share the larger goal of increased global prosperity.

Gopal, S., and Kania, J. (2015). Fostering systems change. *Stanford Social Innovation Review*.

18. A browse through the reports produced within our community of practice over the last five years shows the emergence and propagation of systems change in the social change lexicon. In 2017: "Scaling solutions toward shifting systems" from the Rockefeller Philanthropy Advisors and "Solving the world's biggest problems: Better philanthropy through systems change" from New Profit. In 2018: "The water of systems change" from FSG and "Brokering collaborative systems change" from CYFI. In 2019: "Seven steps for funding systems change" from Ashoka and the systems change "Handbook" from Co-Impact.

Ashoka (2020). Embracing complexity: Towards a shared understanding of funding systems change. *Ashoka Deutschland* and *McKinsey & Company*.

19. Foster-Fishman, P. G., Nowell, B., and Yang, H. (2007). Putting the system back into systems change: A framework for understanding and changing organizational and community systems. *American Journal of Community Psychology* 39: 197–215.

20. System dynamics was developed by Jay Forrester as a methodology for understanding complex systems through mathematical modeling. Forrester was one of the first to use computer-based simulations to model systems for application in industrial process controls and business cycles. His method embodies the *technical approach* we go on to describe, which trusts that with the correct amount of information, we can create models that are effective tools for understanding and controlling systems. However, like those who would take the more *transformative approach*, Forrester cautions against reductionism and reliance on incorrect mental models that don't reflect the true nature of the relationships within the system.

Forrester, J. W. (2013). Modeling for what purpose? *The Systems Thinker*, 24(2).

21. Social innovation researcher Christian Seelos is the director of the Global Innovation for Impact Lab at Stanford University. His contributions to the research on social enterprises, which have deeply informed our own research, are captured well in his book *Innovation and Scaling for Impact*, co-authored with Johanna Mair. Here, they challenge the idea of innovation as a holy grail for creating impact. Rather, they see innovation as a process that involves gains, losses, and learning, and the scaling of innovation as the key to creating impact.

Seelos, C., and Mair, J. (2017). *Innovation and scaling for impact: How effective social enterprises do it*. Berkeley, CA: Stanford University Press.

22. The underpinnings of biologist Ludwig von Bertalanffy's general systems theory mirrors that of Rittel and Webber's wicked problems concept. Taking the living organism as his system, he proposed that the physical laws governing closed systems did not apply to this case as organisms were open, aka general, systems.

von Bertalanffy, L. (1951). Problems of general system theory. *Human Biology*, 23(4): 302–12.

23. As Christian Seelos brought to our attention, a fundamental misinterpretation of the English translation of von Bertalanffy's writings, originally written in German, obscured the intent of his writings. His aim was not to present a unified theory of systems but to propose a new paradigm altogether for how we study, understand, and develop theories about systems.

von Bertalanffy, L. (1974). *Perspectives on general systems theory*. New York: Braziller.

24. Funders like London Funders, New Philanthropy Capital, and Lankelly Chase Foundation feel the challenge of making change actionable, especially when buzzwords like "systems change" muddy the waters. Their guide to systems change addresses this concern by offering a taxonomy for the roots, beliefs, and practices of systems change from a variety of perspectives.

Abercrombie, R., Harries, E., and Wharton, R. (2015). Systems change: A guide to what it is and how to do it. London: New Philanthropy Capital, and Lankelly Chase. https://lankellychase.org.uk/resources/publications/systems-change-a-guide-to-what-it-is-and-how-to-do-it/.

25. The reference to technical and transformative approaches has been covered with slight differences in previous work.

Nilsson, W., Bonnici, F., and Wosu Griffin-EL, E. (2014). The social innovation lab: An experiment in the pedagogy of institutional work. In V. Bitzer et al. (eds). *The business of social and environmental innovation* (pp. 201–12). New York: Springer.

Seelos, C., and Mair, J. (2017). *Innovation and scaling for impact: How effective social enterprises do it.* Berkeley, CA: Stanford University Press.

26. Yaneer Bar-Yam is president of the New England Complex Systems Institute, an independent research organization dedicated to the study of complex systems science. The systems in question range from biological systems to ecological systems to social systems. In his text *Making Things Work*, Bar-Yam explores the tension between the observation that complex problems cannot be solved by a singular actor, and that traditional approaches to organizing for collective action are equally ineffective.

Yam, B. Y. (2005). *Making things work: Solving complex problems in a complex world.* Cambridge, MA: Knowledge Press.

27. We credit Thomas Lawrence, Roy Suddaby, and Bernard Leca for their concept of "work" in the field of institutional theory. This exciting area of scholarship has reinserted individual and organizational agency into institutional theory, highlighting the day-to-day practices and activities that are "aimed at creating, maintaining and disrupting institutions."

Lawrence, T., Suddaby, R., and Leca, B. (2011). Institutional work: Refocusing institutional studies of organization. *Journal of Management Inquiry*, 20(1): 52–8.

Chapter 1

1. Paul Mangelsdorf was internationally recognized for his expertise in plant breeding. His work in the field made him a key consultant to the Rockefeller Foundation (RF) when they enlisted him to assist with an analysis of Mexican food production.

Birchler, J. A. (2014). Paul C. Manglesdorf 1899–1989: A biographical memoir. *National Academy of Sciences.*

2. As the most senior American specialist in soil science in the 1930s, Richard Bradfield served and led a series of domestic and international councils, advisories, and research bodies before joining Mangelsdorf on the RF's agricultural survey in Mexico.

Cline, M. G. (1982). *Agronomy at Cornell.* Agronomy Mimeo No. 82-16. New York: Cornell University.

3. The early career research of plant pathologist Elvin C. Stakman on the stem rust fungus in plants brought him to international prestige as an expert in plant disease affecting wheat and other crops, which led to his selection as a consultant for the RF survey.

Christensen, C. M. (1992). Elvin Charles Stakman 1885–1979: A biographical memoir. *National Academy of Sciences.*

4. In 1967, Stakman, Bradfield, and Mangelsdorf published a book about their experiences conducting the survey in which they re-assert their recommendations and commitment to the idea of agricultural technology as a pathway to human prosperity. They also write: "We came to work and learn together with you." But as Angus Wright notes in a critical essay on the entire process, "the fact that all were trained in the sciences, with virtually no input from social scientists or historians, reflected the unexamined assumption that the solutions to hunger were all to be found in technology. There was no serious attempt to analyze the agrarian reform program" (2012, p. 35).

Stakman, E. C., Bradfield, R., and Mangelsdorf, P. C. (1967). *Campaigns against hunger.* Cambridge, MA: Harvard University Press.

Wright, A. (2012). *A land between waters: Environmental histories of modern Mexico.* Tucson, AZ: University of Arizona Press.

5. Henry A. Wallace came from an agricultural family and developed a passion for corn production as a young man under the tutelage of the botanist George Washington Carver, a colleague of his father's at Iowa State College. In 1926, he founded Pioneer Hi-Breds, one of the first companies to develop mass-produced commercial hybrid corn seed. Despite leaving farming for the world of politics in 1933, Wallace remained steeped in the corporate and scientific discourse in the industry.

Brown, W. L. (1983). H. A. Wallace and the development of hybrid corn. *The Annals of Iowa,* 47: 167–79.

6. In later years, Wallace would regard himself as "the father of industrial agriculture" for his work at Pioneer and subsequent role in the RF's foreign aid programs.

Dowie, M. (2001). *American foundations: An investigative history.* Cambridge, MA: The MIT Press.

7. Connelly, M. R., and Cotter, J. (2003). *Troubled harvest: Agronomy and revolution in Mexico, 1880–2002.* Westport, CT: Greenwood Publishing Group.

8. Patel, R. (2013). The long green revolution. *The Journal of Peasant Studies,* 40(1): 1–63.

9. (Dowie, 2001)

10. (Dowie, 2001, p. 107)

11. Perkins, J. H. (1990). The Rockefeller Foundation and the Green Revolution, 1941–1956. *Agriculture and Human Values,* 7(3): 6–18.

12. (Perkins, 1990)

13. As the owners of Standard Oil, the Rockefeller family was one of the American investors who saw their Mexican business interests pummeled in 1933 when the revolutionary leader Lazaro Cardenas took office. Cardenas seized corporate lands and assets without compensation, a matter that was still tied up in diplomatic discussions by the time RF was considering launching an agricultural program in 1940.

Perkins, J. H. (1990). The Rockefeller Foundation and the Green Revolution, 1941–1956. *Agriculture and Human Values*, 7(3): 6–18.

14. (Dowie, 2001, ch. Food, "Skeptics Ignored", para. 5)

15. (Dowie, 2001, ch. Food, "Skeptics Ignored", para. 7)

16. (Dowie, 2001)

17. (Dowie, 2001, ch. Food, "Surplus and Poverty", para. 13)

18. Researcher Raj Patel notes the similarity in the language used in RF's "Notes on Indian Agriculture" and its Mexico reports. He and Perkins (1990) both zero in on the inside descriptions used with regard to overpopulation: "The villages . . . are as uniform as so many ant hills. Indeed, from the air, where a number of villages may be seen simultaneously, they have the appearance of structures built by creatures motivated largely by inherited animal instincts, and devoid of any inclination to depart from a fixed hereditary pattern. The inheritance in this instance, of course, is social" (Harrar et al., 1952, p. 3).

Harrar, J. G., Mangelsdorf, P. C., and Weaver, W. (1952). Notes on Indian agriculture. *Rockefeller Foundation*.

19. Lele and Goldsmith (1989) and Djurfeldt et al. (2005) in Patel (2013, p. 14)

Patel, R. (2013). The long green revolution. *The Journal of Peasant Studies*, 40(1): 1–63.

Lele, U., and Goldsmith, A. A. (1989). The development of national agricultural research capacity: India's experience with the Rockefeller Foundation and its significance for Africa. *Economic Development and Cultural Change*, 37(2): 305–43.

Djurfeldt, G., Holmen, H., Jirstrom, M., and Larsson, R. (2005). *The African food crisis: Lessons from the Asian Green Revolution*. Wallingford, UK: CABI Publishing.

20. One of the major issues that arose in the wake of the introduction of high-yield varieties (HYV) in Asia was the bias toward regions of greater infrastructure and resources. Researcher Donald Freebairn cites how well-positioned producers with better physical access to markets, high quality soil, and irrigation systems were effectively given preference by the RF programs, leading to increased regional inequality.

Freebairn, D. K. (1995). Did the green revolution concentrate incomes? A quantitative study of research reports. *World Development*, 23(2): 265–79.

21. According to Dowie, "This 'proletarianization' of the peasantry was particularly hard on women, who were even less likely than their male peers to own land. Those unable to find jobs in the countryside moved reluctantly into crowded cities, where many resorted to prostitution" (p. 118).

22. (Dowie, 2001, ch. "Food", para. 3)

23. The century prior to the wars has been called the Progressive Era and was host to some of the most important social movements in human history, including the abolition of slavery in the United States and the women's suffrage movement globally. This period stood in stark contrast to the post-war period as it was marked by a strong distrust in government. Social movements of this period were typically seeking to change government policies.

Holloran, P. C., Cocks, C., and Lessoff, A. (2009). *The A to Z of the Progressive Era*. Lanham, MD: Scarecrow Press.

24. World War II casualty estimates range from 70–80 million people, or 3–4 percent of the population (Brzezinski, 1994). Seventy percent of the industrial infrastructure in Europe was destroyed (Pilisuk and Rountree, 2008). Although displacement estimates vary, one approximation pegs the number at 55 million people displaced as a result of the war (Gatrell, 2007).

Brzezinski, Z. (1993). *Out of control: Global turmoil on the eve of the twenty-first century*. New York, NY: Simon & Schuster.

Pilisuk, M., and Rountree, J. A. (2008). *Who benefits from global violence and war: Uncovering a destructive system*. Westport, CT: Greenwood Publishing Group.

Gatrell, P. (2007). Introduction: World Wars and population displacement in Europe in the twentieth century. *Contemporary European History*, 16(4): 415–26.

25. MacMillan, M. (2009). Rebuilding the world after the second world war. *The Guardian*.

26. As policy researcher Lester Salamon explains, "Indeed, for more than half a century—from the end of the American Civil War in the mid 1860s until the launching of the New Deal in the early 1930s—support for the nonprofit sector became a central part of the conservative ideology that was used to fend off proposals for expanded government social welfare protections" (2001, p. 19).

Salamon, L. M. (2001). The nonprofit at a crossroads: The case of America. In H. K. Anheier and J. Kendall (eds), *Third sector policy at the crossroads: An international nonprofit analysis* (pp. 17–35). New York, NY: Routledge.

27. Atkinson, A. B., and Piketty, T. (eds) (2007). *Top incomes over the twentieth century: A contrast between continental European and English-speaking countries*. Oxford, UK: Oxford University Press.

28. The intellectual institutions of post-war America were far from perfect. Universities and think tanks accepted military-oriented funding from the U.S. government and often provided the intellectual foundations for American imperialism. Nevertheless, the three decades after World War II—when corporate power was checked by a strong labor movement, higher education became broadly accessible, and social services were expanded—were the most democratic in American history.

Sessions, D. (2017). The rise of the thought leader: How the superrich have funded a new class of intellectual. *The New Republic*.

29. Steil, B. (2018, March 22). Ten fascinating facts about the Marshall Plan. *OUPBlog*. Retrieved from https://blog.oup.com/2018/03/ten-fascinating-facts-marshall-plan/.

30. In his landmark text *Political Process and the Development of the Black Insurgency, 1930–1970*, Stanford sociologist Doug McAdam presents a rigorous analysis of the U.S. Civil Rights Movement from which he developed a political process theory of social movements. Based on empirical evidence of the Civil Rights Movement, his model identifies three enablers of effective social movements for the group in question: strengthening of internal institutions and organizations, increased political opportunities, and faith in the efficacy of political processes.

    McAdam, D. (1982). *Political process and the development of the black insurgency, 1930–1970*. Chicago, IL: University of Chicago Press.

31. The end of the post-war golden age in America in the 1970s was marked by an international oil crisis, stagflation, and an economic recession. Unemployment almost doubled over the two years of the recession between 1973 and 1975, the U.S. dollar devalued dramatically, and GDP fell. It was a "perfect economic storm" (Corbett, 2013).

    Corbett, M. (2013). Oil shock of 1973–1974. *Federal Reserve History*. Retrieved from https://www.federalreservehistory.org/essays/oil_shock_of_1973_74.

    Watkins, T. (n.d.). The recession of 1973–1975 in the U.S. *San Jose State University*. Retrieved from http://www.sjsu.edu/faculty/watkins/rec1974.htm.

32. This phenomenon goes by different names, including the *nonprofit industrial complex*, a term coined by the activist group INCITE! Women of Color Against Violence as a critique of the emergent organizing patterns of social change actors. In a collection of essays they published on the topic, the writers and activists explore the failings of the nonprofit model.

    INCITE! (ed.) (2007). *The revolution will not be funded: Beyond the nonprofit industrial complex*. Cambridge, MA: South End Press. https://incite-national.org/beyond-the-non-profit-industrial-complex/

33. Another feature of the post-war boom was the expansion of public funding of social service programs. In the 1950s and 1960s, the American government built on the foundations of the New Deal that followed the Great Depression to introduce a series of legislation and programs that combated poverty and provided assistance for communities. Although these welfare programs were successful in delivering aid to people and communities in need, by 1980 the strain they put on the federal budget combined with the toll of the 1973 recession spurred a political backlash from fiscal and ideological conservatives.

The pattern of political tug-of-war that emerged from this period of social policy development has dominated the discourse ever since.

Stern, M. J. (2013). *Social policy: History (1950–1980)*. Oxford, UK: Oxford University Press.

Berkowitz, E. D. (2005). The 1970s as policy watershed. *Social Welfare History Project*. Meetings of the American Political Science Association. Retrievedfromhttps://socialwelfare.library.vcu.edu/programs/health-nutrition/the-1970s-as-policy-watershed/

34. In a 1994 paper on the nonprofit industry in the 1980s, policy researcher Lester Salamon posited that the "associational revolution" might be altering the relationship between people and governments as much as the nation-state model did in the previous century.

    Salamon, L. M. (1994). The rise of the nonprofit sector. *Foreign Affairs*, 73(4): 109–22.

35. The trend toward privatization has historically coincided with both contraction and expansion of public services. As a route to service delivery, privatization gained a foothold in the 1980s under the Reagan administration's federal funding. But in the 1990s, there was a shift from the use of non-competitive nonprofit contractors to competitive, performance-driven corporate contractors. With this development, the field of providing social services began to mirror the private sector in terms of organizational behavior, incentives, and process.

    Nightingale, D. S., and Pindus, N. M. (1997). Privatization of public social services: A background paper. *The Urban Institute*.

36. Among the forces that pushed the nonprofit model to the fore was the purposeful elevation of privatization by major political powers. "Most visibly, the conservative governments of Ronald Reagan and Margaret Thatcher made support for the voluntary sector a central part of their strategies to reduce government social spending" (Salamon, 1994, p. 114). The more liberal governments of the time, like France and Norway, were equally active in promoting voluntary organizations with their policies.

    Salamon, L. M. (1994). The rise of the nonprofit sector. *Foreign Affairs*, 73(4), 109–22.

37. President Bush's memorable "thousand points of light" description in his 1988 nomination acceptance speech also referred to the role of government. He went on to liken government to any other organization: "part of the nation of communities, not the whole, just a part." Three months later, he won the U.S. presidential election.

    Bush, G. (1988). Address accepting the presidential nomination at the Republican National Convention in New Orleans. *The American Presidency Project*.

38. (Salamon, 2001, p. 19)

39. This critique of the "privatization" of the nonprofit and the rise of the non-profit manager comes from Ruth Wilson Gilmore. In her essay on the topic, she goes on to build the case for funding, not of the projects and portfolios of the nonprofit manager, but the ideas of grassroots organizations who are not constrained by the forms of the NPO.

   Gilmore, R. W. (2007). In the shadow of the shadow state. In INCITE! (ed.), *The revolution will not be funded: Beyond the nonprofit industrial complex* (pp. 41–52). Cambridge, MA: South End Press.

40. Economist Thomas Piketty's *Capital in the Twenty-first Century* explores the forces behind growing wealth inequality. He describes a global shift toward "patrimonial wealth" where inherited wealth is the predominant force in the economy. He explains that although a degree of inequality is fine or even useful, if left unchecked, systemic instability from this increasingly extreme imbalance is inevitable.

   Piketty, T. (2014). *Capital in the twenty-first century.* Cambridge, MA: Harvard University Press.

   LSE. (2014). Five minutes with Thomas Piketty: "We don't need 19th century-style inequality to generate growth in the 21st century." *LSE EUROPP.*

41. Using the United States as a case study, total charitable giving for 2018 comprised $20 billion from corporations, $76 billion from foundations, $292 billion from individuals, and $40 billion from bequests.

   Indiana University Lilly Family School of Philanthropy. (2019). Giving USA 2019: The annual report on philanthropy for the year 2018. *Giving USA Foundation.*

42. A 2013 report produced for the UN gives one of the most accurate views of the size and contribution of nonprofit institutions (NPIs) globally, revealing that the sector was about twice as large as originally conceived by other metrics that grouped large nonprofits in with big corporates. The report points to the substantial role of the industry of social change and the extent to which nations have become dependent on NPIs to deliver social services.

   Salamon, L. M., Sokolowski, S. W., Haddock, M. A., and Tice, H. S. (2013). The state of global civil society and volunteering: Latest findings from the implementation of the UN nonprofit handbook. Working Paper No. 49. Johns Hopkins Center for Civil Society Studies.

43. Rodriguez, D. (2007). The political logic of the nonprofit industrial complex. In INCITE! (ed.) *The revolution will not be funded: Beyond the nonprofit industrial complex* (pp. 21–40). Cambridge, MA: South End Press.

44. Buffett, P. (2013). The charitable industrial complex. *The New York Times.*

45. Social scientists Aaron Horvath and Walter Powell argue that, when combined with the loss of faith in government over the past century, the large role

private philanthropy occupies in providing public services allows it to become "disruptive."

Horvath, A., and Powell, W. (2015). Contributory or disruptive: Do new forms of philanthropy erode democracy? *Stanford Social Innovation Review.*

46. Specifically, Ganz, Kay, and Spicer criticize the tendency for SEE to view social problems as "knowledge" problems with technical solutions. Political approaches, by contrast, see social issues for what they are: "power" problems that require mobilization of people in democratic political processes in order to bring change.

Ganz, M., Kay, T., and Spicer, J. (2018). Social enterprise is not social change. *Stanford Social Innovation Review.*

47. A 2012 study determined that food systems account for 19–29 percent of greenhouse gas emissions.

Vermeulen, S. J., Campbell, B. M., and Ingram, J. S. I. (2012). Climate change and food systems. *Annual Review of Environmental Resources,* 37: 195–222.

48. One of Rittel and Webber's central contentions for the wickedness of social problems was that once practitioners intervene in a system, they have changed it irreversibly. Consequently, they also asserted that would-be social changers must feel the weight of responsibility for their interventions. Where their goal is to impact the system positively, practitioners have no right to be wrong.

Rittel, H. W., and Webber, M. M. (1973). Dilemmas in a general theory of planning. *Policy Sciences,* 4(2): 155–69.

49. (Patel, 2013, p. 29)

Patel, R. (2013). The long green revolution. *The Journal of Peasant Studies,* 40(1): 1–63.

Chapter 2

1. The democratization of South Africa and the process of extending equal opportunities and rights to those citizens previously denied under the apartheid system is widely referred to within the country as "transformation": transformation of political power distribution, of the makeup of organizations, of the wellbeing of communities, of individual access. The events that transpired around the 2015 "Rhodes Must Fall" movement are the eruption of a system that has been transformed in name only, without substantive social change.

South African History Online (2017). Rhodes statue removed at UCT. Retrieved from https://www.sahistory.org.za/dated-event/rhodes-statue-removed-uct.

2. CGTN Africa. (2015). South Africa's controversial Rhodes statue taken down. Retrieved by https://www.youtube.com/watch?v=xt1vzYnyACA (Video incorrectly uses the name Rifumo Moaka.)

3. Fairbanks, E. (2015). Why South African students have turned on their parents' generation. *The Guardian.*

4. Underhill, G. (2013). Man who "insulted" Zuma in limbo. *Mail & Guardian.*

5. Underhill, G. (2013). Mthethwa's sorry "middle finger" story. *Mail & Guardian.*

6. Mupotsa, D. S. (2018). A question of power. In E. Oinas, K. Onodera, and L. Suurpää (eds), *What politics? Youth and political engagement in Africa* (pp. 21–41). Leiden; Boston: Brill.

7. Crowe, T. (2018). Who is Chumani? (Part 1). *Rational Standard.*

8. Patel's description of social change comes from his book *Value of Nothing,* which interrogates the relevance and value of classical economic models in the wake of the 2008 global financial crisis and posits a new approach to how we conceive of value.

   Patel, R. (2009). *The value of nothing: How to reshape market society and redefine democracy.* New York: Picador.

9. The global population in 1900 was an estimated 1.6 billion. As of 2020, the population sits at 7.8 billion.
   http://www.worldometers.info/world-population/world-population-by-year/.

10. Brandwatch has compiled some astonishing figures that reflect the extent to which digital information transfer dominates our current reality. In terms of platforms with the biggest reach, Facebook tops out the list with 2.3 billion users—or 30 percent of the population.

    Smith, K. (2019). 126 amazing social media statistics and facts. *Brandwatch.* Retrieved from https://www.brandwatch.com/blog/96-amazing-social-media-statistics-and-facts/.

11. Glouberman, S., and Zimmerman, B. (2002). Complicated and complex systems: what would successful reform of Medicare look like? *Romanow Papers,* 2: 21–53.

12. Three decades after Bertalanffy wondered whether a generalized theory of systems was even possible, the Nobel Prize-winning chemist Ilya Prigogine seemed to offer an answer in his text *The End of Certainty.* Drawing on his career-defining research in irreversible thermodynamic processes, he explains how the new understandings of natural systems are finally making it possible to move away from the closed system models and study the world as the "open, evolving universe in which mankind lives."

    Prigogine, I. (1997). *The end of certainty: Time, chaos and the new laws of nature.* New York, NY: Simon & Schuster.

13. Wolfram, S. (1988). Complex systems theory. In Wolfram, S. *Cellular automata and complexity. Collected papers* (pp. 491–7). Boulder, CO: Westview Press

Castellani, B. (2018). Map of the complexity sciences. *Art and Science Factory.* Retrieved from https://www.art-sciencefactory.com/complexity-map_feb09.html.

14. In 1980, the World Health Organization (WHO) certified that smallpox had officially been eradicated, making it the first global disease eradication. The process leading up to this milestone in human development was characterized by focused global cooperation with intense local action.

   Koplow, David A. (2003). *Smallpox: The fight to eradicate a global scourge.* Berkeley, CA: University of California Press.

15. Rogers, S. (2011). Occupy protests around the world: full list visualized. *The Guardian.*

16. Women's March. (2019). Mission and principles. *Women's March.* Retrieved from https://womensmarch.com/mission-and-principles.

17. Buchanan, L., Bui, Q., and Patel, J. (2020). Black Lives Matter may be the largest movement in U.S. history. *The New York Times.*

18. Anderson, M., and Toor, S. (2018). How social media users have discussed sexual harassment since #MeToo went viral. *Pew Research Center.*

19. (Grant and Crutchfield, 2008, p. 5)

   Grant, H. M., and Crutchfield, L. (2008). *Forces for good: The six practices of high-impact nonprofits.* San Francisco, CA: Jossey-Bass.

20. (West, 2017, p. 15.) Theoretical physicist Geoffrey West of the Sante Fe Institute has applied his study of universal scaling laws in nature to modeling complex systems that range from organisms to cities. His book *Scale* details the shared structural characteristics that keep these different systems functioning. However, as he acknowledges in this quote, the limitations of the "organization as organism" approach are real and actively being interrogated by complexity scientists.

   West, G. (2017). *Scale: The universal laws of growth, innovation, sustainability, and the pace of life in organisms, cities, economies, and companies.* London: Weidenfield & Nicolson.

21. (West, 2017, p. 16)

22. (Bar-Yam, 2004, p. 85)

   Bar-Yam, Y. (2004). *Making things work: Solving complex problems in a complex world.* Cambridge, MA: Knowledge Press.

23. (Nilsson, 2019, p. 284)

   Nilsson, W. (2019). Social innovation as institutional work. In G. George, T. Baker, P. Tracey, and H. Joshi (eds), *Handbook of inclusive innovation* (pp. 284–304). Northampton, MA: Edward Elgar Publishing.

24. Playboy. (1972). Playboy interview: Saul Alinsky. *Playboy.* Retrieved from http://documents.theblackvault.com/documents/fbifiles/100-BA-30057.pdf.

25. The sociologist William Richard Scott has spent his career studying organizations within the context of the institutional environments, thus contributing to the development of institutional theory. He defined institutions as "social structures that have attained a high degree of resilience. [They] are composed of cultural-cognitive, normative, and regulative elements that, together with associated activities and resources, provide stability and meaning to social life" (p. 48).

    Scott, W. R. (2001). *Institutions and organizations*. Thousand Oaks, CA: Sage.

26. This quote is attributed to de Botton, A.

27. (Mills, 1956, p. 9.) A prominent sociologist in the post-war era, C. Wright Mills brought the concept of "the power elite" into the public consciousness with his book of the same name which theorized that all meaningful power was consolidated in the hands of a centralized, interconnected class of political, military, and economic elites.

    Mills, C. W. (1956). *The power elite*. New York, NY: Oxford University Press.

28. In 1962, the political science researchers Peter Bachrach and Morton Baratz observed a divide over the nature of power. Sociologists, like Mills, viewed power as "highly centralized," while political scientists viewed power as "widely diffused." Their concept of the "two faces of power" side-steps this divide by positing that neither is fully correct but, rather, that power is comprised of decision-making abilities (whether they are centralized or diffused), and the ability to restrict and control the issues about which decisions are made.

    Bachrach, P., and Baratz, M. (1962). Two faces of power. *The American Political Science Review*, 56(4): 947–52.

29. In 1974, the political and social theorist Steven Lukes presented the theory of the "three faces of power." His framework builds on Bachrach and Baratz's dichotomy of decision-making and non-decision-making power with a third dimension: ideological power. One of Lukes' main assertions about this form of power is that it exists where people are dominated by an engulfing system that prevents them from understanding the reasons behind their actions, so embedded is the ideology in the structures around them. This is why Lukes suggests ideological power is the most effective and most insidious: it can enlist the powerless as co-conspirators in their own domination.

    Lukes, S. (2005). *Power: A radical view*. New York, NY: Palgrave Macmillan.

30. Wheatley, M. (2011). Leadership in the age of complexity: From hero to host. *Resurgence Magazine*.

Chapter 3

1. Thomas, K. (August 27, 2018). Personal interview with Cynthia Rayner.

2. After passing a new constitution in 2010 that reshaped the roles of government bodies, Kenya now has two layers of government: national and county.

Coordination between the two bodies has been a major challenge in developing a unified health system, which the country's Health Act of 2017 has sought to address.

> World Health Organization. (2017). Country cooperation strategy at a glance: Kenya. WHO. https://data.worldbank.org/country/KE.

3. Billimoria, J. (March 9, 2016). Personal interview with Cynthia Rayner.
4. (Miller, 2017, p. 141)

> Miller, M. L. (2017). *The alternative: Most of what you believe about poverty is wrong*. Morrisville, NC: Lulu Publishing Services.

5. (Hunt and Benford, 2004, p. 437.) Sociologists Scott Hunt and Robert Benford write that collective identities, defined in one way as a set of shared meanings between a group, "provide cultural contexts for planning, enabling, carrying out, and evaluating individual participation and collective actions" (p. 450).

> Hunt, S. A., and Benford, R. D. (2004). Collective identity, solidarity and commitment. In D. A. Snow, S. A. Soule, and H. Kriesi (eds), *The Blackwell companion to social movements* (pp. 433–58). Malden, MA: Blackwell Publishing.

6. Management consultant Margaret Wheatley explains that the tendency to look for heroic leaders to solve systemic issues is steeped in an illusion that an individual can actually be in control. However, the complexity of these systems means no degree of vision, boldness, or courage will allow a leader to control them in any way. Instead, leaders should be viewed as hosts who acknowledge the complexity and can engage all parts of the system to contribute, and who are awarded the patience and forgiveness of others in the system to do so.

> Wheatley, M. (2011). Leadership in the age of complexity: From hero to host. *Resurgence Magazine*.

Chapter 4

1. RLabs. (2016). Stories of hope—Brent Williams [video]. *YouTube*. Retrieved from https://www.youtube.com/watch?v=Wjczsw1y4WI.
2. De Waal, M. (2012). From Cape Flats to global heights: Marlon Parker, a force for social change. *Daily Maverick*.
3. In his book *Decolonizing Wealth*, social justice philanthropist Edgar Villanueva uses the lens of an indigenous value system to explore how the colonial roots of our current financial and philanthropic institutions continue to shape them in the twenty-first century.

> Villanueva, E. (2018). *Decolonizing wealth: Indigenous wisdom to heal divides and restore balance*. San Francisco, CA: Berrett-Koehler Publishers.

4. (Smucker, J. 2017, ch. Life of the Oppositional Group, "Belonging and 'Therapy'", para. 5.) In his practical guide to leading change movements called *Hegemony How-To*, grassroots organizer Jonathon Smucker advocates a pragmatic view of social change work, insisting that proponents of change take steps to gain power within the existing system.

> Smucker, J. (2017). *Hegemony how-to: A roadmap for radicals.* Chico, CA: AK Press.

5. Youth education and empowerment initiatives feature prominently in the development agendas and budgets of local NGOs, foundations, and government bodies in the Cape Town region. However, the particular outpouring of praise that RLabs has received from the international social change field, city leaders, and, most importantly, members of the local community is unique. It reflects the pride that locals feel for the authenticity of RLab's work, being of and for the people of the Cape Flats.

> https://www.facebook.com/CityofCT/posts/meet-brent-williams-a-reformed-gangster-and-co-founder-of-the-award-winning-soci/1010186812351571/.

6. Sociologists Francesca Polletta and James Jasper define collective identity as "an individual's cognitive, moral, and emotional connection with a broader community, category, practice, or institution" (2001, p. 285). Even if the identity has been defined by outsiders, and in a negative or oppressive manner, collective identity is formed when members identity with positive feelings toward other members.

> Polletta, F., and Jasper, J. (2001). Collective identity and social movements. *Annual Review of Sociology*, 27: 283–305.

7. Social psychologists Lory Britt and David Heiss have explored the process of reclaiming a stigmatized identity extensively in their study of identity politics. In their research, shame is associated with hiding, living in the shadows, and being alone, while pride is linked with expansive behaviors, public displays, and solidarity.

> Britt, L., and Heise, D. (2000). From shame to pride in identity politics. In S. Stryker, T. J. Owens, and R. W. White (eds), *Self, identity, and social movements*. Minneapolis, MN: University of Minnesota Press.

8. UNAIDS (2014). The gap report 2014: Children and pregnant women living with HIV. Retrieved from https://www.unaids.org/sites/default/files/media_asset/09_ChildrenandpregnantwomenlivingwithHIV.pdf.

9. Mitch Besser tells the story of the journey to founding mothers2mothers at the 2010 TEDGlobal conference.

> TED (2010, July). Mitchel Besser: Mothers helping mothers fight HIV [video]. TED.

10. Polletta and Jasper explain that psychological havens are important when developing collective identity because they "supply the solidary incentives that encourage movement participation, but they also represent a 'free space'

in which people can develop counterhegemonic ideas and oppositional identities" (p. 288).

Polletta, F., and Jasper, J. (2001). Collective identity and social movements. *Annual Review of Sociology*, 27: 283–305.

11. Body mapping was developed by clinical psychologist Jonathan Morgan from the University of Cape Town as a therapeutic technique for individuals living with HIV/AIDS.

Gastaldo, D., Magalhães, L., Carrasco, C., and Davy, C. (2012). Body-Map storytelling as research: Methodological considerations for telling the stories of undocumented workers through body mapping. *Creative Commons*.

12. Professor and author Nancy Whittier refers here to the process of consciousness-raising that came out of the women's movement of the 1960s and 1970s. It results in the recognition that one's personal experiences are shaped by larger forces, hence the feminist tenet that "the personal is political."

Whittier, N. (2017). Identity politics, consciousness raising, and visibility politics. In H. J. McCammon, V. Taylor, J. Reger, and R. L. Einwohner (eds) *The Oxford Handbook of U.S. Women's Social Movement Activism*. New York, NY: Oxford University Press.

13. Britt and Heise developed a model for the process of mobilizing collective identity toward change, using the gay rights movement as a specific example. They highlight the role of anger and fear over stigmatization as an important catalyst for drawing members of the identity network into public demonstrations. In the end, the collective public display of their stigma foments solidarity and pride, which are prerequisites for developing a positive sense of that identity.

Britt, L., and Heise, D. (2000). From shame to pride in identity politics. In S. Stryker, T. J. Owens, and R. W. White (eds), *Self, identity, and social movements*. Minneapolis, MN: University of Minnesota Press.

14. The radical feminist and civil rights activist Kathie Sarachild was one of the core members of New York Radical Women (NYRW) during the Women's Liberation Movement. Based on her experiences with pooling at NYRW, which was heavily influenced by the practices of civil rights organizers in the American South, Sarachild has become a champion of consciousness-raising as a radical act for change and the "ongoing political work" of change movements (Ames and Pham, 2019).

Sarachild, K. (1978). Consciousness-raising: A radical weapon. In B. J. Morris and D.-M. Withers (eds), *Feminist Revolution*. New York, NY: Random House.

Ames, M. S., and Pham, E. D. (2019). A radical weapon. *The Crimson*. Retrieved from https://www.thecrimson.com/article/2019/10/31/kathie-sarachild/.

15. Shreve, A. (1989). *Women together, women alone: The legacy of the consciousness-raising movement.* New York, NY: Viking Adult.

16. After a lifetime of work in quantum theory and neuropsychology, theoretical physicist David Bohm was besotted by what he called "the problem of communication" in society at large, stemming from humans' increasing inability to listen to one another, which he felt led to confusion, mistrust, and violence. "Bohm dialogue" refers to a communication practice in which participants freely express something that reflects their individual experience, suspend their belief in this expression as the truth, and openly listen as others express their own experience of something, in order to build something new together.

    Bohm, D. (1996). *On dialogue.* London: Routledge.

    Popova, M. (2016). Legendary physicist David Bohm on the paradox of communication, the crucial difference between discussion and dialogue, and what is keeping us from listening to one another. *Brain Pickings.*

17. Neuroscientist Beau Lotto draws on historic research of philosophers and modern developments in neuroscience to explain how our brains have evolved to make us biologically delusional, incapable of ever seeing reality. His book *Deviate: The Science of Seeing Differently* explores the mechanisms by which our brains perceive information and effectively prevent us from seeing the world as it actually exists. By understanding the limitations of our biology, Lotto posits that we can question our "delusions," seek out more information, and then purposefully deviate from them.

    Lotto, B. (2017). *Deviate: The science of seeing differently.* New York, NY: Hachette Books.

18. Business theorist Chris Argyris developed the concept of "defensive routines" to describe the patterns propagated by people in their interpersonal interactions with others in an organization in order to protect themselves from threats. These patterns include pushing our own ideas to the exclusion of others', managing and working unilaterally, withholding information, and assigning meaning and intentions to the actions of others.

    Argyris, C. (1999). *On organizational learning,* 2nd ed. Malden, MA: Blackwell Business.

19. In his seminal work *The Fifth Discipline,* organizational development researcher Peter Senge introduces the model of the "learning organization" as defined by five characteristics. Learning organizations, which aim to continually evolve in order to achieve their goals, need to develop ways of identifying and challenging the mental models that shape their individual and collective behavior in order to discard or "unlearn" ineffective ones, or embrace and improve useful ones. Systems thinking—the fifth discipline—serves as the underlying blueprint for Senge's conceptualization of the learning organization as it explains how the different levels of individual and collective

behavior interact to create complex patterns that cannot be reduced or analyzed in isolation, but must be taken as a whole.

Senge, P. M. (1990). *The fifth discipline: The art and practice of the learning organization.* New York, NY: Doubleday/Currency.

20. Teasdale, C. A., and Besser, M. J. (2008). Enhancing PMTCT programmes through psychosocial support and empowerment of women: The mothers2-mothers model of care. *Southern African Journal of HIV Medicine*, 9(1): 60–4.

21. Baek, C., Mathambo, V., Mkhize, S., Friedman, I., Apicella, L., and Rutenberg, N. (2007). Key findings from an evaluation of the mothers2mothers program in KwaZulu-Natal, South Africa. Horizons Program Health Systems Trust.

22. Wanga, I., Helova, A., Abuogi, L. L., Bukusi, E. A., Nalwa, W., Akama, E.,… and Onono, M. (2019). Acceptability of community-based mentor mothers to support HIV-positive pregnant women on antiretroviral treatment in western Kenya: A qualitative study. *BMC Pregnancy and Childbirth*, 19(1): 288.

Okonji, E., Sandfolo, S., Myers, A., Scheepers, E., and Schmitz, K. (2014). 2013 Annual evaluation of the prevention of mother-to-child transmission (PMTCT) through peer education and psychosocial support services in Kenya, Lesotho, Malawi, South Africa. *mothers2mothers.*

23. Seelos, C. (2020). Changing systems? Welcome to the slow movement. *Stanford Social Innovation Review*, Winter: 40–7.

24. Isaacs, W. (1999). *Dialogue and the art of thinking together: A pioneering approach to communicating in business and in life.* New York: Currency.

25. (Issacs, 1993, p. 24)

Isaacs, W. (1993). Taking flight: Dialogue, collective thinking, and organizational learning. *Organizational Dynamics*, 22(2): 24–39.

Chapter 5

1. (Miller, 2017, p. 8.) Mauricio Miller documents his journey to founding the Family Independence Initiative in his book *The Alternative.*

Miller, M. L. (2017). *The alternative: Most of what you believe about poverty is wrong.* Morrisville, NC: Lulu Publishing Services.

2. Guidestar (2019). Family independence initiative: Trust and invest in families. *Guidestar.* Retrieved from https://www.guidestar.org/profile/02-0784790.

3. Gerena, J. (June 3, 2019). Personal interview with Cynthia Rayner.

4. (Brafman and Beckstrom, 2006, p. 204)

Brafman, O., and Beckstrom, R. (2006). *The starfish and the spider: The unstoppable power of leaderless organizations.* New York, NY: Penguin.

5. Miller, M. (2016). Lightening talk: Innovations that empower—Family Independence Initiative. Summit on Technology and Opportunity. Stanford Center on Poverty and Inequality.

6. (Miller, 2017, p. 127)

7. (Miller, 2017, p. 150)

8. (Miller, 2017, p. 182)

9. The concept of "social capital" originates with the work of Mark Granovetter on strong and weak ties. It was later popularized by Harvard political scientist Robert Putnam in his book *Bowling Alone*, which detailed the erosion of social capital in America over the last half century and its connection to the decline in civic participation over the same period. The relationship is critical because although social capital is a tangible resource, it can be difficult to quantify and account for in dollars and cents. This makes it easy to forget or discount social capital when designing our organizations and ecosystems, and to instead focus on the clear, visible transactions between people as the drivers of outcomes.

   Putnam, R. (2000). *Bowling alone: The collapse and revival of American community*. New York, NY: Simon & Schuster.

10. As different categories of social capital, "bonding" and "bridging" are used to characterize how the capital is used and by whom. In *Bowling Alone*, Putnam describes bonding social capital—the intra-group asset—as a tool for "getting by," whereas bridging social capital—used between groups—is a tool for "getting ahead."

    Claridge, T. (2018). What is the difference between bonding and bridging social capital? *Social Capital Research and Training*. https://www.socialcapitalresearch.com/difference-bonding-bridging-social-capital/.

11. Our home city of Cape Town launched its Open Data Portal in 2015 following its turn as the World Design Capital for 2014 (http://odp.capetown.gov.za). The initiative demonstrated the city's interest in creating greater transparency and stimulating local entrepreneurship.

    Murray, P. (2017). 40 brilliant open data projects preparing smart cities for 2018. *Carto*.

    Retrieved from https://carto.com/blog/forty-brilliant-open-data-projects-preparing-smart-cities-2018/

12. Social audits are a participation tool that allow ordinary citizens to become more involved in the decision-making around their local governance by evaluating and reporting on public services. Organizations like the Social Audit Network—which grew out of an initiative in Khayelitsha, South Africa, to evaluate sanitation services in the township—offer open source toolkits and guides to empower communities to perform their own audits.

    https://socialaudits.org.za.

13. The Kenya-based organization Ushahidi began in 2008 as an initiative to map the post-election violence taking place around the country. Since then, its mapping tools, which are based on crowdsourced data, have been expanded and adopted by organizations around the world to generate reports on a range of social and environmental issues.

    Ushahidi (2018). Ushahidi: Ten years of impact 2008–2018. *Ushahidi.*

14. Demonstrating the potential high-stakes applications for open data solutions, in 2016 a group of UK-based researchers launched Microreact as a free, cloud-based platform for tracking the ongoing Ebola outbreak as the disease spread in real time.

    Media Team 30 (2016). Online epidemic tracking tool embraces open data and collective intelligence to understand outbreaks. Wellcome Sanger Institute.

15. Miller, M. (June 12, 2019). Personal interview with Cynthia Rayner.

16. Increasing life expectancies around the world are expected to drive spending on geriatric care—which includes home health care—to US$1.4 trillion by 2023. By this time, 12 percent of the global population will be over age sixty-five (Allen, 2019). In the United States alone, the percentage of the population over age eighty-five is projected to double by 2036 and triple by 2049 (Landers et al., 2016). The Netherlands is often positively cited for its handling of these growing patient needs by coordinating health insurers, government, and providers to balance hospital care with home care alternatives (Allen, 2019).

    Allen, S. (2019). 2020 global health care outlook: Laying a foundation for the future. *Deloitte Insights.*

    Landers, S., Madigan, E., Leff, B., Rosati, R. J., McCann, B. A., Hornbake, R., MacMillan, R., Jones, K., Bowles, K., Dowding, D., Lee, T., Moorhead, T., Rodriguez, S., and Breese, E. (2016). The future of home health care: A strategic framework for optimizing value. *Home Health Care Management and Practice*, 28(4): 262–78.

17. Frederic Laloux draws on Buurtzorg's story as part of a discussion of self-management structures in his book *Reinventing Organizations*. His book offers a treatise on a new organizational paradigm for reaching higher levels of collective consciousness through self-management practices and authenticity in the workplace.

    Laloux, F. (2014). *Reinventing organizations: A guide to creating organizations inspired by the next stage of human consciousness.* Brussels: Nelson Parker.

18. Betz, A. (2016). Jos de Blok, the founder of Buurtzorg, speaks of his journey. *Enlivened Edge.* Retrieved from https://www.enliveningedge.org/features/jos-de-blok-founder-buurtzorg-speaks-journey/.

19. The growing hype around Buurtzorg's "upside-down" approach to designing health care has prompted a string of case studies, evaluations, and assessments from different corners of the health-care, public sector, and social change ecosystem over the last decade. One of the more comprehensive studies comes

from consulting firm BCG and their Centre for Public Impact. By their analysis, Buurtzorg scores high across all sub-metrics of impact to indicate that their model has the potential to create better government health services and systems, and to achieve greater public outcomes.

Ćirković, S. (2018). Buurtzorg: Revolutionising home care in the Netherlands. *Centre for Public Impact.*

20. Sheldon, T. (2017). Buurtzorg: The district nurses who want to be superfluous. *The BMJ, 358.*

21. Most of the key cost metrics cited regarding Buurtzorg's operational performance come from the 2015 KPMG study on the organization.

Gray, B. H., Sarnak, D. O., and Burgers, J. S. (2015). Home care by self-governing nursing teams: The Netherlands' Buurtzorg model. *The Commonwealth Fund, 14.*

22. Beadle de Palomo, F. (February 20, 2019). Personal interview with the authors.

Chapter 6

1. The forced eviction of residents in Otodo-Gbame in November 2016 was part of an ongoing effort of the Lagos State authorities to remove informal settlements from the city that began in 2013 and continued through 2017.

Amnesty International (2017). The human cost of a megacity: Forced evictions of the urban poor in Lagos, Nigeria. *Amnesty International Ltd.*

2. Nwannekanma, B. (2016). 10,000 persons rendered homeless. *The Guardian.*

3. The first of the forced evictions Otodo-Gbama on November 9, 2016 alone resulted in the displacement of 4,700 residents.

Amnesty International (2017). Nigeria: Deadly mass forced evictions make life misery for waterfront communities. *Amnesty International Ltd.*

4. Authorities did not just violate community trust with their actions, but legal rulings. Court orders from both 2016 and 2017 directed the state government not to carry out the proposed evictions in Lagos.

Amnesty International (2017). The human cost of a megacity: Forced evictions of the urban poor in Lagos, Nigeria. *Amnesty International Ltd.*

In February 2020, developers announced that they had broken ground on some of the infrastructure projects for the "affordable" luxury residential district that is replacing the informal settlements in Ilubirin.

Ilubirin. (2020). Entrance road to Ilubirin starts on site. Retrieved from https://www.ilubirin.ng/news-details/entrance-road-to-ilubirin-starts-on-site/.

5. "In February 2020, developers announced that they had broken ground on some of the infrastructure projects for the "affordable" luxury residential district that is replacing the informal settlements in Ilubirin.

   Ilubirin. (2020). Entrance road to Ilubirin starts on site. Retrieved from https://www.ilubirin.ng/news-details/entrance-road-to-ilubirin-starts-on-site/."

6. Patrick Geddes was known for his innovative approach to town planning in the early twentieth century that applied theories of biological evolution to those of societal evolution in order to understand how the well-planned public spaces can support the health of people.

   Geddes, P. (1915). *Cities in evolution: An introduction to the town planning movement and to the study of civics.* London: Williams.

7. World Population Review. (2020). Lagos population 2020. *World Population Review.* Retrieved from http://worldpopulationreview.com/world-cities/lagos-population/.

8. The tale of two responses to informal settlements in Lagos was captured by SDI in their publication for the "Know Your City" initiative, which collects the work of organizing slum dwellers in cities around the world. For SDI, the events in Lagos demonstrate that the structures and norms that shape our cities are not pre-determined—they are choices that governments, citizens, and organizations make.

   Chapman, M., and Maki, A. (2018). The cities we create depend on the choices we make: Lagos. In *Know your city: Slum dwellers count.*

   Retrieved from https://www.justempower.org/blog/2018/4/2/read-the-cities-we-create-depend-on-the-choices-we-make-lagos

9. SDI founder Jockin Arputham explained why the typical response that cities have to slum dwellers is so misaligned with the realities of city life. "'City life for the upper middle-class can't survive without domestic help—and where do they come from?' There is no affordable accommodation for them in the city, he points out, causing them to live in slums. The land officially set aside for the homeless in Mumbai, Arputham says, is less than 6 percent, while the requirement, going by their number, should be closer to 60 percent. 'And you blame slum dwellers for your poor planning.'"

   Perur, S. (2014). Jockin Arputham: From slum dweller to Nobel Peace Prize nominee. *The Guardian.*

10. Satterthwaite, D. (2001). Environmental governance: A comparative analysis of nine city case studies. *Journal of International Development*, 13: 1009–14.

11. MacFarlane, C. (2009). Translocal assemblages: Space, power and social movements. *Geoforum*, 40: 561–7.

12. Dalberg is a group of multidisciplinary practitioners who are dedicated to supporting businesses, governments, and nonprofits around the world to achieve "sustainable and inclusive growth."

    Mwangi, J. (2019). James Mwangi on the problem with innovation. *Skoll Foundation.*

13. Among the many awards and accolades SDI has received from the social change community is the Skoll Foundation's Skoll Award for Social Entrepreneurship. The award, which was granted to SDI in 2014, comes with a US$1.5 million investment or support grant for increasing the project's impact over three years.

    Slum dwellers international. *Skoll Foundation.* Retrieved from http://skoll.org/organization/slum-dwellers-international/.

14. (Lindell, 2009, p. 126, 132.) Ilda Lindell describes this organizing strategy across scales as a "glocal movement." She explains that glocal work is important because it elides the debate about which scale is more important for change work and rather demonstrates that transnational activities of the practicing group give power to local movements to influence policy.

    Lindell, I. (2009). "Glocal" movements: Place struggles and transnational organizing by informal workers. *Geografiska Annaler: Series B, Human Geography*, 91(2): 123–36.

15. Patel, R. (May 21, 2019). Personal interview with the authors.

16. (Lindell, 2009, p. 131)

17. (Gasparre, 2011, p. 779)

    Gasparre, A. (2011). Emerging networks of organized urban poor: Restructuring the engagement with government toward the inclusion of the excluded. *International Journal of Voluntary and Nonprofit Organizations*, 22(4).

18. The IMC proved how vital the acts of systematic information gathering and distributing could be to coordinating widespread activities. "Formed by a small crew of activists and housed in a space donated temporarily by a local nonprofit, the IMC functioned as a hub for movement media-making during the protests…As the protests unfolded, the IMC quickly became the most reliable source of information."

    Dixon, C. (2019). WTO shutdown: Remembering for the future: Learning from the 1999 Seattle shutdown. *Common Dreams.*

19. The emergent website that united activists during the WTO protests was Indymedia.org. As activists in other countries began to adopt the IMC model, with 150 IMCs emerging in by the early 2000s, they also began forming their own websites as branches of the Indywire "mothership."

    Glaser, A. (2019). Another network is possible. *Logic*, 8. Retrieved from https://logicmag.io/bodies/another-network-is-possible/.

20. Hennig, B. (2017). *The end of politicians: Time for a real democracy.* London: Unbound.

21. Co-Impact is a global systems change coalition notable for their advocacy of "societal platforms" as a technology-based asset that unlocks systems change. Instead of a one-way solution pipeline from provider to beneficiary, platforms allow players to meet on a decentralized plane where they can design, deliver, and scale a range of solutions fast.

    Ramnath, N. S. (2017). Bill Gates, Nandan Nilekani and the idea of societal platforms. *Founding Fuel.*

22. (CYFI, 2018, p. 13)

    CYFI. (2018). Brokering collaborative systems change. *Child and Youth Finance International.*

23. (CYFI, 2018, p. 39)

24. Billimoria, J. (March 9, 2016). Personal interview with Cynthia Rayner.

25. Sheela Patel is the founder and director of the Society for Promotion of Area Resource Centres (SPARC) and an SDI co-founder.

    Patel, S. (2016). The federation model of community organization [video]. UN Habitat. Retrieved from https://uni.unhabitat.org/new-lecture-release-s03e01-sheela-patel-the-federation-model-of-community-upgrading/.

26. Molokoane, R. (February 7, 2018). Know your city: Slum dwellers count. SDI. Retrieved from http://knowyourcity.info/2018/02/know-city-slum-dwellers-count/.

27. MacPherson, N. (November 8, 2019). Personal interview with Cynthia Rayner.

28. Speaking about the decentralized power made available by technology in their book *New Power*, Jeremy Heimans and Henry Timms address the tension that arises for most of us in the real world as we entertain exciting visions of what new power can bring us, while at the same time being fully immersed in the game of old power.

    Heimans, J., and Timms, H. (2018). *New power: How power works in our hyperconnected world—and how to make it work for you.* New York, NY: Random House.

Chapter 7

1. Mishra, B. (June 13, 2016). Personal interview with Cynthia Rayner.

2. Singh, A. (April 14, 2016). Personal interview with Cynthia Rayner.

3. In 2011, the network Women in Informal Employment: Globalizing and Organizing (WIEGO) conducted a field study of informal workers in Cape Town, South Africa, to better understand their self-organization patterns. Among their findings were the important distinctions between different types of workers that fall into the broad category of "informal worker" according to outside bodies.

Mather, C. (2012). Informal workers' organizing: Research report to the solidarity center. *WIEGO.*

4. One of the galvanizing events for street vendor organizers across the country which has come to epitomize the government overstep of the time, was "Operation Sunshine." One night in November 1996, police in Kolkata took to clearing the pavements of major streets around the city where vendors had erected structures for selling goods and, in effect, "bulldozed the livelihoods of 100,000 vendors to clean up the city for a visit by the UK prime minister" (te Lintelo, D. J. H., 2010, p. 280).

te Lintelo, D. J. H. (2010). Advocacy coalitions influencing informal sector policy: The case of India's national urban street vendors policy. In S. K. Bhowmik (ed.), *Street vendors in the global urban economy.* (pp 275-309). New Delhi: Routledge.

5. Civil rights activist Ela Bhatt founded the Self-Employed Women's Association of India (SEWA) in 1972 as a kind of labor union to protect women in the Indian workforce who overwhelmingly work in the informal sector. As an experienced organizer by the time of the 1990s street vendor ouster, Bhatt was instrumental in coordinating a meeting of international street vendor representatives in 1995 to develop StreetNet and produce the Bellagio International Declaration of Street Vendors, asking governments to establish national policies protecting street vendors (te Lintelo, 2010).

6. One of NASVI's first major actions was to produce a report summarizing the findings of studies it commissioned in seven cities across the country. Beyond giving them an overview of the makeup of their constituents, it also helped them to understand the institution of informal work in the context of the larger economic and political system: why street vending was increasing across cities and how government was problematizing encroachment with extreme bias against vendors. Government's reaction to hawkers was a choice, not an inevitability.

Bhowmik, S. K. (1998). Hawkers and the urban informal sector: A study of street vending in seven cities. *NASVI.*

7. The findings of the NASVI study served as a roadmap for their future work: challenging the accepted paradigm of street vendors as a public nuisance and advocating for national policies that would recognize and protect them as an important part of the economy.

Sinha, S., and Roever, S. (2011). India's national policy on urban street vendors. *WIEGO.*

8. (Singh and Kumar, 2017, p. 7). The National Policy on Urban Street Vendors aimed to "provide and promote supportive environment for earning livelihoods to the street vendors, as well as ensure absence of congestion and maintenance of hygiene in public spaces and streets."

Singh, A., and Kumar, S. (2017). Trade unions in transformation: Towards a better deal for street vendors in India: The case of NASVI. *Friederich Ebert Stiftung.*

9. Singh, A. (June 9, 2016). Personal interview with Cynthia Rayner.
10. Singh, A. (June 9, 2016). Personal interview with Cynthia Rayner.
11. Singh, A. (April 14, 2016). Personal interview with Cynthia Rayner.
12. This is one of the "laws of power" explained by Eric Liu, the founder of Citizen University, which is committed to increasing awareness of power among ordinary citizens in order in increase public participation.

Ted-ed (2014). How to understand power [video]. *TED.*

13. In a study of hundreds of large companies that could be the targets of social critics for their practices of systemic impacts, researchers Mary-Hunter McDonnell and Sarah Soule found "the companies targeted most frequently by activist groups were the most likely ones to create initial responses that led to farther-reaching reforms over time."

Hunter-McDonnell, M., King, B., and Soule, S. (2015). How do activists create change? *Kellogg Insight.*

14. Oscar Mogollón was just one of thousands of teachers across Latin America seeding the unitary school model as part of the unitary complete school methodology (UCSM) promoted by UNESCO in the 1960s.

McEwan, P. J., and Benveniste, L. (2003). A local reform goes global: The politics of Escuela Nueva. In G. Fischman, S. Ball, and S. Gvirtz (eds) *Crisis and Hope.* (pp 93-112). New York: Routledge.

15. Escuela Unitaria was premised on the active learning philosophy developed by famed education theorists Maria Montessori, John Dewey, and Jean Piaget (Rincón-Gallardo, 2019). The Escuela Unitaria program diverged from these methods in two major ways: "(i) all these principles and models are presented in a sequence of work components: demonstration-training-textbooks/(curriculum)-school design-follow up, to be assembled by the teacher, and in that process the teacher is gradually trained on the job; and (ii) the Escuela Nueva has passed the test of large-scale implementation" (Schiefelbein, 1992, p. 47).

Rincón-Gallardo, S. (2019). *Liberating learning: Educational change as social movement.* New York: Routledge.

Schiefelbein, E. (1992). Redefining basic education for Latin America: Lessons to be learned from the Colombian Escuela Nueva. *Unesco.*

16. Colbert, V., and Arboleda, J. (1990). Universalization of primary education in Colombia: The new school programme. *Unesco.*

17. As systems innovation consultant Alex Ryan explains, Oscar Mogollón represents the power of "normal" individuals to shape new norms and models.

Ryan, A. (2016). Scaling innovation: The Escuela Nueva story. *Medium.*

18. Warburg, J., and Gudbergsdottir, E. (2016). Educational model co-created by Prof. Beryl Levinger now a global movement. *Middlebury Institute of International Studies*.

19. A 2017 assessment of student performance in Colombia examined the national standardized test score of 810,000 children across the country. Students in Escuela Nueva programs scored significantly higher than those in other schools, with differences ranging between 10.5 to 23.2 points, which is comparable to the performance difference attributed to a difference of one socio-economic level. More generally, Escuela Nueva models seem to reduce achievement gaps across genders and socio-economic levels (Hammler, 2017). Studies of Escuela Nueva programs in Vietnam (VNEN) show similarly positive impacts on both cognitive and non-cognitive skills among primary school students (Parandekar et al., 2017).

    Hammler, K. (2017). The Colombian Escuela Nueva school model: Linking program implementation and learning outcomes (Doctoral dissertation). Available from https://search.proquest.com/openview/6e43d68bdb79f954a0 9b228b58990d97/1?pq-origsite=gscholar&cbl=18750&diss=y

20. As authors Andy Hargreaves and Michael T. O'Connor explain, "student-centred practices have sometimes been criticized for being an indulgence of educational romantics that do not get results. The evidence of the Escuela Nueva model, however, is that it works."

    Hargreaves, A., and O'Connor, M. T. (2018). *Collaborative professionalism: When teaching together means learning for all*. Thousand Oaks, CA: Corwin Press.

21. Escuela Nueva applies the same principle of student-centered learning to its teachers during their training sessions. This is accomplished through a "learning-by-doing" approach where teachers-in-training visit demonstration schools that already practice the Escuela Nueva model to see it in action.

    Gustafsson-Wright, E., and McGivney, E. (2014). Fundación Escuela Nueva: Changing the way children learn from Colombia to Southeast Asia. *The Brookings Institution*.

22. McEwan, P. (1998). The effectiveness of multigrade schools in Colombia. *International of Educational Development*, 18: 435–52.

23. Psacharopoulos, G., Rojas, C., and Velez, E. (1993). Achievement evaluation of Colombia's "Escuela Nueva": Is multigrade the answer? *Comparative Education Review*, 27(3): 263–76.

    McEwan, P. (1998). The effectiveness of multigrade schools in Colombia. *International of Educational Development*, 18: 435–52.

24. Patrinos, H. A. (2017). How a time-tested education model can prepare students for a high tech future. *World Bank Blogs*. Retrieved from https://blogs. worldbank.org/education/how-time-tested-education-model-can-prepare-students-high-tech-future.

25. Bruce, K. M. (2016). *Pride parades: How a parade changed the world.* New York, NY: New York University Press.
26. Nilsson, W. (2019). Social innovation as institutional work. In G. George, T. Baker, P. Tracey, and H. Joshi (eds), *Handbook of inclusive innovation* (pp. 284–304). Northampton, MA: Edward Elgar Publishing.
27. Based on his discussions with economists and past Escuela Nueva evaluators, policy expert David Kirp estimates that the power of the model is its tethering to democratic values. As he puts it, "Escuela Nueva turns the schoolhouse into a laboratory for democracy."

    Kirp, D. L. (2015). Make school a democracy. *The New York Times.*
28. The "precariat" is a new class of worker that includes freelancers, gig-economy workers, and contractors who are not employees with all the legal protections and benefits that the status confers.

    Standing, G. (2011). *The precariat: The new dangerous class.* New York, NY: Bloomsbury Publishing.

Chapter 8

1. Nesta. (2014). New Radicals 2014—National Change Day. *Nesta.* Retrieved from https://www.nesta.org.uk/feature/new-radicals-2014/nhs-change-day/.
2. The core Change Day activity is pledge-making: a "changeathon" where throughout the day, people, teams, and organizations pledge to take specific actions that will improve or change the way they carry out the work of the NHS. In 2013, 189,000 pledges were made, followed by 500,000 in 2014.

    NHS (2015). NHS change day 2015—making a difference. *NHS.* Retrieved from https://www.england.nhs.uk/2015/03/nhs-change-day/
3. We acknowledge that "measuring" as a term is incomplete and imperfect. There are crucial differences between monitoring, evaluation, and learning ("MEL" in sector lingo) as activities devoted to measuring and understanding social change. However, for the sake of simplicity, we have chosen to use the term "measurement" to encompass all of these activities.
4. One particularly hopeful alternative metric of human wellbeing comes from the United Nations. Since 2012, the UN Sustainable Development Solutions Network has published an annual "World Happiness Report" as part of a broader goal to encourage countries to measure the happiness of their people. Using a measure of the "best possible life" for a person, the report provides rankings of happiness by country and examines the relationship between different systemic variables and national happiness.

    Helliwell, J. F., Layard, R., Sachs, J. D., and De Neve, J.-D. (2020). World happiness report. *Sustainable Development Solutions Network.*

5. The Nobel Prize-winning economist Simon Kuznets introduced the modern conceptualization of GDP as we know it in 1934. Although this econometric was codified with the global adoption of GDP during the post-World War II reconstruction period, Kuznets was clear from the onset about the limitations of national income measures as a welfare indicator. In his initial 1934 report on the use of national income measures, he had stated, "The valuable capacity of the human mind to simplify a complex situation in a compact characterization becomes dangerous when not controlled in terms of definitely stated criteria" (p. 5).

Kuznets, S. (1934). National income 1929–1932, a report to the U.S. Senate, 73rd Congress, 2nd Session. United States Government Printing Office, Washington, D.C.

6. Journalist David Pilling points to other shortfalls of the GDP metric. He writes, "It tells you nothing about whether you can produce the same amount again next year." This is the conclusion driving systems workers to rather look at what is happening in the present.

Pilling, D. (2018). 5 ways GDP gets it totally wrong as a measure of our success. *World Economic Forum.*

7. (Chambers, 2017, p. 72.) A researcher of rural development since the 1980s, Robert Chambers has been an ardent advocate of policy approaches that prioritize participation and place primary actors at the center of the work. Consequently, he is critical of the institutions that push "mechanistic methodologies," namely randomized control trials and systematic reviews, that ultimately collapse the role of primary actors.

Chambers, R. (2017). *Can we know better?* Rugby, UK: Practical Action Publishing.

8. Skoll.org (2016). Michael Porter: Why measuring social progress matters—Skoll World Forum 2016 [video]. *YouTube.*

Social Progress Imperative. (2019). 2019 Social progress index: Executive summary. *Social Progress Imperative.*

9. Speaking in a panel discussion at the 2018 Skoll World Forum on "Impact Measurement: Collaborating for Human Rights", social entrepreneurship researcher Alex Nicholls explains that, given the abundance of measurement tools for solving the "how" issue, all measurement inquiries should start with the "why" question. He said, "Once you ask yourself the question 'why' and answer that strategically, the truth is it might be more than one answer, to appeal to several strategic objectives."

Hogan, K. (2018). Measuring for impact in human rights: What, why, how, and for whom? *Skoll Foundation.*

10. Martin Burt explored the backwardness of the global approach to fighting poverty in his book *Who Owns Poverty?* In a 2019 interview he explained that

what families need is the motivation and skills to address the problems they know they have. "We were told that for people to overcome their poverty, we had to help them love to do what they hated, we had to make it fun."

Militzer, J. (2019). Who owns poverty?: A Q&A with Fundación Paraguaya founder and CEO Martin Burt. *Next Billion.*

11. Berg, L. (April 25, 2019). Personal interview with François Bonnici and Jane Notten.

12. (SDI, 2018, p. 5). SDI (2018). Know your city: Slum dwellers count. *Slum Dwellers International.*

13. Pentland, A. (2009). The water cooler effect: Fewer memos, more coffee breaks. *Psychology Today.*

14. This dimension of Revaluation was influenced by the Tavistock tradition of organizational development. Andrew Harrison is an associate of Tavistock Consulting. https://tavistockconsulting.co.uk/.

15. Robert Chambers concedes that the increased pressure to measure has brought about many good effects. Demands from funders for increased efficiency and accountability incentivize greater care to roll out development programs in a timely and effective manner. "Who can be against these?" he asks. But with the rampant uptake of rigid accountability frameworks—all done in good faith—he fears the pendulum has swung too far in the opposite direction with disastrous consequences. The damage, he says, can be measured in the increasing distance between what practitioners actually do to solve problems on the ground and what they must do to appease funders.

Chambers, R. (2017). *Can we know better?* Rugby, UK: Practical Action Publishing.

16. Since emerging in the late 2000s, impact investment has come to represent the broadest concerted effort within the market to incorporate social and environmental performance into investment decision-making. A 2019 report from the nonprofit Global Impact Investing Network (GIIN) presents the first comprehensive overview of the impact investment market to show that although 60 percent of organizations engaging in impact investing are asset managers, a diverse group of other actors—including foundations, banks, development finance institutions, and family offices—are also participating. The plurality of institutional and individual investment strategies, therefore, demands a plurality of measurement methods.

Mudaliar, A., and Dithrich, H. (2019). Sizing the impact investing market. *Global Impact Investing Network.*

17. Absent a global standard for impact assessment in impact investment, an array of consultants, investors, investees, academics, and nonprofits are involved in the measurement decision on a case-by-case basis.

Bass, R., Dithrich, H., Sunderji, S., and Nova, N. (2020). The state of impact measurement and management practice (second edition). *Global Impact Investing Network.*

18. In 2019, CYFI published a report capturing their "best practices", which they have distilled as five tactics, for others to learn from their process. Importantly, they also include the important but uncommon step of "letting go."

    CYFI (2019). Brokering collaborative systems change. *Child and Youth Finance International.*

19. (Ebrahim, 2019, p. 9.) An expert on measurement strategies in the nonprofit, public, and social sectors, professor Alnoor Ebrahim is an advisor for GIIN and a collaborator with social entrepreneurs at the Schwab Foundation. In his book *Measuring Social Change,* he writes that managers must "be more deliberate about what they seek to achieve and how to measure progress towards it."

    Ebrahim, A. (2019). *Measuring social change: Performance and accountability in a complex world.* Stanford, CA: Stanford Business Books.

20. (Patton, 2010, p. 13.) In his book *Developmental Evaluation,* researcher and consultant Michael Quinn Patton discusses his objective to shift accountability inward, away from the external authorities who have traditionally been charged with independently making decisions. He writes simply that for social innovators, "the highest form of accountability is internal," but that it requires courage to decide that we want to know the truth about the impacts of our actions.

    Patton, M. Q. (2010). *Developmental evaluation: Applying complexity concepts to enhance innovation and use.* New York, NY: Guilford Press.

21. The McConnell Foundation is one organization that welcomed developmental evaluation with open arms. Foundation president and CEO Tim Broadbent summarizes succinctly the journey that systems work demands of funders: "As this Foundation shifted its funding to complex, long-term initiatives that are not so much pre-planned as emergent, the inadequacy of the usual evaluation methods became evident. We need a compass, not a roadmap" (Dozois, Langlois, and Blanchet-Cohen, 2010, p. 6).

    Dozois, E., Langlois, M., and Blanchet-Cohen, N. (2010). DE 201: A practitioner's guide to developmental evaluation. *The J. W. McConnell Family Foundation* and *International Institute for Child Rights and Development.*

22. (Patton, 2006, p. 28)

    Patton, M. Q. (2006). Evaluation for the way we work. *Nonprofit Quarterly,* 13(1): 28–33.

23. (Patton, 2010, p. 13)

24. Siesfeld, T., Evans, R., and Kasper, G. (2017). Reimagining measurement: Enhancing social impact through better monitoring, evaluation, and learning. *Deloitte.*

25. Krauss, A. (2015). The scientific limits of understanding complex social phenomena. *London School of Economics.*

26. The 2019 Prize in Economic Science was awarded to development economics researchers Abhijit Banerjee, Esther Duflo, and Michael Kremer "for their experimental approach to alleviating global poverty." Starting in the mid-1990s, the team began conducting large field experiments in developing countries in order to develop strategies for reducing poverty globally. The randomized controlled trials (RCT) that they pioneered have since become the dominant methodology in their field, drawing both praise and criticism from their peers. Researcher Sanjay G. Reddy summarizes the through-line of most critiques, which once again reflects the same concerns of Chambers, Patton, Krauss, and the two Andrews: "RCTs cannot reveal very much about causal processes since at their core they are designed to determine whether something has an effect, not how."

    NobelPrize.org (2019). Press release: The prize in economic sciences 2019. *The Royal Swedish Academy of Sciences.*

    Reddy, S. G. (2019). Economics' biggest success story is a cautionary tale. *Foreign Policy.*

27. Instead of incentivizing people to reach a target with external stimuli, Dave Snowden says supporting actors should rather "nudge" people to make small movements toward a change by helping them access internal information that they can then decide to act on.

    Butler, N. (2018). Dave Snowden: How to have a lasting impact in a complex world. *Boost.*

    Mattila, N. (2018). SenseMaker is a tool for decision-making in a new kind of world. *Sitra.*

Chapter 9

1. Woodward, C. (2017). Elephants in the box: How can we work together to tackle severe and multiple disadvantages across Greater Manchester. *Lankelly Chase Foundation.*
2. LCF (2018). Manchester. *Lankelly Chase Foundation.* Retrieved from https://lankellychase.org.uk/project-summary/manchester/.
3. Paterson, H. (2017). Frustration and space. *Lankelly Chase Foundation.*
4. Evans, A. (2012). We're all responsible for stemming the rising tide of homelessness. *The Guardian.*
5. Evans, A. (May 22, 2019). Personal interview with the authors.
6. According to Credit Suisse's annual Global Wealth Report 2019, the share of wealth for the bottom 90 percent of people has actually been rising since over the last two decades, increasing from 11 percent in 2000 to 18 percent in 2019. However, the share of the top 1 percent has been increasing since 2007 to 45 percent. Although many factors are involved, one explanation is the growth in

financial wealth outpacing non-financial wealth in the top 1 percent globally, a faction which is weighted toward wealth-rich nations.

Davies, J., and Shorrocks, A. (2019). The evolution of wealth distribution. *Global Wealth Report 2019.* Credit Suisse

7. World Bank. (2018). Net official development assistance and official aid received (constant 2015 US$). Retrieved from https://data.worldbank.org/indicator/DT.ODA.ALLD.KD.

8. Indiana University Lilly Family School of Philanthropy. (2019). Giving USA 2019: The annual report on philanthropy for the year 2018. *Giving USA Foundation.*

9. Mudaliar, A., and Dithrich, H. (2019). Sizing the impact investing market. *Global Impact Investing Network.*

10. One of the most prominent examples of this approach to funding is Gavi, the Vaccine Alliance, which is dedicated to leading global immunization by bringing private and public stakeholders together for "health system strengthening" in low-income countries. Since its founding in 2000, the initiative has gathered megaplayers from the development, health, and government spaces. And yet, Gavi has been criticized for focusing solely on technical solutions to the exclusion of systemic approaches that seek to understand and account for context (Storeng, 2014). Consequently, rather than support the health of the local system to ensure independence, they create greater dependence on global health initiatives like theirs in developing countries (de Jong, 2017).

Storeng, K. (2014). The Gavi Alliance and the "Gates approach" to health system strengthening. *Global Public Health,* 9(8): 865–79.

de Jong, R. (2017). Public–private partnership paradox: The case of Gavi and health system strengthening. *Policies for Equitable Access to Health.*

11. Buffet, P. (2013). The charitable-industrial complex. *The New York Times.*

12. The Aspen Institute. (2015). Anand Giridharadas: The thriving world, the wilting world, and you [video]. *YouTube.* Retrieved from https://www.youtube.com/watch?v=IP7HajXJD3s.

13. The report from the SIX Funders Node retreat in Adelaide is a useful primer in systems change and systems thinking for foundations.

June, J., and Pulford, L. (2018). Taking risks and achieving greater impact: A view from global foundations. *Social Innovation Exchange.*

14. Among the contributors to the "Embracing complexity" report are many of the funders and organizations that we learned from and collaborated with over the course of our own research journey. Their conviction that "solving the most complex challenges humankind faces today requires both a systems change approach and collaborative action by all stakeholders" is a testament

to the undeniable truths of systems change organizations that anyone engaging with them can observe.

Ashoka (2020). Embracing complexity: Towards a shared understanding of funding systems change. *Ashoka Deutschland* and *McKinsey & Company.*

15. Kania, J. (June 9, 2020) Personal interview with Cynthia Rayner.

16. Cape Town Together emerged in March 2020 as a support system for self-organizing community response groups and CANs. Based on variables of infrastructure, economic structure, and geography, local CANs organized a range of different support services for their communities: soup kitchens for school children, sanitation stations, distribution of safe-practices pamphlets, and PPE production and distribution.
https://www.facebook.com/groups/CapeTownTogether/.

Human, L. (2020). How a Cape Town group is helping neighbourhoods fight Covid-19. *GroundUp.*

17. During this time, many reports emerged both praising and critiquing the efficacy of the CAN model. In one notable piece co-authored by our colleague Ralph Hamman, food security researchers observed the high potential for CANs and other local initiatives to respond quickly and deploy effective innovations, but expressed concern for how these efforts can be harmonized and integrated with government efforts.

Hamman, R., Surmeier, A., Delichte, J., and Drimie, S. (2020). Local networks can help people in distress: South Africa's COVID-19 response needs them. *The Conversation.*

18. Scheepers, E. (March 20, 2020). Personal interview with Cynthia Rayner.

19. Bornstein, D. (2018). A call to modernize American philanthropy. *The New York Times.*

20. Australia's Fay Fuller Foundation takes a holistic view of supporting a stronger healthcare system by funding projects across three pillars: enhancing good health outcomes, research of cures for illness and disease, and capacity- and skills-building for good health outcomes. They achieve this by working with a broad cross-section of organizations and services and focusing on building strong relationships with their partner organizations.
https://www.fayfullerfoundation.com.au.

21. The Whitman Institute was founded in 1985 as an operating foundation dedicated to helping people better navigate day-to-day decision-making and problem-solving. When they eventually evolved into a grant-making foundation in 2005, they began to focus on seeding a more collaborative approach to philanthropy among funders. From this evolution, they developed the Trust-Based Philanthropy Project, which "reimagines traditional funder-grantee relationships."

https://thewhitmaninstitute.org.
https://trustbasedphilanthropy.org.

22. The Bertha Foundation focuses on achieving social justice by supporting field collaborations between actors from three spaces: activism, law, and media. They believe that storytelling, radical activism, and an understanding of institutional rules can be used in concert to achieve real change. The Bertha Centre for Social Innovation and Entrepreneurship represents an extension of this mission as a hub for building capacity for social change and knowledge sharing among social change practitioners, organizations, and students in Africa. https://www.gsb.uct.ac.za/berthacentre.

23. Taking a holistic view of the needs of sex workers, the Red Umbrella Fund advances their rights by directly funding local sex worker-led support organizations and facilitating peer-to-peer capacity building. https://www.redumbrellafund.org.

24. Focusing on projects in the middle of their development journey—post-startup but not yet mature—Co-Impact accepts and is transparent about the fact that their funding model is not suitable for most organizations. In their Handbook for systems change, they explain, "We make a targeted set of relatively large-sized grants to well-established efforts to change systems and have impact at scale with rigorously tested, proven ideas." Their aggregation strategy reduces the risk for funders to participate in such large undertakings, and therefore makes it possible for longer-term, deeper systems change projects.
    Co-Impact (2019). Handbook. *Co-Impact.*

25. https://mcconnellfoundation.ca/initiative/reconciliation/.

26. Council on Foundations (2020). A call to action: Philanthropy's commitment during COVID-19. *Council on Foundations.*

Chapter 10

1. In his 2019 book *Psychiatry of Pandemics,* psychiatrist Damir Huremović provides a chronicle of the death and destruction caused by infectious disease from the Athenian Plague of 430 AD, which killed 25 percent of the population in the city state, to the Zika virus of 2015. This chapter ends with speculation about a forthcoming pandemic caused by "Disease X."
    Huremović, D. (2019). Brief history of pandemics (Pandemics throughout history). In D. Huremović (ed.), *Psychiatry of pandemics* (pp. 7–35). Cham: Springer Nature Switzerland.

2. When global anxiety over the pandemic reached a fever pitch in March 2020, South Africa instituted one of the strictest lockdowns in the world. Given the country's high rates of HIV and TB infection, coupled with the high

concentration of households in townships, a swift and intense lockdown was designed to squash the curve entirely. Lines of people, like the ones filmed in the BBC video, waiting for food parcels and soup kitchens became a regular feature of the landscape over the next three months.

BBC News (2020). Coronavirus: South Africans in massive queues for food parcels [video]. *BBC*. Retrieved from https://www.bbc.com/news/av/world-africa-52701571/coronavirus-south-africans-in-massive-queues-for-food-parcels.

3. World Bank (2020). GINI index (World Bank estimate). *The World Bank Group*. Retrieved from https://data.worldbank.org/indicator/SI.POV.GINI.

4. The Nobel-awarded development economist Amartya Sen argued that the provision of human rights or freedoms without the "capability" to participate in those freedoms—both internal and external factors that impact access—these freedoms are empty. Building on this "capability approach" in his 1999 book *Development as Freedom,* Sen claimed that true development is substantiated by the effective freedoms—capabilities—individuals enjoy in a country, rather than any traditional economic metric, such as GDP.

Sen, A. (1999). *Development as Freedom*. Oxford: Oxford University Press.

5. In sub-Saharan Africa, where millions suffer from co-morbidities such as HIV/AIDS, tuberculosis, and hypertension, COVID-19 has posed a disproportionate threat to vulnerable populations in the region. Mentor mothers from m2m—who themselves face greater risks from the effects of COVID-19 as HIV-positive individuals—were able to use their m2m experience to assist with pandemic response efforts.

Beedle de Palomo, F. (2020). Take of two pandemics. *mothers2mothers*.

6. Parker, M. (April 14, 2020). Personal interview with Cynthia Rayner.

7. Marris, E. (2019). Why young climate activists have captured the world's attention. *Nature*.

Curnow, J., and Helferty, A. (2019). A year of resistance: How youth protests shaped the discussion on climate change. *The Conversation*.

8. Buurtzorg Britain and Ireland (2020). Covid-19--what Buurtzorg is learning and what we can learn from Buurtzorg? [video]. *YouTube*.

9. FEN (2020) Newsletter March–May 2020.

10. Wheatley, M. (2011). Leadership in the age of complexity: From hero to host. *Resurgence Magazine*.

11. In a May 2020 issue of his newsletter, Mauricio Miller addressed an important aspect of his mother's story, which had been so fundamental to the founding of FII: racism. Even in the eyes of her more "liberal" community members she found herself looked upon as *needy* and, therefore, *weak*. As a result, "pride and self-respect were the drivers of my mother's resourcefulness that got me through college." Mauricio wields her experiences as an unsparing reminder

that those of us working in the social sector in pursuit of change and justice with paternalistic solutions need to look in the mirror. If we are not working "as peers with the communities of color" or other groups marginalized within the current system, we are not doing good enough.

Miller, M. (2020). Feeding racism. *The Alternative* newsletter.

12. SDI co-founder and former chair Sheela Patel explains how organizations like hers, which represent some of the most in-touch with vulnerable communities, are still rarely consulted by the enormous foundations about what communities actually need. "We don't know where that money goes ... We are not asked what we would like to do with that money," she said. The full webinar from April 2020 focuses on how recovery efforts for COVID-19 can be used to "build back better" the cities hit hardest by the pandemic.

Null, S., Rubnitz, T., and Smith, H. (2020). Cities, battered by COVID-19, remain key to recovery: How can investments be well spent? *The City Fix.*

WRI (2020). Webinar: Build back better: Resilience of vulnerable populations and COVID-19. *World Resources Institute.*

13. Huq, S., and Patel, P. (2020). Transitioning to a better global "new normal." *International Institute for Environment and Development.*

14. As more and more countries began considering plans for reopening parts of their economies in May 2020, street vendors in India received mixed messages from national government and local authorities about whether they could reopen markets and how to proceed. Their experience highlights the communication and coordination failures that stem from poor engagement between primary actors and supporting actors, which were, in this case, government agencies.

Chitlangia, R. (2020). Delhi weekly markets still shut, vendors say "lack of clarity." *Hindustan Times.*

15. As the experience in India indicates, most governments do not have the capacity to reach citizens directly to distribute aid or even provide communications. Organizations like Nidan, who work across a disparate community of street vendors, are needed to provide a singular voice for informal workers and advocate corrective actions that best address the needs of primary actors as quickly as possible.

Mishra, S. (2020). Govt's relief package aims to cover all sections, but lack of data poses hurdle in empowering poor. *News18.*

16. Minimalist and writer Courtney Carver describes our current moment, in May 2020, as being "in between normal."

Carver, C. (2020). Weekend favorites: kindness, skillet cookies and a 4-book giveaway. *Be More with Less.* Retrieved from: https://bemorewithless. com/weekend-favorites-may-23.

17. As of June 2, 2020, the four large countries where coronavirus was increasing fastest were Brazil, the United States, Russia, and Britain—all countries "run by populist male leaders who cast themselves as anti-elite and anti-establishment." There are examples of the contrary—populist leaders who took the virus and scientific evidence seriously—in Hungary and the Philippines. But overall, countries who successfully navigated the virus had more liberal governments led by women, such as Angela Merkel in Germany, Jacinda Ardern in New Zealand, and Tsai Ing-wen in Taiwan.

    Leonhardt, D., and Leatherby, L. (2020). Where the virus is growing most: Countries with "illiberal populist" leaders. *The New York Times.*

18. In the post-COVID world, the World Economic Forum calls on business to, among other things, "mobilize purpose in the common interest." This means embracing multi-stakeholder capitalism and adopting environmentally and socially sustainable practices with more urgency than ever before.

    Lesser, R., and Reeves, M. (2020). 5 priorities for leaders in the new reality of COVID-19. *World Economic Forum.*

19. Taub, A. (2020). Why are women-led nations doing better with Covid-19? *The New York Times.*

20. Sridhar, D., and Majumder, M. S. (2020). Modelling the pandemic. *BMJ.*

21. Hamann, R., Surmeier, A., Delichte, J., and Drimie, S. (2020). Local networks can help people in distress: South Africa's COVID-19 response needs them. *The Conversation.*

22. Writing in another issue of his newsletter in April 2020, Mauricio Miller expressed optimism that "Covid-19 presents a unique opportunity" for making practices of supporting one another across divides of class and race part of the new normal. He calls this "the mutuality society."

    Miller, M. (2020). Continue the spirit of mutuality after the crisis passes. *The Alternative* newsletter.

23. Arkalgud, A. (April 18, 2019). Personal interview with the authors.

24. Nknoyeni, N. (2019). Collective action brings about change. *Mail & Guardian.*

Index

accountability
  Child and Youth Finance
    International 101
  civil society 14
  drive toward 15
  Kenya's community health system 37
  monitoring and evaluation 127,
    133–4, 136
action systems
  collective identity 40, 41, 57*f*, 58,
    65–7, 166–8
  defined 56
Aflatoun 96, 97
agency
  Buurtzorg 80–1
  economies of trust 84
  Family Independence Initiative 70–4
agricultural production 3–6, 16–17
Ahinsu, Celestine 86
Airbnb 93
Alinsky, Saul 28
Amazon 93
Amnesty International 86
AMP Health 33–7
Angana 108
anti-poverty programs *see* Community
    Independence Initiative; Family
    Independence Initiative; Fundación
    Paraguaya
Ardern, Jacinda 237n17
Argyris, Chris 216n18
Arkalgud, Anand 176
Arputham, Jockin 87–8, 130, 188, 221n9
artificial intelligence 14, 24
"Aspen Consensus" 145
Aspen Institute, AMP Health 33–7
associational revolution 12, 13, 207n34
Australia, Fay Fuller Foundation 154–5,
    233n20

Bacharach, Peter 30, 212n28
Banerjee, Abhijit 231n26
Baratz, Morton 30, 212n28
Bar-Yam, Yaneer xxxiii, 27, 202n26
BCG, Centre for Public Impact 220n19
Beckstrom, Rod 71
behavioral economics 14
Bellagio International Declaration of Street
    Vendors 224n5
Benford, Robert 40, 213n5
Berg, Laura 129
Bertalanffy, Ludwig von xxxi, xxxii,
    201nn22–3, 210n12
Bertha Centre for Social Innovation
    xxviii–xxx, 154–5
  community-based health services 45
  Executive Education program 33, 36
  funding 154–5
  safe havens 60–1
Besser, Mitch 58–60, 182
Bhatt, Ela 104, 224n5
big data 14, 24
  monitoring and evaluation 137
  problem-solving 75–7, 76*f*
Big Lottery Fund 142
Billimoria, Jeroo 39, 96–7, 133, 190
Black Power movement 57
Blok, Jos de 79–80, 82, 169–70, 186
Body Mapping 61, 215n11
Bohm, David 63, 152, 216n16
Bohm dialogue 216n16
bonding social capital 74, 218n10
Botton, Alain de 29
Bradfield, Richard 202n2, 203n4
Brafman, Ori 71
Brazil, COVID-19 237n17
bridging social capital 74, 218n10
Britt, Lory 214n7, 215n13
Broadbent, Tim 230n21

Brown, Jerry 69–70, 72
Buffett, Peter and Warren 15, 145
Burke, Tarana 26
Burt, Martin 128–9, 229n10
Bush, George H. W. 12, 207n37
businesses
  drivers of social change 11, 12
  exaggerated influence in democratic
    processes 144
  industry of social change 144
  scale 27
  technical systems change xxxiii
  see also nongovernmental organizations
Buurtzorg xxxvii, 186–7
  COVID-19 169–70
  map xxxviif
  monitoring and evaluation 131, 134, 139
  primary actors 44
  problem-solving 78–83

Camacho, Manuel Avila 3–4
Canada
  Indigenous peoples 157–8
  McConnell Foundation 157–8
  Social Innovation Generation 199n15
capability approach 235n4
Cape Town Together (CTT) 150–2, 175,
    233n16
Cardenas, Lazaro 3–4, 203n13
Carver, Courtney 236n16
Carver, George Washington 203n5
Catalyst 2030: 148–9
Chambers, Robert 127, 228n7, 229n15
Chan, Priscilla 13
Change Day project 123–5, 129–31
charitable industrial complex 15, 145
Child and Youth Finance International
    (CYFI) xxxvii, 190–91
  connection, fostering 39–40
  map xxxvii
  monitoring and evaluation 133–4, 230n18
  platforms 95–7
    for power 99–100
    rituals 98, 99
  safe havens 61
Child Helpline International 39, 96
children
  education see education
  financial empowerment see Child and
    Youth Finance International
  health see mothers2mothers
China, political economy 8

Cilliers, Paul 24
Cities Alliance 91
Citizen University 225n12
civil rights movement 9, 57
civil society
  Bertha Centre 155
  COVID-19 171, 172
  industry of social change 12–13, 14, 15
  reclaiming 173
climate change/movement
  collective identity 41, 168
  disrupting policies and
    patterns 115
  timescales xxviii
  wicked problem xxvii, 176
Clinton, Bill 69
Clinton, Hillary Rodham 28, 69
Co-Impact 157, 223n21, 234n24
Colbert, Vicky 110–14, 194
Cold War 9
collaborative social change 174
collective identity xxxvi, 36, 37–41, 166–8
  and action systems 57f, 58, 65–7
  cultivating 53–67
  defined 56, 214n6
  informal workers 104
  philanthropists 146
  post-COVID-19 recovery 175
  problem-solving 84
collectives
  Buurtzorg 80
  connection 41
  cultivating 51–3, 67
    building a "we" 55–8
    new web of relationships 53–5
    pooling 62–5
    safe havens 60–2
    slowing down 65–6
    from stigma to pride 58–60
  data 75, 76f
  platforms 99–101
  post-COVID-19 recovery 174–5
Colombia
  Community Independence Initiative 74
  Escuela Nueva 110–14
  see also Fundación Escuela Nueva
community action networks (CANs) 150–2,
    175, 233nn16–17
community health see health
Community Independence Initiative (CII)
  connection, fostering 39
  problem-solving 72, 74, 77

community nurses, Netherlands 78–82
  see also Buurtzorg
community organizing
  Alinsky 28
  Cape Town Together 150–2
  Child and Youth Finance
    International 96
  Singh 103
  social change practitioners xxvi
  societal shifts 9
compassionate capitalism 13
complex adaptive systems 22–3, 27
complexity xxvi, xxviii, 18, 31, 164,
    175–6
  approaches to systems change xxxiii
  big data 75
  collective identity 38, 41, 213n6
  context, embracing 41–2, 44
  COVID-19 162, 173
  crisis of 22–5
  defined 21
  economies of trust 84
  funding for partnership
    nurturing 154
    propagating 156
    questions 148, 149, 232n14
    seeding 150
  history of systems change xxxi
  lived experience 66
  mental models 63
  monitoring and evaluation 124, 126–8,
    130, 228n5, 230n21
    deep data 137–9
    invisible value 132
    Revaluation 137
  New England Complex Systems
    Institute 202n26
  organizational principles and
    practices 166, 169, 171–2
  poverty 71–2
  problem-solving 73, 78
  and resilience 53
  and scale 27, 28, 211n20
  see also wicked problems
connection, fostering xiii, 36–41,
    166–8
  camaraderie 56
  defined xlii, xliv
  life experiences 53
  neighbourhoods 82
  philanthropists 146, 149, 159
  see also collective identity

context, embracing xxvi
  Buurtzorg 186–7
  Child and Youth Finance
    International 95, 97, 190
  collectives 57
  embracing xxxvi, 36, 38, 41–4, 166,
    169–71, 176
  Escuela Nueva 111
  Family Independence Initiative 184
  Fundación Escuela Nueva 194
  funding for partnership 146, 157, 161
  monitoring and evaluation 125, 139
  mothers2mothers 182
  Nidan 192
  platforms 94
  power, reconfiguring 47
  problem-solvers 92
  RLabs 180
  and scale 27, 28, 146
  Slum Dwellers International 188
contextual responsiveness 73, 84, 85
  Buurtzorg 78
  COVID-19 166
co-production 141–2, 156
corporate social responsibility 13
COVID-19 162–71
  collectives 57
  food supply chain 16
  post-COVID recovery 172–4, 236n12,
    237nn18, 22
  safe havens 61–2
  South Africa 150–2, 163, 168, 235n2
COVID Response Alliance 174
Crutchfield, Leslie 26, 43
cultivating collectives *see* collectives:
  cultivating
cultural norms *see* norms
cultural turn 40
Czechoslovakia, Prague Spring 10

Dalberg Group 89, 222n12
Darnton, Andrew 123–5, 129–32, 138
decentralized decision-making xxxvi,
    77–8, 171
  COVID-19 171
decentralized networks 169–70
deep data 138–40
deep work and challenges xxvii–xxviii, 18,
    31, 162, 164–5
  Buurtzorg 187
  Child and Youth Finance International 191
  COVID-19 173

deep work and challenges (*cont.*)
  defined 21
  Family Independence Initiative 185
  Fundación Escuela Nueva 195
  funding for partnership 149
  invisible value 132
  mothers2mothers 183
  Nidan 193
  and power 28–31, 164, 165
  RLabs 181
  Slum Dwellers International 189
defensive routines 63, 216n18
Dewey, John 225n15
dialogue 63, 152
Dickey, John 5
discussion 63
Dowie, Mark 5, 6–7, 204n21
Drucker, Peter F. 13, 125
drug users
  South Africa 51–3, 55
  UK 141
Duflo, Esther 231n26

Ebola 219n14
Ebrahim, Alnoor 133, 230n19
Echoing Green 158–9
economic citizenship 40, 96, 97,
  133, 190–1
  see also Child and Youth Finance
    International
economic crises 10–11, 101, 162, 210n8
economic development and growth
  GDP 126
  India 106
  informal economy 104
  post-war period 7, 9
  wicked problems xxvii
economies of trust 83–4
education
  financial *see* Child and Youth Finance
    International
  philanthropists' influence 13
  see also Bertha Centre for Social
    Innovation; Escuela Nueva;
    Fundación Escuela Nueva .
Eijk, Bram van 95
Eisenhower, Dwight D. 8
Elephants Project 141–3, 149, 151, 152
equipping problem-solvers
  data 73–7
  decentralizing decision-making 77–8

economies of trust 83–4
  "knowledge at the edge" 71–3
  positioning problem-solvers 78–80
  sustaining motivation 80–3
Escuela Nueva 194–5
  COVID-19 170
  disrupting policies and patterns 110–14,
    117, 225n15, 226nn19–21, 227n27
  see also Fundación Escuela Nueva
Escuela Unitaria 225n15
evaluation *see* monitoring and evaluation;
  self-evaluation
Evans, Alice 142–3, 148–50, 152–4
Extinction Rebellion 115

Facebook 93, 210n10
Fairbanks, Eve 19
Family Independence Initiative (FII) 5,
  154, 184–5
  connection, fostering 39
  funding for partnership 152
  lived experience 235n11
  map xxxvii*f*
  monitoring and evaluation 134, 139
  problem-solving 68–71, 80
    data 73, 75–6
    decentralizing decision-making 77
    economies of trust 83
    "knowledge at the edge" 71–3
  safe havens 61
  UpTogether 73, 130, 185
Fay Fuller Foundation 147, 154–5, 233n20
feedback loops 32
  funding for partnership 154
  monitoring and evaluation 125, 127,
    133–6, 140
  power 29, 44–5
  problem-solving 73, 78
feminist movement *see* women's
  movement
Floyd, George 159, 172
food security
  COVID-19 163, 172, 233n17
  Green Revolution 3–6, 16–17
for-profit sector *see* businesses
Forrester, Jay xxxi, 200n20
Fosdick, Raymond 4
France
  nonprofits 207n36
  teachers' and students' strike 10
Freebairn, Donald 204n20

Fundación Escuela Nueva
(FEN) xxxviii, 194–5
COVID-19 170
disrupting policies and patterns 109,
112–16
map xxxviif
primary actors 43
safe havens 60
Fundación Paraguaya 128, 139
funding for partnership 141–6, 159–61
nurturing systems work 153–6
propagating systems work 156–9
questions 146–9
seeding systems work 149–53

Gandhi, Rahul 103
Gandhi, Sonia 103
gangs 51–3, 55
see also RLabs
Ganz, Marshall 15, 175, 209n46
Gapminder Foundation 198n8
Gasparre, Angelo 92
Gates, Bill 13
Gavi Alliance 232n10
gay rights movement 115, 215n13
Geddes, Patrick 87, 221n6
Gerena, Jesús 71, 77
Germany, COVID-19 237n17
Gilmore, Ruth Wilson 13, 208n39
Giridharadas, Anand 145
Giving Pledge 157
Global Impact Investing Network
(GIIN) 174, 229–30nn16, 19
globalization
context, embracing 42
informal economy 104
protests 93
Global Money Week 98
glocalization 90, 222n14
Google 93
Gopal, Srik 200n17
governments
associational revolution 207n34
Child and Youth Finance Initiative 39
Colombia 111–12, 113–14
COVID-19 237n17
debt servicing 11–12
India
agricultural program 6
informal workers 103–7, 116
informal settlements 88, 91, 172

Kenya 33–7, 43–4
Mexico 3–4
partnerships 11, 12, 13
philanthropists' influence on 144
post-war social order 7–8
privatization 11, 12
scale 27
social change practitioners'
assumptions 14
social change role 15
social contract 176
societal platforms 100
South Africa
and Bertha Centre for Social
Innovation 155
health system 83
technical systems change xxxiii
transformative systems change xxxiv
UK 141
US
anti-poverty programs 69, 71–2
Mexican agricultural program 3, 4
welfare programs 206–7n33
see also public policy
Granovetter, Mark 218n9
Grant, Heather Mcleod 26
Great Depression 7, 126, 175–6
Great Society 8
Green Revolution 6–7, 16, 17
Groote Schuur, South Africa 58–9
gross domestic product (GDP) 126, 228nn5–6

Hamman, Ralph 233n17
happiness, measuring 227n4
Hargreaves, Andy 112–13, 226n20
Harrar, George 5
Harrison, Andrew 123–5, 129–32, 135,
138, 229n14
Hawken, Paul xxv, 197n2
health
Fay Fuller Foundation 154, 233n20
gains xxv
Gavi Alliance 232n10
home-based care see Buurtzorg
Kenya's community health system 33–7,
43–4, 131
philanthropists' influence 13
smallpox, eradication of 25, 211n14
see also COVID-19; HIV/AIDS;
mothers2mothers
Heimans, Jeremy 101, 223n28

Heise, David 214n7, 215n13
HIV/AIDS
    COVID-19 235n5
    Millennium Development Goals xxvii
    see also mothers2mothers
home-based care see Buurtzorg
homelessness 141, 142–3
Horvath, Aaron 15, 208n45
Hungary, COVID-19 237n17
hunger
    decline xxv
    Green Revolution 6, 16
    Sustainable Development Goals xxvii
Hunt, Scott 40, 213n5
Huremović, Damir 234n1
Hussein, Salim 33–7, 131

impact investments 13, 144, 145,
        229n16
    monitoring and evaluation 132–3,
        229n17
    R3 Coalition 174
    Slum Dwellers International 100
INCITE! Women of Color Against
        Violence 206n32
Independent Media Center (IMC) 93,
        222nn18–19
India
    agricultural program 5–6
    caste system 46
    COVID-19 236nn14–15
    informal economy 103–8, 116, 117, 173,
        224nn4–6, 225n8, 236nn14–15
    "Operation Sunshine" 192, 224n4
    see also Nidan
    informal settlements 87–8
    Ministry of Urban Development 105
    National Policy on Urban Street
        Vendors 105, 224n8
    poverty 103–7
    Street Vendors (Protection of Livelihood
        and Regulation of Street Vending)
        Act 103, 106, 107, 193
    Town Vending Committees
        (TVCs) 45–6, 107, 115, 193
Indigenous peoples 152, 157–8
industrial agriculture 203n6
industrial classification 127
industrial infrastructure, effect of
        World War II on 205n24
industrialization
    agricultural science 5

climate change xxvii
GDP metric 126
industrial process controls 200n20
industrial revolution 8
industry of social change 10–17
    and complexity 38, 42
    vs. fostering connection 41
    funding for partnership 144–5, 156
    "intractability" of social problems 18
    invisible value 131
    monitoring and evaluation 126, 131
    outcomes, focus on 54
    problem-solving 77–8
    scale 26
Indymedia.org 222n19
informal economy
    India 103–8, 116, 117, 173, 224nn4–6,
        225n8, 236nn14–15
    "Operation Sunshine" 192, 224n4
    see also Nidan
    South Africa 223n3
informal settlements 88–91, 98–100, 101
    India 87–8
    Nigeria 86–7, 220n1
    self-evaluation 130
    see also Slum Dwellers International
institutional orientation 7
    challenge 9
institutional theory 212n25
    "work" concept 202n27
International Bank for Reconstruction and
        Development 7
International Monetary Fund 7, 11
invisible value 130–4, 140
Isaacs, William 65
Italy
    COVID-19 168
    social movements 40

Jamiix 53, 54
Jasper, James 214n10
journaling
    Escuela Nueva 113
    Family Independence Initiative 61, 70, 73

Kania, John 21, 149, 200n17
Kay, Tamara 15, 209n46
Kellogg School of Management 109
Kenya
    community health system 33–7,
        43–4, 131–2
    Health Act (2017) 213n2

Lagos State Urban Renewal Agency
    (LASURA) 87
  Ministry of Health 33–7, 43–4
  National Health Insurance 35
  Ushahidi 219n13
King, Martin Luther, Jr 10
Kirp, David L. 117, 227n27
Krauss, Alexander 138
Kremer, Michael 231n26
Kronenberg, Gonnie 79–80, 186
Kumar, Sachin 105
Kuznets, Simon 126, 228n5

labor unions *see* trade unions
Laloux, Frederick 219n17
Lankelly Chase Foundation xxxi, 142–3,
    147–50, 152–5, 201n24
large-scale change 25–8
  Child and Youth Finance
      International 95, 97
  collectives 54
  context, embracing 43
  Escuela Unitaria 110, 225n15
  Fundación Escuela Nueva 113–14
  funding for partnership 157, 160, 234n24
  Green Revolution 7
  linking groups together 91–2
  mothers2mothers 65
  and power 171
  Schwab Foundation 200n16
  Slum Dwellers International 76, 89, 91
  Sustainable Development Goals 127
Lawrence, Thomas 202n27
learning organizations 216n19
Learning Studio 123
Leca, Bernard 202n27
Leland, Olivia 157
Liberia, Community Independence
    Initiative 74
life expectancies xxv, 219n16
Lindell, Ilda 90, 91, 222n14
Liu, Eric 108, 225n12
lived experience
  collectives 54, 56, 57, 66, 67
  context, embracing 43, 44
  economies of trust 83–4
  Elephants Project 141
  Family Independence Initiative 235n11
  funding for partnership 141, 152,
      159, 161
  vs hollowing out of civil society 172
  mental models 63

mothers2mothers 58–9, 61, 64, 83
  nature of social systems 176
  pooling 64
  primary actors xxxv
  of racial injustice 159
  RLabs 64
  safe havens 61, 62
London Funders 199n14, 201n24
longevity xxv, 219n16
Lotto, Beau 216n17
Lukes, Steven 30, 212n29

MacMillan, Margaret 7
Mair, Johanna 201n21
malnourishment xxv, xxvii, 16
Mama Cash 155
management experts 13
Mandela, Nelson 19
Mandela, Winnie 19
Mangelsdorf, Paul 202nn1–2, 203n4
marriage equality 115
Marshall Plan 9
Massachusetts Institute of Technology,
    system dynamics group xxxi
maternal health *see* mothers2mothers
Max-Neef, Manfred A. xxiii
Maxwele, Chumani 18, 19–20
McAdam, Doug 206n30
McConnell Foundation 157–8, 230n21
McDonald, Nicole 157
McDonnell, Mary-Hunter 225n13
McFarlane, Colin 88–9
Mdaka, Rifumo 18
measurement *see* monitoring and
    evaluation
MelJol 96
Melucci, Alberto 40, 56
mental models 63, 64
Merkel, Angela 237n17
#MeToo movement 26, 57
Mexico
  agricultural program 3–5
  Community Independence Initiative 74
Microreact 219n14
Milano, Alyssa 26
military-industrial complex 8
Millennium Development Goals
    (MDGs) xxvii
Miller, Mauricio Lim 68–73, 77, 152,
      184, 236n11
  connection, fostering 39
  COVID-19 172, 175, 237n22

Mills, C. Wright 29, 212nn27–8
Mishra, Bachan 103
mobile counseling app 53, 54
Mogollón, Oscar 110, 111, 225n14, 225n17
Molokoane, Rose 99
monitoring and evaluation 123–5, 140
    deepening the data 137–9
    for meaning 135–7
    pressure to measure 125–8
    shortening feedback loops 134–5
    social audits 218n12
    surfacing invisible value 130–4
    see also self-evaluation
Montessori, Maria 225n15
Morgan, Jonathan 215n11
Morin, Edgar 24
mothers2mothers (m2m) xxxvii, 182–3
    collective identity 58–60
    COVID-19 167, 235n5
    map xxxviif
    pooling 64
    primary actors 43
    problem-solving 75, 82–3
    safe havens 60, 61
    slow movement 65–6
motivation
    Buurtzorg 79–80, 139
    deep data 139
    economies of trust 84
    Family Independence Initiative 73, 78
    fighting poverty 229n10
    Fundación Escuela Nueva 113
    mothers2mothers 82–3
mutual approaches
    COVID-19 175
    Family Independence Initiative 70–5
Mutuality Platform 74
Mwangi, James 89
Mxit 52–3

National Association of Street Vendors of
    India (NASVI) 105–7, 193,
    224nn6–7
    COVID-19 173
National Health Service (NHS), Change
    Day 123–5, 129–31
Netherlands, community nurses 78–82
    see also Buurtzorg
network strategy 88–9, 92
    decentralized networks 169–70
    vs. platform strategy 94f

New Deal 8, 205n26, 206–7n33
New England Complex Systems
    Institute 202n26
New Philanthropy Capital 201n24
New York Radical Women (NYRW)
    215n14
New Zealand, COVID-19 237n17
Nicholls, Alex 127, 228n9
Nidan xxxvii–xxxviii, 192–3
    COVID-19 173
    disrupting policies and
        patterns 104–8, 114–17
    map xxxviif
    power, reconfiguring 45–6
    safe havens 60
Nidan Swachh Dhara Pvt Ltd (NSPL) 108
Nigeria, informal settlements 86–7,
    188, 220n1
Nigerian Slum/Informal Settlement
    Federation 87
Nilsson, Warren 115
Nkonyeni, Ncedisa 176–7
nongovernmental organizations (NGOs)
    Cape Town, South Africa 214n5
    Child and Youth Finance
        International 39
    COVID-19 163, 167
    food parcels, South Africa 163
    industry of social change 12–13
    structural hierarchy 83
    technical systems change xxxiii
    see also businesses
nonprofit industrial complex 206n32
nonprofit management 13, 208n39
nonprofits
    "associational revolution" 12, 207n34
    conservative ideology 205n26
    drivers of social change 11, 12
    Echoing Green 158
    failings 206n32
    financial education curriculum 97
    Gapminder Foundation 198n8
    industry of social change 11, 12–13
    privatization 11, 12
    scale 26
    social change practitioners xxvi
    systems change xxxi
    see also Fundación Escuela Nueva; Nidan;
        RLabs; Slum Dwellers International
norms
    collectives 58

COVID-19 163, 164
and depth 29
disrupting policies and patterns 109, 115,
    119, 225n17
European social model 8
funding for partnership 158
power, reconfiguring 45, 46, 47
and scale 27
social justice activists 9
transformative approach to systems
    change xxxii
Norway, nonprofits 207n36
nurses, Netherlands 78–82
see also Buurtzorg
nurturing systems work 146–7, 153–6, 161

Obama, Barack 28
obesity xxvii
Occupy Wall Street 25
O'Connor, Michael T. 113, 226n20
official development aid 144
oil crisis 11, 206n31
open data governance programs 75
Open Society Foundation 155
organizational principles and
        practices xxxv–xxxviii
    in action 162–4
    COVID-19 pandemic 162, 165–73
    deep challenges 164–5
    "in between" normal 173–5
    window of now 175–7
    Buurtzorg 186–7
    Child and Youth Finance
        International 190–1
    Family Independence
        Initiative 152, 184–5
    Fay Fuller Foundation 154
    Fundación Escuela Nueva 194–5
    funding for partnership 148, 152, 154,
        158, 161
    mothers2mothers 182–3
    Nidan 192–3
    RLabs 180–1
    Slum Dwellers International 188–9
organizational scale 27
    funding for partnership 160
    Schwab Foundation 200n16
Organization for Economic Co-operation
        and Development (OECD)
    big data 75
    Global Money Week 98

Organization of the Petroleum Exporting
    Countries (OPEC) 11
outcomes-based financing 13, 14

Palomo, Frank Beadle de 83, 167
Parker, Marlon 51–6, 60, 167
participatory processes
    Cape Town Together 150–2
    Child and Youth Finance
        International 95, 96–8, 99, 100–1
    COVID-19 167
    disrupting policies and patterns 106–8,
        111, 115, 119
    Elephants Project 141–2
    Escuela Nueva 111
    funding for partnership 141–2,
        150–2, 158
    monitoring and evaluation 124
    NHS Change Day 227n2
    Nidan 106–8
    platforms 93–4, 101
    power, reconfiguring 46
    primary actors 228n7
    safe havens 214n10
    Slum Dwellers International 89, 90,
        92, 98–9
    social audits 218n12
partnerships
    Bertha Centre for Social Innovation xxviii
    Child and Youth Finance
        International 101
    Family Independence Initiative 77
    funding see funding for partnership
    industry of social change 11, 12
    Kenya's community health system 34, 36
    monitoring and evaluation 132
    scale 26–7, 42
    Slum Dwellers International 88, 91, 100
    technical systems change xxxiii
    transformative systems change xxxiv
Patel, Raj 17, 21, 90–1, 204n18, 210n8
Patel, Sheela 98, 172, 223n25, 236n12
paternalization 172
Paterson, Hannah 142
patterns see social patterns
Patton, Michael Quinn 135–6, 230n20
Petrus Community 142
philanthro-capitalism 13, 145
philanthropy
    collaborative 156–7
    colonial roots 213n3

philanthropy (*cont.*)
  funding for partnership 143–6
  nurturing systems work 153–6
  propagating systems work 156–9
  questions 146–9
  seeding systems work 149–53
  Green Revolution 3–7
  industry of social change 11, 12,
    13, 14, 15
  mindset 77
  monitoring and evaluation 132
  and power 109
Philippines
  agricultural program 5–6
  Community Independence Initiative 74
  COVID-19 237n17
Piaget, Jean 225n15
Piketty, Thomas 208n40
Pilling, David 126, 228n6
Pioneer Hi-Breds 203nn5–6
platforms, promoting 86–9, 102
  collaborating with flexibility 94–5
  defined 93
  linking groups together 91–4
  vs. network strategy 94f
  observing rituals 98–9
  from outrageous to acceptable 96–7
  for power 99–101
  vertical and horizontal 89–91
policy *see* public policy
political economy
  COVID-19 162, 173
  GDP metric 126
  India 104–7, 224nn6–7
  industry of social change 11
  Mexican agricultural program 5
  and skills 114
  South Africa 19
  upheaval 8–9
  US 206n31
Polletta, Francesca 214n6, 215n10
pooling 62–5, 67
population, global 23, 210n9
Porter, Michael 127
post-COVID recovery 172–4, 236n12,
    237nn18, 22
poverty
  COVID-19 162
  global approach to fighting 228n10
  Green Revolution 4, 6
  India 103–7

  intergenerational 96
  levels xxv
  Millennium Development Goals xxvii
  Sustainable Development Goals xxvii
  urbanization 87
  US 68–73, 77
  see also see Community Independence
    Initiative; Family Independence
    Initiative; Fundación Paraguaya;
    informal economy; informal
    settlements; Slum Dwellers
    International
Poverty Stoplight 129, 134
Powell, Walter 15, 209n45
power 108–9
  accountability as a relationship of 134
  COVID-19 163
  decision-making 30, 45, 212n28
  deep challenges 28–31, 164, 165
  defined 29
  disrupting policies and patterns 119
  dynamics *see* power dynamics
  elite 212n27
  Family Independence Initiative 71
  funding for partnership 142–6, 160–1
    nurturing 155–6
    propagating 158
    questions 148
    seeding 149–52
  glocal movements 222n14
  ideological 31, 45, 108, 212n29
  informal workers 103
  non-decision-making (agenda-setting)
    30, 45, 212n29
  of "normal" individuals 225n17
  of philanthropists 13, 146
  platforms for 99–101
  politicized nature of xxvi–xxvii
  post-war period 7
  questions to explore 115–16, 116f
  reconfiguring xxxvi, 36, 38, 44–7, 115,
    166, 171–3, 176–7
    invisible value 133, 140
    philanthropists 146
  Slum Dwellers International 91
  social issues as problems of 209n46
  sociological versus political science view
    of 212n28
  street vendors, India 106–7, 108
  transformative approach to systems
    change xxxii

power dynamics
  disrupting policies and patterns 119
  funding for partnership 148, 161
  reconfiguring 31, 38, 44–7
"precariat" 117, 227n28
pride, transforming stigma into 58–60, 67,
    214n7, 215n13
Prigogine, Ilya 24, 210n12
primary actors, defined xxxv
private sector *see* businesses
privatization 11, 12
  industry of social change 12–13,
    207nn35–6
problem-solvers, equipping 68–71, 85
  data 73–7
  decentralizing decision-making 77–8
  economies of trust 83–4
  "knowledge at the edge" 71–3
  positioning problem-solvers 78–80
  sustaining motivation 80–3
professionalization 11, 13
  vs. economies of trust 83–4
  of health system layworkers 65
  hollowing out of civil society 172
propagating systems work 146–7,
    156–9, 161
public education *see* education
public health *see* health
public policy
  and power 109
  Child and Youth Finance Initiative 133
  Colombia, education 110, 112–14
  deep challenges 165
  defined 109
  disrupting 114–19
  Elephants Project 141
  evidence-based 138
  financial education 97, 98
  glocal movements 222n14
  India 103, 105–8, 173, 224nn5, 7, 225n8
  Kenya 34, 35–6
  mothers2mothers model 66
  nonprofits 207n36
  philanthropists' influence 13
  post-war era 205n23
  primary actors 228n7
  scale 26
  slum dwellers 88, 89, 91
  US 11, 206–7n33
  see also governments
Putnam, Robert 218nn9–10

R3 Coalition 174
racial justice 172
  collective identity 41, 57–8
  Echoing Green 158–9
  scale 25
  timescales xxviii
radical containers 141, 149, 153, 161
randomized controlled trials
    (RCTs) 138, 231n26
Reagan, Ronald 207nn35–6
Reconstructed Living Labs *see* RLabs
Reddy, Sanjay G. 231n26
Red Umbrella Fund 155–6, 234n23
reporting cycles 134–5
Revaluation 125, 129–31, 136–7, 229n14
  dashboard 131*f*
  shortening feedback loops 134
Reyes, Art, III 173
Rhaman, K. Sabeel 172
"Rhodes Must Fall" movement 18,
    20, 209n1
Rittel, Horst W. xxvii, 17, 198n9,
    201n22, 209n48
rituals 98–9, 102
RLabs xxxvii, 180–1
  collective identity 39, 53–6
  COVID-19 167
  map xxxvii*f*
  pooling 64–5
  problem-solving 75, 83
  safe havens 60
Rockefeller family 4, 203n13
Rockefeller Foundation (RF) xxxi, 4–7, 16,
    17, 202nn1–3, 203n6
Rodriguez, Dylan 14
Roosevelt, Franklin D. 3, 4, 197n1
Rosling, Hans xxvi, 198n8
Russia, COVID-19 237n17
Ryan, Alex 225n17

Sachs, Jeffrey xxvii, 199n10
safe havens 60–2, 67
  platforms 101
Salamon, Lester 12, 205n26, 207n34
Sarachild, Kathie 62, 215n14
scale xxvi, xxviii, 18, 31, 164
  collaborations 174
  and complexity 27, 28, 211n20
  connection, fostering 39
  context, embracing 42
  COVID-19 173

scale (*cont.*)
    defined 21
    economies of trust 83, 84
    Escuela Nueva 110
    Fundación Escuela Nueva 112–14
    funding for partnership 146,
        149, 156–7
    glocal movements 90, 222n14
    illusion of 25–8
    invisible value 132
    monitoring and evaluation 127
    organizational principles and
        practices 166, 168
    platforms 223n21
    problem-solving 85
    social capital 74
    see also large-scale change;
        organizational scale
Scheepers, Ella 115, 151–2
Schwab Foundation for Social
        Entrepreneurship xxix–xxx, 174,
        199n13, 200n16, 230n19
scientific orientation 8, 15
    challenge 9
Scott, William Richard 212n25
seeding systems work 146–7, 149–53, 161
Seelos, Christian 65, 201nn21, 23
self-determination 89–91, 98–9
Self-Employed Women's Association of
        India (SEWA) 224n5
self-evaluation 128–30, 140
Self Worker Movement 117, 193
Sen, Amartya 235n4
Senge, Peter 63, 217n19
SenseMaker 138–9
sex workers 155–6
Shaban, Lubna 95
shared understanding 52–3, 62–5, 67
    see also collective identity
Singh, Arbind 45, 103–7, 117, 192
Skoll Foundation 222n13
slavery, abolition of 205n23
slow movement 65–6
Slum Dwellers International
        (SDI) xxxvii, 188–9
    awards and accolades 222n13
    big data 76
    COVID-19 172
    invisible value 132
    "Know Your City" 76, 221n8
    map xxxvii*f*
    monitoring and evaluation 130, 132, 134

platforms 87–9, 95, 97, 221n9
    linking groups together 92, 93
    for power 99, 100, 101
    rituals 98–9
    vertical and horizontal 89–91
    power, reconfiguring 46
    Urban Poor Fund International 100
    slum eradication schemes 86–7
    small data 76*f*
    informal settlements 130
    problem-solving 74, 75
    Slum Dwellers International 98–9
smallpox, eradication of 25, 211n14
Smucker, Jonathan 54, 214n4
Snowden, Dave 138–9, 231n27
Social Audit Network 218n12
social audits 75, 218n12
social behavior
    complexity 22
    disrupting policies and patterns 109
    industry of social change 14
social capital 74, 218n9
social change xxv–xxxviii, 21–2, 31–2, 175–7
    ambitious aims 37
    Bertha Centre 234n22
    changing conceptualization 11
    Child and Youth Finance
        International 95
    collaborative 174
    collective identity 40
    collectives 54
    complexity 22, 25
    context, embracing 44
    core work 38
    COVID-19 and recovery 164, 174–6
    defined xxxiv
    depth and power 28–31
    disrupting policies and patterns 110,
        112, 115–16
    funding for partnership 145
    nurturing 156
    propagating 157, 158
    questions 148–9
    seeding 151
    Green Revolution 6
    industry of *see* industry of social
        change
    measuring and understanding
        see monitoring and evaluation
    Mexican food production 3
    organizational principles and
        practices 166, 167, 169, 171

post-war psyche 7
power, reconfiguring 45
pragmatic approach 214n4
problem-solving 71
scale of *see* scale
South Africa 20, 209n1
statistics, limitations of 162
technical approach 9, 10, 165
trajectory 154
transformational approach 10, 165
social change practitioners, defined xxvi
social entrepreneurship 230n19
    Billimoria 96
    capitalism 145
    COVID Response Alliance 174
    Echoing Green 158
    Harrison 123
    industry of social change 13, 14
    Schwab Foundation xxix–xxx,
        200n16
    social change practitioners xxvi
social impact assessment 132–3
social impact investing 13, 14
social innovation
    accountability 230n20
    Arkalgud 176
    Bertha Centre *see* Bertha Centre for
        Social Innovation
    Echoing Green 159
    funding 147, 159
    limited coverage of academic
        literature xxix
    scale and context 28
    Seelos and Mair's view of 201n21
    social change practitioners xxvi
    Social Innovation Generation 199n15
Social Innovation Exchange (SIX) 147,
    148, 149
Social Innovation Generation 199n15
social investors 144
social justice
    activism 9–10
    safe havens 61
    Bertha Centre 234n22
    collective identity 168
    number of organizations concerned
        with 197n2
    and paternalism 236n11
    reimagining 176
social media 14
    Child and Youth Finance
        International 98

large-scale change 25–6
shared understanding 52–3
social patterns
    defined 109
    disrupting 114–19
Social Progress Imperative 127
social services 9
    Bertha Centre for Social
        Innovation xxviii
    Family Independence Initiative 68–73,
        75–6, 77
    industry of social change 11–14
    US 11, 205n28, 206–7n33
societal platforms 93–102
Society for Promotion of Area Resource
    Centres (SPARC) 223n25
Socion Advisors 176
Soule, Sarah 225n13
South Africa
    apartheid, legacy of xxix, 18–19,
        20, 151
    Cape Town
        Bertha Centre *see* Bertha Centre for
            Social Innovation
        Cape Town Together 150–2,
            175, 233n16
        Open Data Portal 218n11
    COVID-19 150–2, 163, 168, 235n2
    gang and drug culture 51–3, 55
    Groote Schuur 58–9, 182
    informal economy 223n3
    Poverty Stoplight 129
    protests 18
    Slum Dwellers International 99
    social audit 218n12
    transformation 209n1
    wealth inequality xxix, 163
    see also mothers2mothers; RLabs
Soviet Union, political economy 8
Spicer, Jason 15, 209n46
Sridhar, Devi 174
Srinivasan, Viji 104
stagflation 11, 206n31
Stakman, Elvin C. 202–3nn3–4
Standard Oil 204n13
Stellenbosch Centre for Complex Systems
    in Transition xxix
stigma
    HIV 64, 167
    sex workers 155
    transforming into pride 58–60, 67,
        214n7, 215n13

Stockholm Resilience Centre xxix
StreetNet 104
street vendors 103–7
COVID-19 173
see also Nidan
Suddaby, Roy 202n27
supporting actors, defined xxxv
sustainable capitalism 145
Sustainable Development Goals
(SDGs) xxvii, 127
system leadership 177
Child and Youth Finance
International 96
COVID-19 and recovery 164,
173–4, 237n17
disrupting policies and patterns 115–17
Fundación Escuela Nueva 114
Nidan 105, 108
funding for partnership 145, 148,
149, 158–9
hosts vs. heroes 41, 213n6
organizational principles and
practices 166, 169, 171, 172
power, reconfiguring 46, 47
slow movement 65
Slum Dwellers International 89
systems change 17, 21
Bertha Centre's Executive Education
program 33
Child and Youth Finance
International 95
collaborative 95, 133
definitions xxx–xxxi, xxxiii, xxxiv
exploring xxviii–xxx
funding for partnership
Co-Impact 234n24
Lankelly Chase 143
propagating 159
questions 147–9, 233n14
seeding 152
history of term xxxi–xxxii
measuring *see* monitoring and
evaluation
platforms 89, 223n21
power, reconfiguring 45
reimagining 176
SIX Funders Node 147, 232n13
technical vs transformational
approaches xxxii–xxxiii, 200n20
work, lack of emphasis on xxxvi
systems thinking
learning organizations 216n19

popularization xxxi
SIX Funders Node 232n13
systems work xxv–xxvi, 21, 175–7
Buurtzorg 186–7
collectives 54
complexity, scale, and depth 31
COVID-19 164
deep challenges 165
defined xxxiv
Family Independence Initiative 184–5
Fundación Escuela Nueva 194–5
funding for partnership 159–61
Lankelly Chase 143
measuring *see* monitoring and evaluation
mothers2mothers 182–3
Nidan 192–3
nurturing 146–7, 153–6, 161
organizational principles and
practices 166, 169, 171
philanthropists 146
policies and patterns 109
power, reconfiguring 46–7
principles and practices xxxv–xxxviii,
xxxviii*f*, 33
problem-solving 75
process 37–8
propagating 146–7, 156–9, 161
RLabs 180–1
seeding 146–7, 149–53, 161
Slum Dwellers International 188–9
social capital 74

Taiwan, COVID-19 237n17
Taub, Amanda 174
Tavistock Consulting 229n14
technology entrepreneurship *see* RLabs
Thatcher, Margaret 207n36
third sector 13
Thomas, Kisimbi 33–7, 43, 131
Thomas, Stacey 154
Thunberg, Greta 168
Timms, Henry 101, 223n28
town planning 221n6
trade unions
decline 14
teachers 111, 112
trust
bridging social capital 74
Buurtzorg 131
collective identity 41
cultivating collectives 54, 56, 61
economies of 83–4

funding for partnership 152–6, 159
mothers2mothers 167
Tsai Ing-wen 237n17

Uber 93
undernourishment 198n6
UNESCO
   Escuela Nueva 110
   unitary complete school methodology
      (UCSM) 225
UN Habitat 91, 101
unions *see* trade unions
unitary complete school methodology
      (UCSM) 225
United Cities and Local Governments
   Africa (UCLGA) 91
United Kingdom
   COVID-19 168, 237n17
   drug users 141
   Elephants Project 141–3, 149, 151, 152
   homelessness 141, 142–3
   Lankelly Chase Foundation xxxi, 142–3,
      147–50, 152–5, 201n24
   National Health Service (NHS), Change
      Day 123–5, 129–31
   nonprofits 207n36
   Rockefeller Foundation xxxi
   stagflation 11
   Thatcher administration 207n36
United Nations
   big data 75
   climate action 168
   establishment 7
   "World Happiness Report" 227n4
United States
   aging population 219n16
   Apollo 8 mission 10
   Black Power movement 57
   civil rights movement 9, 57
   COVID-19 237n17
   Echoing Green 158–9
   Escuela Nueva 117
   Great Society 8
   imperialism 205–6n28
   King's assassination and protests 10
   Marshall Plan 9
   and Mexican agricultural program 3
   New Deal 8, 205n26, 206–7n33
   nonprofits 12, 207nn35–6
   Occupy Wall Street 25
   philanthropy 144, 208n41
   post-war psyche 8

poverty 68–73, 77
racial justice 25, 158–9, 172
Reagan administration 207nn35–6
recession (1973–75) 11, 206n31,
   206n33
slavery, abolition of 205n23
social capital 218n9
social movements 9, 206n30
social services 11, 205n28, 206–7n33
stock market crash (1973) 10
Vietnam War 10
wicked problems 199n9
women's movement 25, 62, 215n14
   see also Family Independence Initiative
University of Cape Town (UCT)
   protests 18
   Bertha Centre *see* Bertha Centre for
      Social Innovation
University of Waterloo Institute for Social
   Innovation and Resilience
      (WISER) xxxv
UpTogether 73, 130, 185
urbanization
   Green Revolution 6, 16
   informal settlements 87, 91
   street vendors 105
Urban Poor Fund International (UPFI) 100
USAID 111
Ushahidi 219n13

values
   collective identity 40
   conservative 9
   COVID-19 163, 164
   deep challenges 28, 29, 164
   disrupting policies and patterns 109, 115,
      117, 119
   Escuela Nueva 227n27
   Fundación Escuela Nueva 114
   monitoring and evaluation 132, 136, 137
   organizational principles and
      practices xxxv
   power, reconfiguring 45
   process of change xxxiv
   and scale 27
   social justice activists 9
venture capital 100
venture philanthropy 13
Vietnam, Escuela Nueva programs 226n19
Vietnam War 10
Villaneuva, Edgar 53, 152, 213n3
visible value 132

Wallace, Henry A.   3–4, 203nn5–6
water cooler effect   131, 139
wealth inequality   144, 145, 176
    forces behind   208n40
    philanthropy   11, 13
    post-war period   7
    South Africa   xxix, 163
Weaver, Warren   4–5
Webber, Melvin   xxvii, 17, 198n9,
        201n22, 209n48
"we-ness" see collective identity
West, Geoffrey   27, 211n20
WhatsApp   61–2, 152
Wheatley, Margaret   31, 171, 213n6
Whitman Institute   154, 233n21
Whittier, Nancy   62, 215n12
wicked problems   xxvii, 199n9,
        201n22, 209n48
    bonding social capital   74
    hunger   16
    power   31
    proliferation   176
    scale   28
Williams, Brent   51, 53–6
Women in Informal Employment: Globalizing
        and Organizing (WIEGO)   224n3
Women's March   25
women's movement
    consciousness-raising   62, 215n12

pooling   62
suffrage   205n23
Woodward, Christopher   142
World Bank   7
    big data   75
    Colombia's Escuela Nueva policy   112
    Green Revolution   6
    structural adjustment programs   11
World Economic Forum
    post-COVID-19 recovery   174,
        237n18
    Schwab Foundation for Social
        Entrepreneurship   xxix–xxx, 174,
        199n13, 200n16, 230n19
World Health Organization (WHO)   60
World Trade Organization (WTO), protests
        against   93, 222–3nn18–19
World War I   7, 175
World War II   7, 175
Wright, Angus   203n4

youth
    empowerment see RLabs
    financial see Child and Youth Finance
        International

Zimmerman, Brenda   23
Zuckerberg, Mark   13
Zuma, Jacob   19–20